Mabel

A Biography of Mabel Dodge Luhan

Also by Emily Hahn

Mabel

A Biography of Mabel Dodge Luhan

by Emily Hahn

Illustrated with photographs

HOUGHTON MIFFLIN COMPANY
BOSTON 1977

Copyright © 1977 by Emily Hahn

Library of Congress Cataloging in Publication Data

Hahn, Emily, date
  Mabel : a biography of Mabel Dodge Luhan.
  Bibliography: p.
  Includes index.
    1.   Luhan, Mabel Ganson Dodge, 1879–1962.
  2.   United States — Biography.
CT275.L838H34   973.9'092'4 [B]   76-58905
ISBN 0-395-25349-7

Printed in the United States of America
V   10 9 8 7 6 5 4 3 2 1

The author is grateful for permission to reprint from the following: *Earth Horizon* by Mary Austin, copyright 1932 by Mary Austin, copyright © 1960 by Kenneth M. Chapman and Mary C. Wheelwright. Reprinted by permission of Houghton Mifflin Company. *Indians of the Americas* by John Collier, copyright © 1947, 1975 by John Collier. Reprinted by arrangement with The New American Library, Inc., New York, N.Y. *Music at Midnight* by Muriel Draper, copyright 1926 by Muriel Draper. Reprinted by permission of Harper & Row, Publishers, Inc. *A Victorian in the Modern World* by Hutchins Hapgood, copyright 1939 by Hutchins Hapgood. Reprinted by permission of The Estate of Hutchins Hapgood. *John Reed: The Making of a Revolutionary* by Granville Hicks, copyright 1936 by Granville Hicks. Reprinted by permission of Granville Hicks. *My Young Years* by Arthur Rubinstein, copyright © 1973 by Arthur Rubinstein. Reprinted by permission of Alfred A. Knopf, Inc. *Shadow and Light: The Life, Friends and Opinions of Maurice Sterne* edited by Charlotte Leon Mayerson, copyright 1952, © 1965 by the Estate of Vera Segal Sterne. Reprinted by permission of Harcourt Brace Jovanovich, Inc. *What Is Remembered* by Alice B. Toklas, copyright © 1963 by Alice B. Toklas. Reprinted by permission of Holt, Rinehart and Winston, Publishers. *Fragments*, Volume Two by Carl Van Vechten (New Haven, Yale University Library, 1955), copyright 1955 by Carl Van Vechten. Reprinted by permission of Donald Gallup, Literary Trustee.

Dedicated to
MILTON AND BUNNY CANIFF,
with love

Acknowledgments

Much of the material in this book comes from the Beinecke Rare Book and Manuscript Library, Yale University, especially the papers of Mabel Dodge Luhan. The author wishes to thank the Library staff for having given her access to the papers. She is particularly grateful to Donald Gallup, Curator of American Literature, for his guidance and advice.

Obviously she has drawn heavily, as well, on information given her by her good friend Alice Henderson Rossin, formerly Mabel's daughter-in-law.

Mabel's series of four books called, collectively, *Intimate Memories*, as well as two others, *Lorenzo in Taos* and *Winter in Taos*, supplied the outline. Persons who have been generous with their help include Paul Horgan, Muriel R. Hanson, Stacy May, Henriette Harris, James Parton, Dorothy Brett, Herman Kahn, the late Mrs. Mary Ames and the late Spud Johnson. The author owes thanks, too, to Curtis Harnack, Director of Yaddo, and his wife, Hortense Calisher, also Yaddo itself, where she found peace and space in which to assemble her notes.

Illustrations

Mabel

A Biography of Mabel Dodge Luhan

Chapter One

PEOPLE BORN after the First World War might reasonably ask who on earth she was — Mabel Ganson Evans Dodge Sterne Luhan, to give her all her names. It will help if we consider her as an original who refused to be held back by the conventions of her era. She was married four times, widowed only once, and was divorced twice before divorce was the ordinary experience it is today. A rich woman, for a time she maintained a salon in New York at which she entertained a number of people not customarily found on the guest lists of the rich — labor leaders, revolutionary artists, Bolsheviks, Margaret Sanger. Mabel was one of the first Americans to be psychoanalyzed. But it was her fourth marriage which attracted the most attention, even more attention than did her much-publicized friendship with D. H. Lawrence, for the man she married, and stayed with for the rest of her life, was an American Indian.

It is a general idea that most rebels in the United States come from the broad, boring plains of the Middle West. But Mabel was born much nearer to exciting Manhattan, in Buffalo, New York, the only child of Charles and Sara Cook Ganson. Her grandfathers on both sides were bankers, a fact that was the chief reason for the match, according to Mabel's ex-daughter-in-law, Alice Henderson Rossin.

"Mabel's parents should never have married each other," she said. "They weren't suited, but it seemed such a good thing to combine the banking interests that their parents went ahead and fixed it up anyway. Of course in those days people didn't get divorced, no matter how miserable they were together, so the Gansons stuck it out."

Yet Mabel, born in 1879, told in *Background* that one of the members of her parents' circle actually did break the rule and get a divorce decree. It was such an unusual thing that the woman didn't know how to behave about it: she had no pattern to follow. At last she put on deep mourning, ordered a closed carriage, and drove from house to house, announcing the divorce to her friends and showing them her papers. Of course such conservatism was not peculiar to Buffalo, though Mabel seems to have thought it was: she tended always to look on her native city as a backwater. But the fact was that the Ganson circle would have been stuffy anywhere, being rich and complacent and self-contained. The Ganson bank was based in Buffalo, but Sara's grandfather had created the little town of Bath, a hundred miles away, and the family house was still there. Sara's father, however, had long since built himself a house in New York City, on Seventy-eighth Street and Fifth Avenue, far uptown, across the street from the Metropolitan Museum of Art. It was something of an adventure for Mabel to visit Grandma and Grandpa Cook in New York, and at stated intervals she did so. Buffalo was her home: she lived in Buffalo and went to school there.

"As originally planned by Joseph Ellicott, the plan of Buffalo somewhat resembled that of Washington, but the plan was much altered and then not adhered to," says the *Encyclopaedia Britannica* of 1910.

Buffalo today has broad and spacious streets, most of which are lined by trees, and many small parks and squares. The municipal park system is one of unusual beauty, consisting of a chain of parks with a total area of 1030 acres, encircling the city and connected by boulevards and driveways. The largest is Delaware Park . . . Buffalo is widely known for the beauty of its residential sections, the houses being for the most part detached, set well back from the street, and surrounded by attractive lawns.

The article goes on to give details about the manufacturing industries of the city, but that sort of thing never interested Mabel. Enough to say that she was born on Delaware Avenue in one of those attractive houses set back from the street.

The Erie Canal's western terminus was at Buffalo. As the *Britannica* continues, "In 1832 Buffalo obtained a city charter . . . In that year, and again in 1834, a cholera epidemic caused considerable loss of life . . . Grover Cleveland lived in Buffalo from 1855 until 1884, when he was elected president, and was mayor of Buffalo in 1882, when he was elected governor of New York State." I quote all this to show where Mabel fitted into the time scheme of things. She was five years old when Cleveland was elected President, and it was not really a long time since Indians had been a part of the local scene. There is a monument in the town's Forest Lawn Cemetery to the Seneca chief Red Jacket (1751–1830), who had been friendly to the whites of Buffalo, and, as we shall see, Mabel always had a good opinion of Indians.

Her mother, Sara, was pleasure-loving and vivacious, an exacting, efficient housekeeper, a handsome woman with the dark red hair all the Cook girls possessed. She was exuberantly healthy. Charles, on the other hand, was a highly neurotic man. He had trained for the law but didn't practice it, had been asked by his father to work at the family bank but refused, and now spent his days in an office he rented downtown. Nobody knew how he filled in his time there, though it was rumored that he "wrote." Probably he concentrated on his hobby: the flags of the world. Flags fascinated him, and he became an authority on their patterns, history, and use. Whenever important foreigners visited Buffalo, Charley Ganson hoisted the appropriate banner on his private flagpole that stood on the front lawn: for example, he flew the British flag during a visit paid to the town by Oscar Wilde. Moreover, Ganson designed a private flag for himself, which he flew whenever Sara went to New York to visit her parents, lowering it to half-mast when she returned. Charley was frank about hating his wife; nevertheless he became violently jealous if she showed even the slightest polite interest in another man. Then he made scenes, which she treated with icy contempt — though they scared Mabel to death.

All her life Mabel liked to keep journals, and when, as a woman, she went in for psychoanalysis, she had already covered reams of paper with her memoirs. Her analyst encouraged her to dig deeper, so she wrote and wrote and wrote about her parents, until her resentment filled volume after volume. In the end she published four books of reminiscence, with enough material remaining to fill another fifteen if she had wished to do so. In *Background*, she told how as a small child, even as a baby, she was conscious of the emptiness of the Ganson house, where there was no warmth, no love, nothing for her spirit to feed on. Before she was old enough to find friends outside the family, said Mabel, she was perpetually lonely and bored, yet at the same time terrified that her mother would leave home for good. Not that she loved her mother, but she feared being left alone with her father, whose black moods were awe-inspiring. Possibly the loneliness of her childhood explains why she was so remarkably gregarious in adult life, avoiding as much as possible any kind of solitude.

Once, she remembered, Sara took her to New York for some reason, she did not know why. It was (and is) a long train ride from Buffalo, but at last they arrived, in the evening. Instead of going to her Grandpa Cook's house, they stayed at the Fifth Avenue Hotel, where her mother, evidently by prearrangement, met a number of friends in a holiday mood. Sara put Mabel to bed in a hotel room, told her to be good and go to sleep, and left her. For hours Mabel lay awake, in fear of something she did not understand. Why had her mother gone away? What could she be doing? What shameful secret was she hiding? Mabel would have us believe that she was mysteriously aware of sin, and suspected her mother of adultery, but we must not be too quick to accept this theory of childish instinct. It is more likely that something her father said during one of his many quarrels with her mother implanted the seed in the child's mind. In any case it was a storm in a teacup: Sara was merely attending some blameless family party.

If half Mabel's stories about her father are true, it is no wonder that he became a legend in Buffalo. Often, she said, he decided that he could no longer tolerate life at home, and rushed out of the house to find refuge with his widowed mother, who lived only four blocks away. Grandma Ganson was always delighted to welcome him. Of course he could stay, she said, and sent him up to his old room, but a moment later Charley would descend again, declaring as he prepared to go home that he couldn't live in a room where there was no running water. After several such occurrences, Grandma Ganson decided to surprise him, and had running water with a bath installed on the second floor. The next time her son arrived in his tempestuous way, she sat in her living room chuckling as he ascended the stairs. But down he came, as furious as ever.

"I can't use that thing!" he shouted. "The hot water runs in the cold-water faucet!" And off he went.

Every Sunday, Fred Pratt came to dine with the Gansons. Fred was Charley's oldest friend: they had been at college together and had spent the same year studying in Germany. But one Sunday Fred aroused his host's ever-alert suspicions by talking with what Charley considered too much enthusiasm to Sara. Charley sat with them on the veranda, growing glummer and glummer, until at last he got up and stamped indoors, slamming the door behind him. Sara, who was by nature silent, did not mention this, but went on chatting with Fred, and he too remained unperturbed until Charley reappeared, a stamped, addressed envelope in his hand.

"You will receive a letter in the morning," he told Fred. Then, in full view of his guest, he walked down the street to the mailbox, posted the missive, and returned. Afterward he sat with Sara and Fred on the porch and made conversation pleasantly enough. But in the morning when Fred received the letter he learned from it that he was not to come to the Gansons' house anymore, because, said Charley, he was having too much fun with Sara. Nor did he come, at least for several months.

"That Charley Ganson!" said Buffalo indulgently.

Mabel's stories of her mother fail to carry conviction. She tells of how embarrassed she was one Sunday morning when she found Sara still in bed, surrounded by newspapers and in tears. "I feel so blu-u-ue," Sara quavered. To hear her mother express emotion of any kind flabbergasted the child, who was not used to hearing her talk at all. Nobody in the Cook family was exactly chatty, said Mabel, but Sara was worse than all the others, so stubbornly silent that her father once lost his temper and beat her for it. So often does Mabel tell us how coldly repellent Sara was that it comes as a shock to hear from Mrs. Rossin that this same woman was adored by her grandson and great-grandchildren as a charming old lady, always ready to laugh and take part in family expeditions.

As the years went by, Mabel lost her emotional dependency on these unsatisfying parents and collected around her a group of friends her own age. One of her many diaries has survived in the possession of her favorite friend, Mary Forman, who later married Conger Goodyear and later still became Mrs. Ames.

"*Written only for Mary Forman*" is scrawled across the top of the front page. "*And not for anyone else. M. Ganson — June 21 — —94. Richfield Springs.*"

She was fourteen years old, going on fifteen. Her parents had decided to try the waters at the little spa, and Mabel was reluctant to accompany them. Spas, she wrote, were all the same — dull, dull, dull — but that summer, at least, she seems to have found it all engrossing enough. Her first entry gives a good picture of what life was like for privileged Americans in the early nineties. They traveled in force: "Mama, Papa, three maids, two dogs, one parrot and ten satchels, three trunks etc." They had taken a house to live in, and when Mabel's pony Cupid had been brought to join the party and she had acquired a kitten, she felt well settled. Cupid was very important in Mabel's life: she had a pony-trap to drive him in, and she used to take her friends all over Buffalo in that fashion, a Yorkshire terrier sitting on the pony's back. She went on much the same at Richfield Springs. People looked with disfavor on the girl because she drove so recklessly fast, but she seems never to have had an accident.

The diary prattles about Bob, the boy she was interested in: it is really a long letter to Mary, her confidante at the time. But there were other interests than Bob:

This morning took a drive with Mamma and went and saw Dr. Ransom . . . Gave me something for my skin and told me about the sulphur baths. They have swimming baths, too, with a swimming master, and I am going in swimming every day. I have to get up early and go to the Hotel and take a glass of cold sulphur water ¾ths of an hour before breakfast, and some other things.

This afternoon Agnes & I went to "Chas. Lee's Great London Show"!!!! and had the gayest time!!! Never saw anything so "country" in my life.

On June 25 she went out for a "bum" with a friend, Lizzie.

First we went to the Hotel, for the night we first came we both had caught sight of a mighty handsome young clerk in the office . . . Then we went into the parlor and fussed around. And then came back through the office he *smiled* at us when we went through and we smiled back. Exciting ! ! ! ! ! . . . I will try and describe the clerk, and then will find out his name and tell you.

He must be about 24. Has straight dark brown hair parted in the middle. Enormous BLUE eyes rather deep set in his head. A clear skin. Lot of tanned and pink. *And* such a mouth! . . . His profile is EXACTLY like that picture in Sherlock Holmes . . .

There are inserts, souvenirs of games and parties: one record of "Consequences," badly creased, and a few dance programs — "March, Lancers, Two Step, Paul Jones, and the Boston Post." She mentions tennis, croquet, cards, and a lot of driving. She was fond of Huyler's candy. All in all, the girl obviously was not bored, and in spite of everything she was to say later, she seems to have got on well with Mama at that time. She must have forgotten how amiable Sara was when it came to writing her memoirs years later.

In Buffalo Mabel attended the school for girls that was approved by "everybody" — that is, the women of Mrs. Ganson's circle. It was a day school, which left her free for such social life as was permitted to girls her age. The young people in the neighborhood had their parties, attended by ever-shifting groups, and for a long time Mabel was passionately, if blamelessly, in love with Bob Rumsey, who was for the most part uninterested in her because he was enamored of Mary Forman. No hearts were broken in this blameless game, though for a few days Mabel was blissful because Conger Goodyear was able to report that Bob had put her name first on his list of the girls he liked. What rapture! Even though she knew that her honored position was merely temporary, she was happy.

She seems to have enjoyed a considerable amount of freedom, though it was no more than that possessed by her contemporaries. Inevitably there were clashes now and then with her father, who trusted nobody, least of all his daughter: when she was only six or seven he had warned her against playing kissing games at parties, and his sense of proper decorum made him ever more watchful once she was older. But Mabel sloughed this off without worrying. What was more serious was that Sara must have complained about her to Grandma Cook in New York.

That redoubtable lady was not easily ignored: she always knew exactly what her daughters should do, and her daughters paid attention to her lectures. She spent every morning, without fail, at her desk, writing to the three of her four daughters who lived away from home, in Auburn, Bath, and Buffalo. (Georgie, the fourth and favorite, had brought her husband home and lived with her parents on Seventy-eighth Street.) Grandma Cook's letters were filled with painstaking advice on many subjects — housekeeping, husband management, and the rearing of children. In all these matters her daughters seem to have obeyed her implicitly: at any rate, Sara did. Unfortunately, Grandma Cook did not like Mabel, and Mabel returned the compliment: she said Grandma was mean, cross, and domineering.

When Mabel was sixteen her grandmother decided that she

should go to boarding school because, as she wrote to Sara, the child was very strong willed and needed discipline. Sara was going to have trouble with Mabel if she wasn't careful, added Grandma Cook; she had a queer look in her eyes.

Sara always heeded her mother, and Mabel was speedily entered as a student at Miss Graham's Young Ladies' Boarding School in Manhattan. All the Cook girls had attended Miss Graham's school in their youth, mainly because Miss Graham had herself been at school with Grandma Cook. As was to be expected, Mabel hated it. She complained that the place was stuffy, and it probably was, especially for a girl who had hitherto spent most of her time out of doors in Buffalo's fresh air. All her schoolmates were boring, said Mabel, until at last her attention was caught by a girl named Mary Shillito. The others thought Mary odd, and laughed at her. She was appallingly shy and nervous, given to eating her nails down to the quick, and she could hardly speak English. She had been brought up in Paris, where her father, who with his wife came from Cincinnati, represented some large commercial firm. There was another Shillito girl, slightly older than Mary, who had been placed in another select young ladies' boarding school across town; this girl, Violet, and her sister had been deliberately separated so that they would learn English faster. It was for this reason, to learn English, that they were spending an academic year in exile in America, but the separation, said Mabel, was cruel, for the sisters were very dependent on each other. At least Mary depended on Violet. She never stopped talking about her.

The strangeness of Mary's situation attracted Mabel, as anything out of the ordinary always did. Europe, a French accent, and all the rest were irresistible, and she went out of her way to cultivate Mary Shillito. They had long talks, mostly about Violet, whom Mary was permitted to meet now and then on weekends. Violet too hated her school, said Mary, but she was philosophical about it, as she was about most things. She counseled Mary that one must accept everything; that there is always a reason even though it might not be obvious at the time. The Shillito girls, Mary explained, led a secluded life at home, with their governess and their own suite of rooms in their parents' apartment, quite apart from the rest of the household. Their parents? Mary dismissed them scornfully, saying that her mother was a cow and her father a pig. They had not the least idea, for example, what a jewel they had there in Violet, who was like nobody else in the world . . .

Mary, homesick and lonely, talked on and on, and Mabel listened in fascination. In fact, she became so wrapped up in the Shillito saga that it was with mixed feelings that she heard at last from her mother: since she was so unhappy at Miss Graham's, she would be permitted to stay at home after the Christmas holidays. It was wonderful news, of course, but — it meant losing touch, Mabel feared, with Mary and the fascinating world she represented. No, said Mary reassuringly, they would correspond. Why shouldn't Mabel persuade her mother to bring her over to Europe in the summer, to hear the Wagner at Bayreuth as the Shillitos were going to do? They were to be thus rewarded, said Mary, for having been good girls and learned English.

Mabel got to work immediately on Sara, and found it remarkably easy to persuade her. Sara was pleasure-loving and always ready for a jaunt: only Mabel's youth, one feels, had hitherto restrained her desire to travel abroad. The older Cooks had been to Europe more than once and had bought dozens of pretty things — paintings, vases, marbles, and even a husband for their lovely daughter Georgie, named Carlos de Herédia. Mabel had always thought Uncle Carlos a romantic if pitiable figure, dangling around the New York house with nothing to do, no way to pass the time. Her grandparents, she knew, thought little of Carlos, but Georgie had wanted him, so they let her have him. Apart from that, Europe seemed a good place to the Cooks, a place that people in their walk of life almost had to visit from time to time. In such a spirit the American Mrs. Leonard Jerome had taken her three beautiful daughters to France and England, and married off Jennie to Lord Randolph Churchill. The Cooks had a connection of sorts with the Jeromes. One of Jennie's cousins, Eva Thompson, was married to a lawyer in Grandpa Cook's bank, and often came to stay with the Gansons. Having assured herself of Grandma Cook's approval, Sara readily consented to take Mabel to Paris and Bayreuth.

In Paris, mother and daughter went to the Hôtel Meurice, because the Cooks always stayed there. Mary Shillito came over the next day right after breakfast to pick up Mabel and take her home. Mabel was surprised at the change in the girl, who was not at all the nervous, uncertain young creature she had been at Miss Graham's: she was poised, self-confident, and inclined to be patronizing to her old friend. Of course she was no longer dressed in the ugly school uniform of New York. Her simple, elegant clothes made Mabel conscious that her own costume was completely

without charm. The two girls set out in the Shillitos' open carriage, its fat black horses driven by a coachman in livery. If Mabel
looked around and noticed Paris as they went, she has not mentioned it. Her whole attention was on the approaching meeting, so
long deferred, with the wonderful Violet. They went straight up to
the sisters' suite in an elevator, and it seemed to Mabel as they
rose that Mary too was excited, trembling a little in anticipation of
the great moment of meeting. She herself may possibly have felt a
little breathless.

The elevator stopped, and there was Violet at last. Was Mabel a
little disappointed at first? Surely nobody could have lived up to
the advance description Mary had given of her sister, and Violet
seems not to have made much of an impression just then. As
Mabel put it, Violet came gradually into one's perceptions, opening
slowly like a flower that reveals its beauty only bit by bit.

In her diary, Mabel went into immense detail describing this
new friend. She had had practice: she often listed a person's attri-
butes, as in this description of a girl at Richfield Springs.

> Name. Alice Howe.
> Age — 15 yrs. Goes to N.Y. often.
> Size — small.
> no. of sisters — 4.
> She's the oldest.
> Youngest — 8 yrs.
> Color eyes, grey blue.
> Beautiful complexion.
> Bad nose.
> Large mouth.
> Tannish brown straight hair in one braid.
> Small hands & feet.
> Dresses to her ankles.
> In winter lives in Summit, New Jersey.
> She was quite nice on the whole . . .

She gave Violet the same treatment. At first glance Mary's sister
seemed all brown and dusky, a "red-brown" girl with a flat, slender
body that swayed backward a little. Hair soft and dark, done in a
knot on top of her head. Eyes red-brown, slanted up a little at
corners. Mouth drawn over slightly projecting teeth (which were
not, however, as bad as Mary's). Nose sensitive, small and high-

bridged and delicately pointed. "Delicious" hands. Violet, said Mabel, completely understood everyone and forgave them. She knew everything intuitively, yet had a very unusual intelligence, teaching herself Italian so that she could read Dante at sixteen, learning Greek so that she could read Plato and the dramatists, and studying higher mathematics at the Sorbonne "for the beauty." If this studious tabulation does not give us an all-together idea of Violet's quality, it is not the fault of her friend and admirer. Mabel loved Violet, and — she says — knew she would love her forever because of her "genius." Violet, in turn, loved Mabel and knew her thoroughly — at least, so Mabel believed — with a knowledge that accepted everything that was to come. Violet knew, for example, that Mabel would leave her without a pang when the time came; Mabel would drop her if it suited her. She understood Mabel's nature and loved her anyway.

Well, perhaps. Mabel loved to find deep, inner meanings that would probably have surprised her companions if they had heard of them, but this is the first clear mention in *Background* of her lesbianism, though earlier in the book she goes into considerable detail, scandalizing her readers, about what might be called a breast complex or fetishism.

Under the influence of the Shillito girls Mabel read French authors — Alfred de Musset, George Sand, Sainte-Beuve, Flaubert, De Vigny — for the first time. Violet played on their little piano — Chopin, Beethoven. Mary would weep when Violet played Beethoven. Through her new friend Mabel learned something of the Greek classics and then a few of the moderns, but, as she wisely noted of this instant education, "the great lack was humor."

In due course Mabel was presented to the elder Shillitos, who, as Mary said, did not know what they had in their house in the person of Violet. While not exactly a cow, as Mary described her, Mrs. Shillito was lazy, and her husband, thought Mabel, was really dreadful — small and fat, with a piglike profile and a habit of complaining querulously all through his meals. One had to be careful not to let him know what erudite subjects Violet was studying at the Sorbonne, as he would have been alarmed (he was extremely conventional). For example, the Shillito parents had forbidden their daughters to have anything to do with an acquaintance who lived on her own upstairs, a young woman who wrote and published poetry. The Shillito girls had played with this girl, Pauline, when they were all children together. But Pauline, because she lived alone, was no longer *comme il faut,* said Mr. Shillito, and that was that. Sometimes, however, Violet crept upstairs and visited her for a few stolen minutes.

Looking back, Mabel marveled at the way the Shillito family lived in separation. The girls were thought of by their parents as good docile young creatures, not too beautiful but with a certain Parisian elegance. Their father paid for their governesses, their concerts and opera tickets and books and photographs, then left them to themselves while he and his wife lived their own lives in the larger rooms of the apartment. It was the way *jeunes filles* were brought up in those days, commented Mabel.

After talking and speculating for hours on the habits of the demimonde and Mr. Shillito's no doubt bad morals, the girls resolved to see something of the night life of Paris for themselves. Mary and Violet told their parents that they were to dine with the Gansons and see a play, while Mabel told Sara the same story in reverse. Then the three of them drove to the Café de la Paix, hired a private room upstairs, and ordered dinner with a bottle of wine. They went on to the Comédie Française, where they hired a *baignoire* — a box enclosed by a grille — and watched the play. Nobody caught them out in this wickedness.

While Mabel was absorbed by the Shillito girls, her mother kept herself amused. Her brother-in-law Carlos had a sister in Paris, Rosita de la Barre, who was always ready to take her rich kinswoman shopping, and there were other compatriots with whom she could lunch and dine. Sara, in a genial mood, readily consented when Mrs. Shillito asked if Mabel could visit them at the Château Pierrefonds, in the country, before they all went on to Bayreuth.

The girls were lodged in a little stone farmhouse connected with the chateau but not actually a part of it. Mary occupied the dressing room, and Mabel and Violet shared a bed in the other room, where, as might be expected, something of an amorous nature took place — not much, but Mabel never forgot it. She reached out and cupped Violet's left breast with her hand. "I love you," murmured Violet, and Mabel whispered in reply, "And I love you." All night they lay like that.

How often this love passage was repeated we are not told. They all went to Bayreuth — where Violet interpreted the symbolism of

Wagner's operas to the other girls — and then everything was over, at least as far as Mabel was concerned. The Shillitos returned to Paris, but Sara Ganson insisted on a sojourn at a spa to rejuvenate her health, and Mabel had to go along. She was very unhappy. She missed the Shillito girls, and there was nothing to do at the baths — nothing, that is, but drink the nasty waters when Sara noticed pimples on her face. Any hope she might have entertained of a farewell visit to Paris was soon dissipated, for Sara decreed that they were to go straight back to Buffalo. How Mabel hated her mother for that!

Back home, her parents decided that their daughter, now seventeen, had time for one last year's schooling before her debut. For the finishing process they decided on another boarding establishment, this time at Chevy Chase, Maryland. There, if we are to believe Mabel, she amused herself by influencing the music teacher, who was hesitating between studying her art further in Munich or marrying an insistent suitor who seemed admirably eligible. Mabel plumped for music rather than domestic bliss, and argued for it so passionately that the nitwit teacher submitted. One night she rushed into the girl's room and fell on her knees by the bed, where she burst into tears.

"I have sent him away," she sobbed. "It hurts so!"

At these words, says Mabel, she felt a thrill of delight, though she did not know why. The story is outrageous enough to be true, but even if it isn't, the fact that she told it, like the dreams the analysand makes up on the couch, is a significant guide to her character. There can be no doubt in the mind of anyone who follows her career that Mabel enjoyed the kind of power that comes from meddling in other people's emotional lives.

She found another sort of power after she left Chevy Chase to live at home. She was a pretty girl and men admired her. She discovered that she was able to upset them to her heart's content. For some reason she seemed to attract older men rather than the boys with whom she had grown up, but the man who claimed most of her attention was the downright ineligible, because married, Seward Cary.

One of her early childhood memories was the sight of her next-door neighbor Emily Scatchard, dressed in white with a bridal veil, going off to church to be married to Seward, but she was seventeen or eighteen when she first really noticed him. He was passionately addicted to horses, which he broke and trained to draw carriages. He loved the danger of the pastime, and sometimes took his small daughters with him on his adventures, making them climb around behind and on top of the trotting animals. His recklessness attracted Mabel, and she joined him in mad escapades, helping him break "green" horses and trying them out. She even cut her hair short to look as much as possible like Cary, this at a time when no other girl would have dared to wear such a fashion. Nobody ever suspected her of wrongdoing with Seward, she said, least of all his wife, Emily, and the world was right in its lack of suspicion. She was perfectly safe with him. Their friendship was not tainted with sex, possibly because she was not "ready" for it, and turned away from his infrequent, halfhearted passes. One wonders, however, what the terrible-tempered Charley Ganson had to say about it all.

Then her eighteenth birthday approached, and with it her debut, the coming-out ball that was de rigueur for any girl of her class. Tremendous preparations were necessary. The Gansons invited Violet Shillito for the occasion — she and Mary were fortunately in Cincinnati, undergoing their own debut — and Violet came and stayed. Mabel, however, was too busy going to parties and dating and all that to pay much attention to Violet, and this lapse haunted her conscience later. All the girls of her set in Buffalo came out in the same place, a club on Delaware Avenue. Mabel was not daring enough to object to the club, but she made up her mind to do something original, at any rate: she would have a new kind of background for the old ballroom. Her former art teacher, Miss Rose Clark, agreed to do the decoration and create a "baronial" effect. This was achieved with phony family portraits painted in the style of Rembrandt and Velázquez and framed in black. Banners and coats of arms enclosed the lights. Carpenters made the furniture, old-looking settees and chairs and tables, equally black to match the hanging picture frames. The attendants were dressed in medieval costumes. It was certainly an original decor, the most "artistic" setting it had ever been her doom to adorn, wrote Mabel scornfully, obviously forgetting the Villa Curonia she later occupied for some years in Fiesole.

Rosita de la Barre had Mabel's dress made in Paris. A photograph of the debutante wearing it serves as the frontispiece for *Background* — Mabel in white satin with a small waist, as she herself describes it, with billowing folds of white net covered with hyacinth petals and dewdrops, and in her hair a couple of tall hyacinth flowers. What she does not describe is the round face, surprisingly pretty with its arched dark brows and half-smile.

The ball lasted well into the small hours, until Charley Ganson lost patience and stamped out to the middle of the floor and hissed at the musicians in their balcony. Taking the hint, they broke into "Home, Sweet Home," and the guests laughed and clapped and then went home. Good old Charley Ganson, what a character he was!

Sara and Mabel drove up the street the short distance to their house.

"Well, that's over with," sighed Sara, sailing into her room and leaving her daughter to mount one more flight of stairs.

Chapter Two

IT IS NOT CLEAR why Mabel waited two years after her debut to marry, but perhaps in Buffalo a debutante didn't have to flaunt an engagement ring during her first year after coming out. At any rate, Miss Ganson seemed quite unperturbed about her single status, and went on enjoying herself in her usual manner. The story of how she finally came to be married at the advanced age of twenty-one is hard to swallow, but anything is possible, and perhaps it happened just as she told it in *European Experiences*.

Though Karl Evans was not the boy next door, his family lived quite close to the Gansons' house. His father was president of the Anchor Line Steamboat Company, which had offices down on the waterfront. Mr. Evans Senior tried to put all his sons — he had a lot of children — into the firm, and Karl, the youngest, had a nominal position there which suited him as well as any. He neglected his duties a good deal of the time, however. What he liked was the active outdoors life, hunting and boating and driving. All his acquaintances seem to have accepted the obvious fact that he would never be a serious money-grubber — it was just one of those things. Buffalo looked on him as a charming ne'er-do-well, and liked him in spite of it. Mabel said he had a "rugged" face, a long upper lip, and a crooked smile.

He found Mabel attractive because she shared his tastes. He called her "Peg," and told her how impressed he had been by the sight of her breaking horses with Seward Cary. Peg and he would make a good pair, he said, and Mabel placidly agreed with him, concealing her conviction that it wasn't as simple as that. She did like horses and speedboats and dogs and such, but she also loved reading and art — "strange, beautiful things for houses," as she put it. He seemed amusing to her, she recollected, rather like a nice dog. The only interesting thing about Karl, in her opinion, was that he had spent months in the Indian Territory and had been taken in by the Indians and treated as one of themselves. Mabel liked him when he dressed up in Indian buckskins; they suited his dark skin and white teeth.

This was all very well, but in spite of his lighthearted courting of Mabel, Karl was engaged to another girl in Buffalo, a beautiful blonde named Elsie. Her father, while sharing with his contemporaries a low opinion of Karl's abilities, had indicated a willingness to let Elsie marry him, even though it probably meant that he would have to support his son-in-law. But now that he knew Mabel, Karl didn't love Elsie anymore. He told Mabel this, and said it was awkward, since Elsie was really serious about the engagement.

As it happened, he could not have hit on a better method to interest the new object of his affections. In her memoirs, Mabel admitted that she never felt the validity of anybody else's claims on what she might want, so the fact that Karl was engaged to another girl enhanced his desirability for her.

One evening, knowing that Karl was at Elsie's house, she telephoned and summoned him and he came over immediately, running from the house to meet her at the Gansons' front gate. He told her that Elsie had tried to stop his leaving. She stood across the stairs, but he pushed her out of the way so hard that she fell down and began to cry.

"I want you," said Mabel in reply — not out of love, she explains, but merely from a desire to prove her power. When Karl immediately suggested that they become engaged, she consented — to keep him from Elsie.

Charley made a scene when she got home that night. No daughter of his, he said, was going to run around with the no-good Evans boy. Mabel answered defiantly that she would run around with Karl as much as she liked because she was engaged to him. Her father would probably have worked himself up to a heart attack if she had not seen her mother's warning gesture and obeyed it, getting out of the room in haste. She went to bed delightfully intoxicated by her new sense of power — and in the matter of Karl, that was as far as she intended to go. An engagement is one thing; marriage is quite another. For the moment she found it pleasant enough to go on seeing Karl in secret, since her father had forbidden it, but Karl had other ideas.

One day he suggested that Mabel and one of her friends, Charlotte, go with him on a little jaunt through the countryside in a trolley car. Karl had a good friend, an older man named Jack Piper, who, when Karl was a little boy, had taught him to shoot, and who was now, by courtesy of Mr. Evans, the motorman-cum-conductor of the only car on a trolley line that ran between two villages in Niagara County, near the Evanses' country house. The villages were only two miles apart. At one of them, Lewiston, was a little church that Karl assured Mabel was awfully pretty and well worth seeing. As for Jack Piper, he was wonderful, said Karl. He always carried his rifle with him, and stopped the trolley to blaze away if he saw any game crossing the tracks. It sounded amusing, so Mabel fixed it up with Charlotte, and the two girls met Karl one Sunday morning and went by train to the end of the trolley line. They were introduced to Piper, a tall, weatherbeaten, saturnine man, and the jaunt began. Laughing and chatting, the three young people, the car's only passengers on the way to Lewiston, filled in the time — though Jack Piper saw no game — until the car halted at the other end of the line. Up on the hill was the church, and they could hear the bell ringing and see people coming out. The service was evidently over, and the members of the congregation started down to the car on their way home.

"Come on, Peg," said Karl. There would be just time enough to see the church and yet catch the homeward trip, he explained, so they hurried. Into the church they went and up to the chancel rails — and there, still in his robes, stood the minister with a book in his hand.

"Good morning, Mr. Evans," he said. "Is this the young lady?"

The next thing Mabel knew, she was kneeling by the side of the kneeling Karl being married, with Jack Piper standing behind her to keep her from running away if she had tried and Charlotte bursting with excitement. Evidently Karl had already acquired the necessary license. Mabel protests that she didn't really want to be married, but what was she to do? She was scared into it, she implies. Jack Piper looked very fierce . . . That is the way she tells it, and it may be true. She didn't go in for tears or recriminations afterward: they ran downhill, laughing, and got into the car and chuffed back along the rails to Buffalo. Mabel was a bride.

It was probably fear, pure and simple, that kept the young people from telling their elders the secret right away, but they did not leave the marriage dormant. Married people have houses, so Mabel started looking for a suitable house. One day she saw a tiny white house with an amusing peaked roof. Karl liked it too, and rented it. Then Mabel sold a ring and with the money bought some simple furniture and a lot of paint, and she set to work decorating. In a puzzling passage, she says that everyone who came to see them during the following fortnight laughed at her work, because nobody in Buffalo had ever before painted chairs and tables with such bright colors. It is puzzling because we are not told why, if the marriage was supposed to be such a secret, their friends dropped in to see Mabel painting the furniture? However, she insisted in *European Experiences* that her parents had no idea of her marriage — and, again, it may be true. Nevertheless, one of these days, she and Karl agreed, they would have to confess. His parents offered no real threat. They would be only too glad that one of the brood had left the house. But the Gansons were a different matter, and neither Karl nor Mabel wanted to face them. Then Karl had an idea: Dr. John Parmenter. He was a very wise, kind man, said Karl, and had always been the Evanses' family physician and friend. He would think of something, never fear. So they telephoned him and met him at Charlotte's.

Mabel was favorably impressed by Dr. John, a big, blue-eyed man who looked healthy yet sensitive. The young Evanses told him the facts and asked him to communicate them to the Gansons, smoothing things over with Sara if he possibly could. He was ready and willing to do it, though he scolded Mabel. Couldn't she see that her mother would be very hurt by her lack of confidence? Yes, he would tell Mrs. Ganson, but the children must stand by and be ready to face her after he had broken the news. That evening after dinner, Dr. Parmenter dropped in on Sara Ganson — we are not told where Charley was, but he was absent — and when he gave the signal, Karl and Mabel appeared. Dr. John had done his work well. Mabel's mother cried a bit, but was ready to make the best of things. Only Mabel would have to be married again, at Trinity Church, she said firmly, otherwise nobody would believe the girl was really married.

She had her way, and Mabel was well and truly wedded, all over again, by *three* church dignitaries: Grandma Ganson's minister, Sara's High Church priest, and the Bishop of New York State. Mabel wore ivory satin and had six bridesmaids. Her Grandfather

Cook came all the way from New York to give her away because Charley Ganson was suffering from a bad case of gout and had to stay in bed — it was possibly a diplomatic illness. Nevertheless, nobody in Buffalo could possibly have doubted any longer that Mabel was indeed married. None of the three weddings that followed was so firmly and repeatedly sealed.

Soon after her first, dubious marriage the bride experienced orgasm, which took her completely by surprise. In spite of her various experiments with sex, she had never heard of it, and she wrote of it as a transformation that felt like silent, fiery fountains falling on black velvet — not at all a bad description. She admitted, however, that she did not include Karl in these feelings. It was as if it had happened to her alone. Karl did not matter; he was just a casual stranger who lit the fires within her and then passed by.

Then fate overtook her. She was pregnant and she felt dreadful. Dr. John was summoned. He found her listless, and declared that she shouldn't live in the little house any longer because it was damp. Mrs. Ganson found another house on Delaware Avenue, and while it was being prepared the young couple lived with Grandma Ganson. Soon Mabel's condition gave cause for increased alarm. She was showing unmistakable signs, said the doctor, of a miscarriage, and he called in a specialist to help it along.

Mabel thoroughly enjoyed her convalescence, which was comfortably lazy and, of course, very long, for in those days women were kept in bed — at least women whose parents were as rich as Mabel's — for weeks and weeks after female troubles like hers. She was in no hurry to get up.

Dr. Parmenter called every day, and she received him wearing red camellias in her hair. She remained in bed, spoiled but flourishing, until the new house was ready and she and Karl could move into it.

The account now skips an undefined period of time until she was again pregnant. One supposes this development did not take place too soon after her first venture, but through it all her attitude was quite different, no doubt because she was in better health from beginning to end. All through the months of gestation she was as lazy as could be, and later she looked back with regret on those endless days of pure well-being. Sometimes she sewed but oftener she just sat, luxuriously sniffing the aroma of some pansies she had in a pot close by, and otherwise doing nothing. Karl had acquired a red Packard, the first automobile in Buffalo, and now and then when he came home from the Anchor Line office she would consent to be driven out to take the air, but she didn't really like the horseless carriage. She preferred her room, and grew quite lyrical writing about her time of waiting.

Perhaps, she said, those were such happy days because she was, for the first and only time in her life, *contributing* to the earth. She was doing what was most wanted of her — wanted, that is, by nature. All the rest of life, the passion and storm and beauty and pleasure and pain, matters not a bit to nature, who wants only reproduction. That was what Dr. Parmenter had said, commented Mabel. Nothing so dramatizes the fact that her pregnancy took place more than seventy years ago than those few pages. Mabel actually argued that, though it might sound like a long indulgence in laziness, hers was the way to make a good baby. John, she said triumphantly, weighed thirteen pounds at birth and looked three months old. Strangely, she seems not to have attributed to the baby's size the fact that she had a very difficult birth, and needed more than one remedial operation afterward, but — perhaps significantly — John was the only baby she ever had.

When, going into labor, she told Parmenter she was scared, he naturally laughed at her, saying that she was going to have a fine party. It was not a fine party. Little by little the pains became worse until she was in agony — an "outrageous" pain, she said, and the doctor hurried to give her chloroform.

When it was over and she woke up, she was overwhelmed with sadness, though she didn't know why. In vain did the doctor congratulate her on her thirteen-pound boy; Mabel didn't want to look at the child. And when Karl carried the baby in, joyfully saying that he was a wonder, and put him down next to her on the bed, all she could think was, I don't like it, by which she meant not little John particularly, but the whole system. Inwardly she was weeping. For days she lay there and refused to take an interest in anything. She had no milk, and John was put on a bottle, but he thrived on it. He thrived on everything. He was full of vitality, but his mother had none. At last she got over actively disliking him, but even then she didn't feel any love for him, and she felt sorry for him because of it.

What Mabel did not tell her readers was that she had fallen in love with Dr. Parmenter and he with her, which probably explains her mixed-up maternal reactions.

A year passed, and one day Mabel had an operation that she needed as a result of John's difficult birth. Ten days later she was lying in bed feeling sorry for herself, and expecting to be there at least another four days or so, when Dr. Parmenter arrived early in the morning with bad news. Karl had been duck-hunting with a companion at dawn, and the other man had accidentally shot him in the back. He lay seriously ill in the hospital, asking to see her. She must get up and walk, the doctor told her, no matter how ill and weak she felt.

"Somehow," she said dramatically, they managed to dress her, and then, because her feet were all pins and needles, Dr. Parmenter carried her downstairs to the waiting car. She got to the hospital in time, but only just. Karl spoke to her, saying it wasn't his friend's fault, and then he died. Charley Ganson, in the meantime, had also died, so now she and her mother were both widows, Mabel wrote. John was nearly a year old and she was about twenty-two, she added. The word "about" in this context is characteristic: Mabel was always imprecise about dates, and she was even less precise at this point. For a year or two, she said vaguely, life went on on Delaware Avenue, but then she had a nervous breakdown. Sara sent her to Europe "for a change," along with John and two nurses, one for him and one for her. In fact, it was quite a bit later when they sailed — 1904, when Mabel was twenty-five. She says that she set out rather sadly, without interest in anything.

Why not? Why the tragedy? We might well ask, because Mabel often said that she and Karl were not suited. She implied, if she didn't say outright, that she never loved him. She mentioned that he had stayed away from the house, following his own pursuits, and she certainly gave the impression that this did not distress her unduly. After all, according to her, he had tricked her into marriage in the first place, so why all this grief over his death?

The answer is that Mabel had compunctions about telling the full story. When she set out to publish her memoirs — not to write them; she had been happily and uninhibitedly writing them for years — she resolved to spare certain persons who figured largely in the original version, especially those who were still alive and would certainly be embarrassed by her revelations. However, having made up her mind to follow this praiseworthy program, her methods left much to be desired. Her editing was hasty. She wielded the blue pencil like a butcher's cleaver, so that yawning gaps have been left in the material. At this point in the narrative, for example, she erased all mention of the Parmenters, and if one doesn't know the true story the effect is mystifying. We have no way of knowing that Mabel and John Parmenter had a passionate love affair. We see only that a year and a half elapsed, inexplicably empty of any incident whatever, and that the time ended with that nervous breakdown she mentions.

The facts were, of course, otherwise. Mabel and John were in love, and Mabel was reckless about taking what she wanted. After all, as she herself said, she had absolutely no compunctions about people's claims on each other, a generalization that applied to Dr. John's wife, among others. The affair scandalized Buffalo, until in the end Mrs. Parmenter threatened to drag it into the open by taking it to the divorce court, upon which the lovers began to see reason. Such a case would, of course, ruin the doctor, and Mabel reluctantly agreed to give him up. Sara Ganson did what any mother of her financial standing would have done: she packed up her daughter and the child and sent them out of the country, presumably to stay away until the scandal blew over.

Of all this Mabel has said nothing, but there is no doubt that she was very unhappy.

Aboard ship, she moped. She would lie all day on a chaise longue on deck, tired out, she said, though we might call it sulking, while John, two and a half, trotted around making friends. With the two nurses in attendance, he took all his meals in the salon, but his mother ate from trays, always on deck. It was July and the weather was beautiful, but she was too depressed to make the effort to move about. However, on the last night before the ship's arrival at Le Havre, she was bored enough to consent to dine with the other passengers. She didn't put it that way: she said that her nurse had begged her to do so, as it was such fun, and she went to please the woman, wearing a white China silk dress. At this period Mabel always wore white, her dresses invariably made in the same style. It wasn't a fashionable style, but she thought it suited her: a full skirt, a belted waist, and the neck cut round.

Reports say that she was very pretty at that time, in an unconventional way.

There was a stranger at the table she shared with the nurses, a young man who seemed pleased by her appearance. She liked him, too. He had a good face, she thought, with an open brow and kind blue eyes. After dinner they sat together on the deck, chatting. His name was Edwin Dodge. He was an architect from Boston, and was on his way to revisit Paris, where he had studied architecture at the École des Beaux-Arts. Mabel enjoyed talking about houses, and they got on very pleasantly together.

She assumed that she had seen the last of him when the ship docked in the morning, that being the way of most shipboard acquaintance. Mary Shillito and her father were there to meet her at Le Havre. Both Violet and Mrs. Shillito were dead — Mabel does not go into details about these events — and what with her friends condoling with Mabel on the loss of Karl, and Mabel condoling with them on their double bereavement, Edwin Dodge was lost in the shuffle. From the corner of her eye Mabel saw him lift his hat politely and depart; then she was being organized by the Shillitos, who took her with her party to Paris where she had rooms — at the Meurice, of course.

The next morning Mabel woke up full of energy and went out and bought herself a hat and cape, which she described in full detail years later. The hat, she said, was broad-brimmed, black, and transparent, with two black ostrich feathers drooping over the brim in back; it went admirably with her white silk dress, especially after she found the little short cape of changeable taffeta. As any woman would, she put on these things in the shop, and was so bedecked when she ran into Edwin Dodge at the very door of the Meurice — for it seemed that he was staying there too.

Their chat was interrupted by Mary Shillito, who had come to lunch; she looked surprised and disapproving that her old friend had made a new friend so soon.

Tearfully, over their luncheon, Mary told Mabel some details of Violet's death. Violet had joined the Catholic church during her last days — as had Mary after her — under the influence of a great friend, Marcelle Senard, of a wine-growing family in Burgundy, whom she had met at the Sorbonne. Marcelle was an amazing girl, said Mary enthusiastically, as strong-minded as a man, brilliant, and beautiful. She had loved Violet so dearly that she had devoted all her time, her very life, to easing the patient's sufferings, and now she was impatient to meet Mabel because Violet had talked of her so much. Indeed, said Mary, Violet had *bequeathed* Mabel to her friend, begging her to take care of Mabel when she returned to France.

Now Mabel was here and Marcelle, who had been alerted, awaited her impatiently at the family chateau down in Burgundy.

"You must go now," declared Mary. The thought crossed Mabel's mind that her once timid, neurotic friend had certainly gained a measure of authority since Violet's death, now that she alone was responsible for the care of her sorrowing father. Mabel was not sure that the change was all that convenient for herself. Did she really want to rush off to some unknown family in Burgundy before she'd had a chance to enjoy herself in Paris? But Mary was talking, saying that she would come along, except that she had to accompany her father to the country for a bit. Never mind, she would follow soon and join the party in Burgundy. Mabel would not need the nurses, she said, she must get rid of them. Marcelle would take care of everything once they got to the chateau.

Mabel did not say yes or no. Then Mary changed the subject and asked about the man she had seen with Mabel. She warned her friend: Mabel was too young, she said, to pick up strange men. Again Mabel was noncommittal, but that evening she went out to dinner with Edwin and had a delightful time.

But when he suggested a repeat for the following evening, she had to tell him, however regretfully, that she was already engaged. She had asked the Shillitos to dine with her. Dodge was downcast. He implored her to put off the Shillitos — surely she could plead a headache or something? After due consideration, Mabel thought she could. After all, it would be lovely to go somewhere with Edwin and dine out of doors. She wrote to Mary regretting her indisposition, and that evening she and Edwin went up the Seine to dine at the loveliest imaginable little white pavilion. Unfortunately, as they entered and looked around for a table, she found herself staring straight into the affronted faces of Mary and Mr. Shillito.

There was nothing to do, simply nothing. Mabel bowed slightly to them, then hurried after Edwin to a table around the corner of the veranda, where they dined in miserable embarrassment. Worse was to follow, for when Mabel returned to her rooms she found half a dozen boxes of flowers all over the place. Mary had sent a note with the first one, telling her poor darling friend to get better as soon as possible, and saying that she was sending flowers every so often, just to console Mabel.

Mary arrived in the morning, dressed all in black, to administer retribution. Her eyes filled with tears, she brushed aside Mabel's apologies to tell her, in trembling tones, that her father had passed judgment. For him, he said, Mabel was now déclassé — but that young man, he had added, knew his Paris.

The enormity of what she had done dawned on Mabel, and she agreed humbly to go to Burgundy at once, as Mary insisted. A two o'clock train? Certainly. It was a rush to arrange everything, to get the tickets, to relieve her own nurse of her duties — for, Mary or no Mary, Mabel had no intention of going to Burgundy without someone to take care of John — and packing, but by lunchtime all was ready and Edwin, when he breezed cheerfully into the dining room, was faced with a *fait accompli*. He was downcast. However, he said, he would see them off on the train. No, said Mabel, he mustn't. Mary was coming back to do that. But Edwin insisted, so he and Mary stood side by side, waving, as the two o'clock train pulled out of the station.

The anecdote Mabel told about what followed between the two who were left behind sounds like another tall story — but, again, it might have happened. As the train disappeared, Mary and Edwin walked out of the station together. Mary's manner now changed. With Mabel safely out of the way, she found it in her heart to be reasonably gracious. She said, in friendly tones, that Mabel looked very young to be a widow.

Edwin is alleged to have been surprised. "Is she?" he demanded, and Mary assured him that she was.

"Didn't you know it?" she asked him.

"No, I didn't know a thing," said Edwin, and stood there staring as she drove away. Then he hurried to a café and started to write a letter.

Could Mabel really have been so sedate and silent that she never even mentioned this important fact about herself to her new friend? Yes, it is possible. Like Sara, she was of a silent disposition, a better listener than talker. It was one of her charms.

Marcelle met the party when they arrived at the village. A good-looking, dark-haired young woman, she was rather austere, but she made Mabel welcome at the chateau. It was what Violet had wished. They talked a lot about Violet, and they seemed drawn to one another. She knew that Marcelle liked her, perhaps, she hazarded, because she was so unlike herself, dressed only in white silk, and looking absurdly young, yet widowed, with that big, growing son.

They passed the day very gently in Burgundy, eating and drinking much of the time. They always had three different kinds of Senard wine at dinner, so it was probably fortunate for Mabel's liver that she heard from Edwin on the second morning, begging her to come back to Paris. It was the letter he had written after hearing that she was a widow, and it throbbed with excitement. Reading it, Mabel was suddenly impatient with the rich, sluggish existence at the chateau. Paris called her — Paris and whatever excitement waited for her there.

She wanted to go. She was determined to go. However, she knew she must play it carefully. Marcelle already suspected that the letter spelled a threat. Mabel was sorry for Marcelle, because she knew that her own coming had brought a breath of life to the French girl: she herself represented something both Marcelle and Mary wanted. But she was not satisfied to play the role they had assigned her. She had to return to Paris.

That day, however, she said nothing about her plans. The next morning another letter arrived from Edwin, and this time Mabel said to the waiting Marcelle that she had to go to Paris; something had turned up there. Of course Marcelle suspected the truth, and she argued and fought valiantly, but Mabel was more than a match for her. Within herself Mabel felt a new strength. For months she had been passive, quiescent, but now her true strength of character reasserted itself. In the end, of course, she won the argument — even Marcelle, for all her determination, could hardly keep the other woman prisoner — and on the fourth day after her arrival Mabel departed.

But she would return, she said, certainly she would return; she and Mary and Marcelle would all have a holiday in the mountains. As an earnest of good faith, she left John and his nurse with the Senards in the chateau. Then, with a light heart, she rode off toward Paris and her second marriage.

Chapter Three

TOO IMPATIENT to wait for Mabel to arrive in Paris, Edwin Dodge traveled down to a way station and met her train. Once aboard, he asked her immediately to marry him, and she accepted — though in her memoirs she asked herself, rather plaintively, why, and seems to have had no firm answer. Because he was so good to John? Perhaps, said Mabel, or perhaps she merely had the idea of building a new life, for which Edwin would do as well as any other man to protect her. According to her story, she didn't love him and told him so frankly. But she did accept him on the understanding that she was doing so because she needed him around to help her in general. They agreed that they would work together to make something new and beautiful, though this is vague. We are left to infer that Edwin as an architect offered her a vista of countless rooms to decorate, but we must not take too seriously Mabel's word for her lackluster attitude. Later events no doubt colored her memories.

Edwin at least had no misgivings, and they set about making plans. Certainly, said Mabel, he must go to America as soon as possible, to meet her relatives and tell them the news. To the conventional Bostonian Edwin this seemed exactly the right thing to do, and he agreed, but he was puzzled by her next stipulation, that he must also go and visit the Senard family in Burgundy and announce the engagement to Marcelle in person. The Senards? Edwin could not see why he had to do it. Surely they weren't so important as all that to Mabel, he expostulated. But he did not hold out long. If his beloved wanted him to go, that was enough. Edwin went to Burgundy.

Earlier, during the tempestuous time that Mabel was on the verge of leaving the Senards to go and meet Edwin, Marcelle had said something significant. Pleading with her guest not to rush off to Paris, she declared that if Mabel simply had to have men — a taste she herself found incomprehensible — she could provide them, really attractive men with depth and finesse and charm. Mabel caught her meaning. She was referring, of course, to the priests who had converted the Shillito girls to Roman Catholicism. The realization gave Mabel a pleasurable *frisson* of dread mixed with temptation. Episcopalians were like that in the world of the Gansons. Sara, who was very High Church — and, indeed, later gave the money to build a chapel for her favorite priest — shared her contemporaries' firm conviction that the Roman Catholic church was the Scarlet Woman. Edwin Dodge was of the same mind. He must have realized that, to Mabel, conversion had all the charm of forbidden fruit, and when, during his interview with Marcelle, he asked her what she had in mind for Mabel and she promptly replied, "The Church," he said — to quote from his report to Mabel — that his heart froze within him. He was quick to insist that Marcelle leave his intended bride alone while he was away in Buffalo. She must not try to convert Mabel. Marcelle promised.

"And she kept her promise," recorded Mabel. One detects here a note of disappointment: she would have loved to have been tempted to conversion. After Edwin returned from America Marcelle assumed that all bets were off, and when the Evanses and he spent their long-deferred holiday in the Alps with Mesdemoiselles Seward and Shillito, Marcelle reverted once more to the forbidden topic. Every night when they were going to bed she invited Mabel to come to her room, and there in the quiet of the night she prayed over her guest. Edwin was *furious* when she told him about it.

"I'm going to get you out of here," he declared, and he did. There were terrible scenes with Marcelle, but he got her out. It is clear that Mabel simply loved the whole thing.

Grandma Ganson came over for the wedding in Paris at the *mairie*, and then the couple went off to Biarritz for their honeymoon.

It was early in October, late in the season for the ocean, and cold. Mabel's account of her wedding night is anything but rapturous, but we must make allowances, for her writings are accompanied, always, by an afterthought, the need to explain and justify her fourth and final marriage as the biggest step she ever took in her life. Each time she invited reminiscence, pen in hand, she was impelled to assess her present situation all over again. Well, here I am, she seemed to be telling the reader, and I was right. It's good, it was worth it! I was never really happy until now. My earlier ventures did not make me happy, but this one does. Even when she looked far back and thought of Karl, her youthful husband, it was necessary to explain that she had never fooled herself for a minute. She had been *tricked* into marrying him; it wasn't her fault. It was the same when she wrote of Edwin, though there is some compunction in her dedication of *European Experiences:* "For Edwin . . . long-suffering and always so kind . . ." In spite of his kindness, Mabel could not give due credit to her second husband because she had to pay her meed to her final marriage. She was honest with Edwin, she must have argued with herself as she wrote. Edwin was warned, so he had no right to feel aggrieved with the way things turned out. It was never right for Mabel, not after that first night. This is the last definite thing we are told about Mabel's malaise in her marriage.

She did not spare herself in describing her conduct at that time. She didn't even try to be cheerful. Everything met with her disapproval; everybody in the hotel was criticized.

She was haughty, silent, and disagreeable. She would spend hours dressing up in her Paris trousseau, changing her shoes several times a day. She began buying immense quantities of things, including hundreds of dollars' worth of silk shawls from China, which later appeared in her New York apartment and in a novel by Max Eastman. She shopped and shopped, moped and moped. Even the good-natured Edwin was at last forced to admit that all was not well with his wife when she snarled at him for making some innocuous remark.

"Well, if this is marriage, excuse me!" said Edwin. These were strong words, and both the Dodges must have been relieved when the honeymoon ended and custom permitted them to get on with the business of living. With Biarritz behind them, they embarked on a search for a satisfactory villa on the Riviera, for Mabel complained of feeling unwell, and it was decided by the doctors that she needed a few months in a mild climate. Unfortunately none of the villas they looked at pleased the difficult lady. There was no nuance about any of them, she complained to Edwin. Even the flowers planted around these blond houses displeased her, puffing out their perfumes with such abandon. She found the sea insincere, and declared that the Riviera lacked privacy. And the awful furnishings! Nevertheless they took one of the places, though Mabel didn't care for it. Too many flowers surrounded it, she said.

With nothing to do but smell flowers and take care of her health, Mabel was bored. Edwin played tennis at the club every day, but his wife had no taste for such pursuits; instead, she carried on a long correspondence with Marcelle about the Roman Catholic faith, and when this palled she declared herself even more ill than usual, so that Edwin sent for the doctor. Once, however, she felt a little better than usual and actually walked down toward the club to meet Edwin on his way home. What happened then she told with a gleam of humor — Mabel was not without humor.

Edwin caught sight of her at a little distance, and didn't seem to recognize her at first. When he did, he said, "My God, Mabel! You're short! I thought you were tall."

Mabel was dismayed — her secret was out. She hadn't wanted Edwin to realize that she was short. It spoiled her act, she said, and kept her from dominating him. It took weeks before she could build herself up again in his eyes.

Meantime her misery continued. One night, when it was even deeper than usual, she called on the dead Violet to come to her aid, to give her some sign that she was near and understood Mabel's unhappiness. A moment later in the dark and the silence she heard a sound — china clinking on china, and a trickle of water. Lighting a candle, Mabel found a tiny puddle of water in the corner near the jug on the dressing table. She took it as that much-desired sign from Violet, and was comforted. Mabel always had a weakness for the supernatural.

The winter was marked by a visit from her mother and Rosita de la Barre, Aunt Georgie's Parisian sister-in-law. Sara Ganson was delighted to find her daughter so comfortably settled with her new husband in a pretty house, and Edwin made a good impression on her. She called him "Dodge," and, Mabel disapprovingly noted, grew flirtatious with him. So did Rosita — after all, he was the only man around. Rosita kept him busy showing her into and out of carriages, lighting her cigarette, or picking up her dropped gloves, whereas Sara, whenever she got the chance, held him firmly by sallies of laughter and shouting attempts to be funny, as Mabel scathingly wrote. Whatever happened to that cold, silent woman on Delaware Avenue?

"She was charming, a *warm* person," insisted Alice Rossin. "Once John said that Grandma [i.e., Sara] was the only person he ever loved."

But then, Mabel on the Riviera was jealous of both women. She admitted it. She wrote that she made life miserable for poor Edwin merely because he seemed to enjoy his popularity with her relations — surely a blameless reaction — and she was so unpleasant to her mother and aunt, merely by being dignified and silent, that she froze them. They left at last, wondering what had gone wrong.

When winter ended and the villa grew too warm for comfort, the Dodges carried out the plan they had always entertained, to go to Florence. They went by way of the Alps — "Beyond the Alps lies Italy!" Mabel taught John to say, pointing dramatically in the proper direction — where they stopped for a time, and Mabel felt herself to be much better, that is, happier. They would live forever in Florence, it was understood, and carry out that pledge they had made to each other — to create something new and beautiful — but the idea of newness did not survive their first few days in the city. Antiquity bewitched them. Leaning on the windowsill of her hotel room, Mabel exulted in the scene of the Arno at twilight, curving away into the distance past lamps that lit palace façades across the road. She saw Giotto's tower against the sky, and sniffed for the first time the odor characteristic of Florence, of old stone, damp box, and laurel.

"I will make you mine," she vowed to the city.

She had already rushed to the shops before sunset and brought back a few objects, which she lovingly described — a gold box, a miniature, a crucifix, even a square of velvet (faded orange) on which to place these things. That evening she lay on a couch and exulted in her imaginings — the air, she said, was thick with memories. Next morning, brisk as any other American tourists, she and Edwin set out to find a place to live. Their first errand, of course, was to establish friendly relations with the bank. The Englishman in charge of it, Charlie Eyre, was most receptive. In no time at all he had taken them home and presented them to his wife, Eva. Through the Eyres, the Dodges were soon acquainted with a large number of the foreigners and Italians who comprised the city's society, and their intimacy with Charlie Eyre and his wife went further than that; during their search for a suitable house, Mabel and Edwin actually moved into the Eyre house, the Villa Pazzi, without unseating its owners, and paid all the expenses of running it for their entire visit.

Mabel loved Florence. Every day she investigated it, wholly enchanted at first with the mysterious palaces, the enticing doorways leading she knew not where. But in time she found it almost too easy to get into those houses. Every time she entered a fresh door that opened to her, every time some little mystery was solved, she lost a small world. The truth was never as attractive as the story she had made up about it, and she declared that she was never again to know Italy as well as she had during those first days of ignorance.

The fact is, she was greedy. She had a tremendous zest for experience — her daughter-in-law said that she was very small, but a dynamo. "She used to wear flat shoes at the time I knew her," said Mrs. Rossin, "and she had a special walk: she would turn on her heel, pivot you know, because she felt so full of energy."

One day the Eyres invited the Actons — Arthur Acton, a cousin of the historian Lord Acton, and his American wife — to tea to meet their new friends. Mrs. Acton was exquisitely pretty, and it seemed to Mabel that Edwin was infatuated with her. Mabel saw something sinister in the way he waited on the lady, bringing her a cup of tea and cakes, and lingering — at least so it seemed — to chat with her. Abruptly, Mabel dashed from the room and took refuge in her bedroom, where Eva Eyre, who had followed, found her in floods of tears. Eva had to comfort her. No, no, said Eva, she had noticed nothing. She didn't think there was anything in it . . . But Mabel went on weeping. Not long afterward she succumbed altogether to an attack of what she called "nerves." The doctor they summoned examined her and declared that she was still badly torn from John's birth, and must go under the knife. Surgery took place in due course, and Mabel nearly died of the hemorrhage that followed, but she was a sturdy woman and she pulled out of it. Moreover, her recovery had a wonderful side effect — she was never jealous of Edwin again. At least, that is what she said, but we have reason to doubt it. Mabel, all her life, was a very jealous woman.

Once recovered, she set out with Edwin on a serious search for a house. It took a long time, for she had firm ideas. She said she wanted a sunny house, and this was not easy to find, since nearly all the villas had been built for coolness in the summer and faced north or east, whereas the Dodges intended to spend the winter in theirs. True, the villas of Fiesole and Settignano faced south, but they were crowded together, sometimes sharing walls with their neighbors. Mabel wanted space, grandeur. She would be a queen, with plenty of land around her. Most of the villas they saw did not live up to her concept; they seemed insignificant. Admittedly, they had more significance than any house she had occupied before, in America, but regardless, they would not do.

What they found at last was the Villa Curonia at Arcetri, near the Eyres in their Villa Pazzi. Mabel, who still loved it years after she left, described it: perched on a high round hill in the bottom of a topographical bowl, it was a long house running east and west, with the width of two large rooms.

They agreed on a division of responsibility, financial and otherwise. Edwin paid for the house as it stood, an ancient shell; he was in charge of its reconstruction. Mabel supplied the furniture and did the decorating. Years later, when the Dodges were divorced, she took what she wanted from the villa, but it remained Edwin's property. Really, said Mabel, he was in luck. It was something for a young architect, only recently out of the Beaux-Arts, to have a lovely old house like this to work on, to add to, and to restore. Out of some obscure sense of guilt, in her memoirs, she gave him full credit for the work and an interesting discovery he made while doing it. The entrance of the villa as they found it did not please either of them. Edwin noticed a curving crack on the wall, guessed what it might be, and began chipping the plaster away, uncovering a buried courtyard of "the best Brunelleschi type" — a perfect *cinquecento cortile*, two stories high. Sometimes when restoring these old houses, said Mabel, people found pearls and tapestries and similar treasures hidden away and forgotten, but what could be more thrilling than to find a courtyard buried in one's house? They enclosed it and made a hall of it.

Room by room, with obvious affection, Mabel led her readers through the Villa Curonia. "And she did create beautiful rooms," said Alice Rossin. "Wherever she went she made them lovely. Out here in Taos, for instance, she mixed everything — Italian, French, Indian things — but it always looked exactly right."

However, Mabel did not stay close by Edwin's side as he worked in the villa. As the days went on she met people everywhere, by the score, and one of them caught and held her attention — the

Marchese Bindo Peruzzi de Medici. A marquis *and* a Medici — what could be more enchanting! To be sure, he was notoriously poor, and notorious for other reasons as well, but he was beautiful, Mabel thought, like a figure in an early Italian painting. It was not long before she had the whole story, for nothing is easier, in Florence, than to garner gossip. Bindo's mother was American, from New England, the daughter of a sculptor who brought her over to Florence. Pen Browning, the only child of Robert and Elizabeth, had been in love with her, but she preferred the Marchese Peruzzi, and small wonder considering what a peculiar little man Pen Browning was. ("Lives of great men all remind us, we should leave no sons behind us," said Edwin of Pen.) Widowed, the *marchesa* found herself almost penniless. She had two sons, Bindo, the elder, and Ridolfo, a slender, quiet boy. Bindo was a brilliant youth to begin with, endowed with everything but fortune. As an officer in the army he lived in Rome and ran heavily into debt, but that could be said of ninety per cent of his fellows. What ruined him was that he was homosexual and it was found out. A first court-martial absolved him, but an enemy accused him again, and this time Bindo refused to go through another trial. Instead, he resigned his commission and retired to Florence, where he lived near his mother. Most people cut him dead — unless he cut them first.

Only a few friends, including Eva and Charlie Eyre, did not accept his ostracism and insisted on speaking to Bindo no matter what had happened. Mabel was much smitten with his appearance, and when she heard the story she insisted on Eva's introducing them. At first Eva demurred, rightly supposing that the conventional Edwin would not approve, but Mabel laughed at her doubts and had her way. She and Bindo became friends. She pushed the acquaintance, called to take tea with him, bought a little pony and cart from him, and sometimes went driving with him through the outskirts of town — for Bindo wanted to be careful of her reputation, no matter how heedless she might be. Away from him, she listened eagerly to the talk of the town — how the *marchesa* had been to the pawnbroker to sell yet another lot of silver or lace in order to keep the house going, and all the rest of it — but it made no difference in her feelings for Bindo. Even when he told her all about the scandal that had been his undoing, and admitted that he was guilty of what they said, Mabel accepted his guilt. He spoke of "that fatal feeling" that sometimes overpowered him: "I don't know what it is; it's as though I grew blind, and didn't know anything any more — and then, suddenly, I see red and I am lost ..." Mabel willingly believed this highly colored account. Wasn't he a Medici? The last of the Medici, as she romantically called him, forgetting his little brother Ridolfo.

"Oh, Bindo, what can I do to make it easier?" she cried once, and he replied, "You do make it easier." Mabel thought him heroic.

The *marchesa* was pleased that a woman of the respectable world had taken a fancy to her problem son, and sometimes she invited the Dodges to dinner; they went, and entertained her in turn, though Mabel didn't care too much for her. Then one day Bindo dropped in on Mabel and sat there in gloomy silence until she asked him what the matter was. After some hemming and hawing, he admitted that his family was in trouble over money. His mother had signed a note which would fall due in a few days, and they hadn't anything with which to pay it. Mabel didn't know what to do. Always generous, she longed to offer Bindo the necessary sum, but she knew Edwin wouldn't approve, and if she dipped into the family account he was sure to know. Then she thought of a way out. Her pearls, of course — the pearls that Grandpa Cook had given her on the occasion of her formal marriage to Karl Evans. Edwin didn't keep an eye on such personal possessions. She ran and fetched them, put them into the gold box she had bought that first day in Florence, and handed it over to Bindo, saying, "Here, take them and sell them."

He protested in a gentlemanly way, but Mabel insisted, and at last he put the box in his pocket. As she wrote later, he stared at her intensely, as if he wanted to express gratitude and affection, but she also detected "a fiendish look of derision." It was all very fast, but she would never forget the satanic spirit she saw then in his eyes.

Here her love for the supernatural overwhelmed her. Where you and I would simply have seen Bindo trying not to laugh, she saw Satan. At least, however, she did see something — she was no fool. It made no difference in her feeling for Bindo, and she went on seeing him more and more often, which fact was not lost on the Florentines. Edwin was so busy out at the Villa Curonia that he was probably the last person to notice the growing friendship between his wife and a man he was certain to disapprove of. He does not seem to have minded even when Mabel brought Bindo to see the villa. But the occasion made her think. She reappraised Edwin. Drawing at a table in one of the rooms, he looked very New England, she reflected, "nice, as men go," but he looked out of place in his surroundings, whereas Bindo, graceful and aristocratic, appeared to suit the old house much better.

"It will be a beautiful place," said Bindo, and Mabel cried impulsively, "I wish we could live here together."

Did Edwin overhear? It seems likely. But perhaps his suspicions were aroused in another way, perhaps the *marchesa* boasted too often in society that her son could, after all, love a woman. Almost anybody might have warned Edwin. At any rate, he began to resent Bindo, and he spoke to Mabel about it, saying that he didn't care for the fellow and wished she wouldn't spend so much time with him. Mabel promptly invited Bindo and his mother to dinner. This precipitated a real row between the Dodges, for Edwin overheard Mabel telling Bindo that she would not let "them" separate her from him, come what may. After the guests had gone, Edwin made an announcement: he was going away. He was going to visit England and America, and Mabel could come with him if she liked — it was up to her. Anyway, he was going, and he left her to think it over.

All the rest of the night she thought. She knew Edwin meant what he said, and she admitted to herself that he had some right, at least, on his side. Though she and Bindo were not lovers, the appearance of an affair was almost equally abhorrent to Edwin. She knew, then, that she didn't want her marriage to fall apart; she wanted a house with a husband in it, a father for John, and a peaceful life. She would go with Edwin, but she felt sick about leaving Bindo to his fate.

Edwin was not generous in triumph. He forbade Mabel even to telephone Bindo, and she hints that he intercepted a letter she wrote.

Eva Eyre tried to comfort Mabel when she wept. One couldn't love Bindo, at least a woman couldn't, she said, and she went on to tell Mabel that Edwin thought the *marchesa* and Bindo were planning to marry him to her because with a rich wife he might recover his position. Mabel refused to believe it and was still woebegone when she and Edwin left for London. According to her version, she was well enough amused in England. Through Mabel's old friend Eva Thompson, the Dodges met Lady Randolph Churchill and

Winston and all their connections. But no matter where she went or whom she met, she thought always of Bindo. With Edwin's surveillance somewhat lifted, she did manage to write to him from England. Then they sailed for America, and in Buffalo, though Mabel had dreaded going home again, her spirits lightened. She had not been there since her departure in 1902, and it was fun showing off her husband and meeting those of her friends, and seeing the new babies and all the rest of it. Buffalo wasn't so bad, after all.

A party was given in their honor, a kind of wedding breakfast for the Dodges, who had not received one before because they were abroad; and one of the guests remembers a characteristic anecdote. All through the breakfast, it seems, Mabel was getting up and moving a pot of tulips that stood on the windowsill, now to a shady place and then to a patch of sunlight. She did this several times until at last her hostess said, "What on earth are you doing, Mabel?"

"I'm teasing the tulips," she said.

Was Sara married again by this time? Probably, though it is hard to pin down the dates of her two marriages after Charley's death. Her second husband was a retired admiral, Reeder, who had a weakness for drink. (Mabel once sent him, for Christmas, a silver cup incribed "General Reader." Regrettably, that was the kind of joke she liked.)

The Dodges were in Buffalo for what Mabel remembered as a couple of months. Then, by way of New York, they set out for Florence again, the Villa Curonia, and perhaps Bindo, though Mabel was aware that she had almost forgotten him at last. She was eager to return, to get on with the decorating of the villa. However, she began to think about Bindo when they were nearly arrived in Florence, and Edwin was sensitive enough to realize it. He said, sharply, that Mabel was to have nothing to do with the Peruzzis, and that if she met Bindo in the street she was not to recognize him. She was to cut him dead. A bargain is a bargain, and Mabel did not protest.

It was seven days before she was put to the test. She had just come out of the bank and gone to her carriage when Bindo drove toward her. They looked at each other as his carriage passed, but she never smiled or moved. The next morning Edwin came into her room where she was having breakfast in bed and told her the news: Bindo had shot and killed himself. "And a good thing, too," he added.

Ever since then, Mabel wrote, for Bindo's sake she had liked and been friendly with homosexuals. In this she was ahead of her time.

Chapter Four

FURNISHING THE Villa Curonia released something in Mabel. Ordinarily she wrote with intense interest about houses and their rooms and how they were decorated, but never did she speak with such love as when she talked of the Florentine house, especially of the *gran'salone*, or drawing room. View by view, detail by detail, she listed its beauties — the window that looked out toward Florence with its stone window frame, the fourteenth-century fireplace that she was so proud of having found. She filled the room with a few large pieces of very carefully chosen furniture and added a number of the little things she was always collecting — flashes of metal, glints of crystal. A special touch in this room was an enormous fifteenth-century *pharmacia*, a drugstore counter, on which was placed a wooden figure of the Indian god, or goddess, Kali-Shiva-Vishnu. Ridiculous? It sounds so, and could have been, but probably it was not. Mabel had an eye, and no less an expert than Roger Fry, the English art critic, told her that her Indian carving was a grand find.

The *padrona's* bathroom was no less extraordinary. One had to go down three tiled steps to reach the huge tub. Over it, in the ceiling, was a trap door that led to Edwin's bathroom on the floor above, and a silken ladder was hidden just under it, hanging on a golden hook. The idea was that the master of the house could, if he wished, descend to his wife's domain more expeditiously and romantically by the ladder than he could walk around by way of the corridor and stairs. It was just a whim, said Mabel airily, just an idea that she and Edwin had had one day during the renovation of this part of the house; but, alas, Edwin never used the ladder except on that first day when it had just been put up, to see if it worked. It worked all right, but the occasion displeased his wife.

As he climbed down toward her bathroom, she noted with distaste that his coat rode up and his shoes looked too awfully modern on the silk rungs. Edwin was hopelessly Bostonian, she mused, and he made everything commonplace. (Mabel had not enjoyed their recent visit to Boston, where she met Edwin's people and found them stuffy — much too American, in her estimation.)

Mabel herself, however, fitted admirably into the Curonia, she was sure. Jacques Émile Blanche, one of the many artists who delineated Mabel at one time or another, painted her portrait sitting in the *gran'salone,* clad fittingly in apricot and orange silk and wearing a turban — Mabel said she was wearing turbans well before the Russian ballet started the style — with John kneeling beside her, like a page. Two photographs of the little group, one a direct snapshot and the other of the Blanche painting, give us the idea in *European Experiences,* whereas another photograph, of Edwin and John in a garden, is revealing. Edwin does indeed look very correct in collar and tie, gazing seriously into the camera — not at all a husband, one would say, for that exotic lady in her drawing room. At least Mabel was coming to that conclusion, often remembering how Marcelle had prophesied that the marriage would not be a good one. Perhaps Marcelle was really a sorceress who could foretell the future! Certainly there was something in what she had said.

Thinking it over in retrospect, Mabel decided that the trouble was in Edwin's nature. He was *superficial.* He seemed to avoid introspection, whereas she loved it. He was amusing and light-hearted, he made a joke of everything, and this offended her. However, he was not always around to irritate his wife. Now and then he went to America and elsewhere to work on commissions, leaving Mabel free to get on with the undercurrents that he avoided.

It was probably during one of these absences that his wife's eye lit on Gino. We are not told just how or where she first saw him, or in fact much about him at all except that he was a beautiful young man, blond, and presumably a peasant. His hair turned up about the edges of his cap, like that of a Florentine page of an earlier century. Mabel thought he looked like one of the figures she had seen in many Florentine paintings — and, as we have seen, whenever Mabel identified a man with an Italian painting, trouble was in store. This case was no exception. She hired Gino as a chauffeur so that she could look at him all she wanted. He would drive her at a mad pace through the city and countryside, Mabel constantly urging him to go even faster. Once they sailed past a young woman and she waved to them. "My wife," said Gino in explanation. No matter; Mabel was able to forget wives. She thought and thought about Gino; she was obsessed with him. Whatever she did — going to parties or entertaining at home or shopping — she thought only of Gino. She made up romantic stories of how he had come to possess his particular type of beauty. His breed might have been fathered long ago in Tuscany by one of the Austrian grand dukes, which would account for his unusual coloring. As she explained, she had to believe he was royal. She couldn't have been in love with a mere chauffeur.

Even so, the idea of actually taking him to bed revolted her sense of social correctness. She told herself over and over that he was really nothing to her, but it didn't help her to sleep. She told herself further that this was ridiculous, that she was too proud, too fastidious, to fall in love with her chauffeur — and in such a frantic way, too. But there it was: she couldn't get Gino out of her head. She thought of suicide as a way out, and tells a story of how she ground up pieces of a glass bottle, mixed them with figs, and swallowed the lot. Did it really happen? We shall never know. At any rate, she admitted that the glass did not harm her in the slightest.

Well, she had tried. Now she decided to go the other route and have the man. There lived in the Villa Curonia a woman she called "Tante Rose" — Rose Clark, who had been a teacher of Mabel's in the art class of her Buffalo school. Tante Rose served as housekeeper, companion, and sometime teacher for John. Mabel now took her along as a sort of unwitting chaperon, and bade Gino drive them up into the nearby mountains, to spend the night in a cottage there. Once arrived, Mabel saw Tante Rose safely to her room and then turned to send Gino a smoldering glance. He understood, and as soon as everything was quiet he came to Mabel's room. But, alas, after all this scheming Mabel found that she couldn't, she really couldn't, and Gino was turned away.

Back in the city, in despair she tried suicide again. She got hold of a bottle of laudanum and drank it off, nearly but not quite dying of it. The household had a bad fright, but she survived; and even as she explained to the doctor that it had happened because she was very unhappy, she realized it was no longer true. She was not unhappy at all. Violent action had cured her. She was still alive and glad of it. Of course, however, the story of the attempted suicide got out, and for a little time it was the talk of Florence. One night a young Franciscan came up to the villa and serenaded her, and sent her an illuminated parchment on which was written, "I send my song up to your heart, hoping only to lessen your pain." Who could help loving Italy?

Nevertheless, sometimes Mabel simply had to get out, and when such a mood overtook her she went to Paris for a change. Marcelle had by this time moved in with Mary, since Mr. Shillito had died, leaving his daughter very rich and in possession of the apartment. It was not really exciting to spend time with Mary and Marcelle, they were so correct and stiff and religious. They were also very proud of Marcelle's collection of Old Masters, twenty rather dreary paintings that Mabel didn't take to at all. So it was a relief to go to a party on the Left Bank given by a new friend, the American Janet Scudder, who was a sculptor and lived in Paris. Mabel made a lot of new acquaintances there, including Roger Fry; she took him to see Marcelle's paintings and he declared they were all fakes, which pleased her.

Even so, Mabel continued to see Mary and Marcelle. It was a habit, and they were old friends, after all. She even took Edwin to visit them again in the familiar chateau in Burgundy. Edwin was bored and didn't stay long, but Mabel didn't go away with him, for she was at work on a new project, the sentimental capture of Marcelle.

As she put it, she began to throw a little net around the other woman, concentrating on her, until at last, she wrote triumphantly, she managed to light a fire in Marcelle, who shed the crust of reserve she had built around herself. They met night after night. By day Marcelle moved around the chateau like a new woman, glowing and laughing, until Mary grew alarmed. One night she came to her friend's room and found Mabel there, and a terrible scene resulted. Mary, said Mabel, was unable to understand the genuine innocence of the emotion she and Marcelle experienced.

How really innocent it was she does not explain, but she declared that she had not been unfaithful to Edwin. Mary, however, did not believe this. As her guest remarked, more in pity than anger, Mary's mind was full of dreadful images of deeds she had read about and blushed over, and she almost, though not quite, turned Mabel out of the chateau. Through all the racket Marcelle smiled and smiled, now and then telling Mary, in gentle tones, to be quiet. As might be imagined, the rest of the household, especially the servants, were startled, and a fellow guest rebuked Mabel for "upsetting the *ménage.*" Nobody believed in the women's innocence, said Mabel sadly, so she took Marcelle off to Aix-les-Bains for several days alone, away from all the noise. Then it was time to rejoin Edwin, and she sent her friend home.

Save for such refreshing interludes, however, Mabel was in Arcetri or Florence, liking it well enough. Like the other residents, she indulged in a good deal of gossip, and filled the days with social doings and hunting for art pieces. That was what they all did, she said scathingly in her memoirs; art was their life.

It is doubtful if she felt such scorn at the time. During the early years she was content to be one of the crowd, filling the house with art objects, vying with her acquaintances when it came to uncovering or discovering new treasures, and proud of her beautiful house. As long as she was preparing the Villa Curonia she could feel that she was creating something important. It was only afterward, probably, that her excitement died down and she felt the need of something new, and became restless. But when she wrote about it, the wisdom of hindsight (and her psychiatrist) colored her recollections. The Curonia, she felt, was a career in itself — but was it enough? No, she decided, it was not. She had created a setting for herself out of a lack of love. Out of longing she had furnished the villa, and in time she felt caught and entangled by it, having built a prison around herself.

Mabel let her memory wander freely as she wrote her memoirs about the people of Florence and the visitors who stayed at the Curonia. They were a mixed array. She devotes many pages to Muriel Draper, the American whose husband, Paul Draper, sang German lieder and with whom Mabel remained in touch for many years; but it is the story of Marguerite Michel that lingers most stubbornly in the mind. Mabel loved ghost stories, and out of Marguerite she wove a good one. Marguerite was a tall, sickly creature who had lived in the Curonia in its earlier days, when it belonged to the Baroness de Nolde. Marguerite had taught the baroness's children and loved her employer, really loved her, so that she would sit on a bench in the garden all afternoon merely in hopes of seeing her adored one returning home. Now that she was back in the villa, nominally as John's governess — though that doesn't seem to have come to much — she transferred her love to Mabel. Mabel liked being adored, but as time went on she resented Marguerite's jealousy, which extended to everybody in the world (except Edwin) who so much as talked to her mistress. Her scowls and bad temper got on Mabel's nerves until she took to teasing the governess, with the help of friends who were in on the secret. They pretended to take liberties with each other, and at last Marguerite's health gave way under the strain. Her heart was bad anyway; she had to go into the hospital in Florence. When she left, she said she would be back.

She died in the hospital, and, sure enough, soon Mabel grew aware of a strange, oppressive atmosphere in the Villa Curonia. Maud, a friend who was lodged in what had been Marguerite's room, complained of having had a bad night. She said that a long, cold foot seemed to be trying to push her out of the bed — a strange enough experience, one would think, and we can hardly blame her for insisting that she be given another room. We cannot understand the next woman who slept in that bed, Janet Scudder. In spite of an experience similar to Maud's — with the added discomfort of a mysterious something trying to pull her bedclothes off — Miss Scudder for some reason didn't insist on changing rooms, but suffered nightly for a whole fortnight, though every day, in the words of the song, she grew pale, and paler. At last she left abruptly and went back to Paris, declaring that she would never stay in the Curonia again. Marguerite's spirit then remained peaceful until another woman, Constance Fletcher, stayed in her room for the night and actually heard her speak. They talked, and Constance said it was a beautiful experience. Then there seems to have been a lull in the ghost's activities, but once when an Indian holy man, "the Swami," was staying in Marguerite's old room, Mabel told him about it and he agreed. Yes, there was an unquiet spirit in the place, and he knew it, but it didn't bother him. However, since it seemed to bother other people, he was willing to get rid of it. On his last night at the Curonia he sealed up the windows as the household watched, and lit a lot of sticks of incense, murmuring an incantation as he worked. On leaving the room, he stuffed up all possible cracks. Dead people's spirits could not bear sweet odors, he explained, which is why we surround the dead with flowers.

After that, Marguerite did not reappear until one hot summer when Edwin was away. The house was full of Mabel's friends when the ghost began cutting up. This time it wasn't simply a question of trying to kick people out of bed; it behaved like a poltergeist. Everyone but Mabel, who was bubbling over with excited laughter, said they would have to leave the Curonia altogether unless something was done about Marguerite, and one of the women suggested exorcism. Mabel sent for a priest, who came right over and performed the ceremony. She loved it.

For a time she had as a guest the illustrious Duse and her "companion," a young Italian girl who dressed as nearly like a man as was possible in that more constricted age. She was only twenty-three, but had already written a play in which Duse appeared, electrifying Rome, and now she made a determined sexual assault on Mabel, arguing that her genius had to be released and she could not do it alone. Mabel, she said, had the key. Mabel resisted, but Edwin in all innocence complained that he didn't get a wink of sleep with those women next door. They were fighting all night, and he wondered if the girl wasn't brutalizing Duse in some way.

Gordon Craig, too, was an acquaintance of the Dodges. One day Mabel had a half-serious idea, while talking to him, of putting on a tremendous pageant in Florence which should go on and on and on, with all the inhabitants dressed in fifteenth-century clothes and all the restaurant cooks preparing the food of an earlier day. Craig took fire at the notion, and after they had parted he went on elaborating it. He wanted Mabel to work with him, giving up all her time for a year, but she turned him down and he took offense. It is an interesting anecdote, not because of the people involved, but because it was not the last time Mabel thought in terms of pageants.

It was in Paris, probably through Janet Scudder, that Mabel met Gertrude and Leo Stein, in those days living together, brother and sister on the best of terms, at 27, rue de Fleurus. Gertrude had done some writing, but was still willing to take a back seat to her brilliant brother. A friend of theirs named Hutchins Hapgood, not yet one of Mabel's circle, wrote at length of Leo and Gertrude in his memoirs, *A Victorian in the Modern World.*

"Whenever I think of Leo Stein, I like him better than when I am with him," he wrote. "He couldn't leave the slightest subject without critical analysis. He and I argued the livelong day." This refers to a period aboard a ship in the Pacific when Hapgood, like

Leo, was going on his *Wanderjahr* after the university. "He was almost always mentally irritated. The slightest flaw, real or imaginary, in his companion's statements, caused in him intellectual indignation of the most intense kind. And there seemed to be something in him which took it for granted that anything said by anybody except himself needed immediate denial or at least substantial modification." Mabel, who retained to the end a fondness for Leo, described him as ramlike in appearance, with his long nose and receding chin.

As for Gertrude, "Hutch" Hapgood met her in Europe with her brother after the trip to Japan was long over. They were sitting one night by the romantic castle of Heidelberg, by the light of the full moon. "Gertrude Stein at that time seemed to me an extraordinary person," wrote Hutch; "powerful, a beautiful head, sense of something granite. I felt in Gertrude Stein something wholly intense . . . a deep, temperamental life-quality, which was also inspiring." At that time, he added, she was utterly devoted to Leo; "she admired and loved him in a way a man is seldom admired and loved; it was a part of her profound temperament."

He met them again in Florence — how Americans used Europe as a playground in those pre–world war days! — and spoke of the "weighty and stalwart Steins," who were living in a villino at Settignano. "They appeared sometimes at the Villa I Tatti," wrote Hutch, mentioning the famous residence of Bernard Berenson, "dressed in long monkish gowns of brown cloth, with sandals on their bare feet, and with the air of authoritative prophets." By "weighty," the writer explained, he referred not to Leo's intellectual habit of mind but to Gertrude's physical size. Fifty pages later he mentioned the Steins again as having settled in at rue de Fleurus, "a little house and most attractive studio." He continued,

Gertrude was still absorbed by the great enthusiasm of her life, namely her brother Leo. He was the master. They had an independent income, which enabled them to give themselves up to an intelligent devotion to literary and artistic things. I think that Leo Stein was the discoverer, if one can use that word, of two of the young Paris painters, Matisse and Picasso . . . Leo and Gertrude bought some of their paintings at a time when a few francs seemed momentous to the artists.

Mabel reminds us that Leo had already discovered Cézanne, and bought some of his works. He insisted that people really look at these paintings. At the rue de Fleurus, when the studio was full of guests who had dropped in just for laughs, he would stand up before the funny pictures by the moderns and obstinately hold forth with messianic fervor until some, at least, of the laughing company were converted. Mabel was one of these. Little by little she was convinced, and she even took on Leo's self-imposed duty to show the world. Later, in Florence, she spoke about it to Blanche, but he was not receptive, and she decided, sadly, that he was middle-aged and incapable of learning new things. In those days at the rue de Fleurus, she said, Gertrude simply sat in the living room among the others. Listening to Leo, sometimes she seemed a bit puzzled, even though in her own way she too was trying to break the mold and create something new.

Mabel described Gertrude as physically prodigious, with "pounds and pounds" of firm fat piled up on her bones. She used to roar with laughter, a laugh like a beefsteak, said Mabel, who was no doubt inspired to this simile because she had seen Gertrude eat five pounds of rare steak at a sitting, while her friend Alice B. Toklas would toy daintily, catlike, with one little slice. Mabel witnessed a part, at least, of a now famous drama, describing how Alice entered the Steins' lives and made herself indispensable to Gertrude, and how, little by little, Leo was displaced until he removed himself from the rue de Fleurus. For a while Mabel stayed friends with both sides. In the end, for reasons that will shortly be apparent, she broke off with Gertrude — or, rather, Gertrude broke off with her. But Leo remained her friend and kept in touch with her through her various changes of home and husband, and he wrote her long letters about his internal life, mental and physical, and his psychoanalysis and all sorts of matters. For the moment, at any rate, Mabel liked Gertrude enormously, and invited her with Alice Toklas to visit her at the Villa Curonia. Gertrude was no stranger to the Curonia; during her earlier stay in Florence she had sometimes walked over, with or without Leo, to drop in on Mabel. She would arrive all in a sweat, said Mabel, and as she sat there, fanning herself with her hat, she seemed positively to steam. Her clothes stuck to her great legs when she stood up, and without shame she simply pulled them away. Yet, said Mabel, there was nothing repulsive about her. On the contrary, she was attractive.

Staying in the villa, Gertrude settled down to work as she did at home, always at night. To Mabel's delight, one of her works turned out to be "Portrait of Mabel Dodge," which begins, "The days are wonderful and the nights are wonderful and the life is pleasant." What follows is not as clear, but the general impression is — well, at any rate, the work does not give the impression that Gertrude disliked the Villa Curonia or its *padrona;* on the contrary. It ended, for what it is worth, "There is not all of any visit." Later, Edwin Arlington Robinson, who refused to take seriously the works of Gertrude Stein, wrote to Mabel, "How do you know it is a portrait of you at all?" But Mabel had no doubts. She had the "Portrait" printed and bound with Florentine wallpaper, and kept a large supply on hand to give to friends. In the meantime, she was carrying on one of her not-quite-affairs with Paul, John's tutor, a blond young man she found fresh and attractive. Gertrude's room was next to Mabel's summer bedroom, which was inconvenient when Paul came to attempt the *padrona*'s virtue because she knew that the writer was wide awake, sitting at her desk. Their arms around each other, the almost-lovers lay on the bed, Mabel muttering under her breath, "I can't, I can't, I can't," until the moonlight waned and Paul went back to his room, leaving Mabel unassuaged. Gertrude, perhaps influenced by her work on the "Portrait of Mabel Dodge," began paying special attention to her hostess. Mabel's coquettish response was only halfhearted until there came a day when Gertrude, at the lunch table, sent Mabel "a strong look," so powerful, said Mabel, that she still remembered it keenly as she wrote her memoirs.

Unfortunately Alice saw the exchange and ran out of the room. Gertrude, recalled to herself, followed her friend out and came back to say that Alice was feeling the heat and wouldn't have lunch. The incident marked the beginning of the end as far as Mabel and Gertrude were concerned, though for some time no break took place. In her memoirs, *What Is Remembered*, Alice mentioned Mabel with a certain amount of malice, as for example in this story: "Mabel's little son by her first husband said he wanted to fly and stood on the balustrade of the terrace stretching out his arms. Mabel encouraged him, saying, Fly my dear, fly if you want to. But the boy did not, he stepped down. Edwin said to Mabel, There is nothing like a Spartan mother."

It was 1912, which made it ten years that the Dodges had lived in Florence, when Mabel took stock of herself and her life there. She did not quite tell herself — not yet — that she had used up Florence and the Curonia and was ready for something else because she wasn't quite sure what that might be, but she was not contented anymore. In one respect, however, she had a glimmering of the trouble. Of all the factors that irritated her, the outstanding one was her husband, Edwin. He got on her nerves. He laughed too much at instead of with people. When he was at table with her guests, she felt that he limited the talk because he wasn't sophisticated enough, and his facetiousness irritated her more and more. When he was there, moreover, he kept *looking* at her. It was not to be tolerated. We will never know whether Mabel first mentioned divorce to the doctor she was currently consulting, or he to her, but the word was spoken at least once, and she was thoughtful.

Divorce would not be easy for several reasons, and Mabel had many misgivings before making up her mind about it. She knew that she would be up against considerable opposition from people friendly to Edwin, including her son and her mother. John liked Edwin, and Sara had always approved of him. And her approval changed to outright fondness after the affair of her second husband, Admiral Reeder.

Mabel was a bit acid about the admiral, saying that Sara had met him in a hotel somewhere and married him. She described him as short and square, with a short, square white beard. He was attracted by her mother's opulent good looks, her healthiness, and her money, said Mabel in addition, and Sara, she declared, liked him because he was so *clean.* But theirs was not an untroubled marriage. Sara was bossy by nature, and when the admiral proved to have a roving eye she became more than ever domineering until once, when they were staying in Florence within a short distance of the Curonia, the admiral disappeared outright. It was Edwin who tracked the recalcitrant man down to a hotel in Rome, where he had passed out in his bedroom surrounded by empty beer bottles, and brought him back to his tearful wife — Edwin, always good-natured, was always ready for such little errands. No, Sara would not like the idea of her daughter's leaving Dodge, nor would a lot of other people in Buffalo, where he was popular. Still, Mabel was never one to be put off her chosen course of conduct by public opinion. She had not quite made up her mind, but she was not far away from it.

Another matter, too, needed attention. John was now twelve or thirteen — Mabel's dates of such details tend to be vague — but he was old enough to go away to school, and she could not decide where to send him. She had thought, earlier, that he would go to England, where so many sons of other rich families were sent, but now she wondered if that was the right thing to do. She had been reading H. G. Wells, and his works gave her misgivings about the state of affairs in Britain. At last she wrote to Wells himself, apologizing for taking such a liberty with a man she didn't know and asking his advice. Some of her statements in the letter make us open our eyes wide. She was, she said, in sympathy with socialism as an idea — this daughter of banking families, whose initial outlay in furnishing her villa had been either thirty or forty thousand dollars, she was not sure which. She went on to explain that her son John would have a lot of money someday and she wanted him to know what to do with it. Yet she could hardly, she said, keep him from the ordinary conventional education most boys got. Did Wells know of any good school for boys that would supply an education that embodied socialistic philosophy?

The letter must have irritated Wells. He replied only briefly, saying that he was in a similar predicament, not knowing what school to select for his own boys, but he supposed America was the right place for a rich young American.

This settled it for Mabel. The seer had spoken, and she had to take John to America. She tells us that the prospect dismayed her. It was often said by her compatriots in Florence that they wouldn't live in their native land for any inducement that might be offered them, and Mabel felt that she ought to share their attitude. She hated America, she told herself. She had come a long way to get away from Buffalo and its dull, grubby men and women, its streetcars, cigar stores, and baseball games. But John had to go to an American school, so she must leave the beautiful Villa Curonia.

Of course this was nonsense and she must have realized it. A woman of Mabel's resources could surely arrange it if she wanted to continue living abroad. John was to be in a boarding school in any case, and all she needed to do was come back with him and settle him in, bringing him to Florence during vacations. However, it suited her to pretend reluctance, perhaps because she was inwardly confident that in New York it would be easier to get rid of Edwin. Not that she said as much, even to herself. Weeping, she explained to Edwin that for John's sake they had to move. Sobbing, she made a careful selection of such goods as might come in handy in the house she meant to take in New York. Brokenly, she arranged that Domenico, the Curonia's major-domo, would come to America to run their house, and at last they all boarded their ship and sailed away. Even then Mabel kept up her pretense. As they crossed the Atlantic, whenever she was on deck she sat with her face toward the Old World, refusing to look ahead to the New, and when they arrived in New York harbor she took John by the hand and led him to her favorite place on the stern deck, bidding him look back toward Italy, lost beyond the horizon.

"Remember, it is *ugly* in America," she told him emotionally. "America is all machinery and money-making and factories — it is ugly, ugly, ugly!"

But John, stubbornly turning his head toward New York, merely said, "*I* don't think it's so ugly."

What Edwin had to say is not on record.

Chapter Five

MABEL HAD AN EYE not only for bibelots but for people. During her years at the Curonia she tried, with considerable success, to gather into her orbit famous people, as well as those on the way to fame. Later, of course, some of them wrote about Mabel, not always kindly, and this poses the question of why she had gone to so much trouble to collect them in the first place.

"I thank God I've never been a famous hostess," said a friend of mine recently after reading a book about Lady Ottoline Morrell. "As far as I can make out, nobody thanks you for your hospitality. People come and live comfortably under your roof, and make free with your food and drink — they live far better than they would at home — and then go away and write nasty things about you. It's always open season on hostesses."

Still, we need not pity Mabel on this score. There is nothing of the victim about her; when it comes to catty memoirs, she more than holds her own. Moreover, she usually gives what seems a truthful picture of a situation, in that she scores off herself as well as her guests.

Why did people come to stay with her — apart from the fact that she made them comfortable, of course? She has said herself that it was because she was such a good listener. She never talked very much; she preferred to sit there in silence, listening, and for this reason people poured out their hearts to her. Of course hers was a conscious pose. She liked to think of herself as a sphinx.

"In her haunted villa sat Mabel Dodge," wrote Muriel Draper in her lively book *Music at Midnight*. She went on:

In the nobly arched fourteenth-century courtyard of it stood Edwin Dodge, her architect husband, greeting her guests and leading them through one perfectly proportioned room after another until they reached an inadequate flight of stairs, down which they stepped into the less perfectly proportioned room he had added to the villa. Once in the room, the slightly unbalanced scale upon which it was built, the "rich man's red" brocade with which the walls were covered, disappeared in the definite visible atmosphere that Mabel Dodge always created about her within four walls.

There she sat.

Mrs. Draper recollected, accurately, that Jacques Émile Blanche was painting Mabel's portrait, but her memory failed when it came to what the sitter was wearing at the time — deep red velvet and black feathers, she said. Deliberately she telescoped many days into one, putting Janet Scudder into the villa simultaneously with Gertrude Stein (whom she amusingly described as writing Mabel's portrait at the same time that Blanche was painting it) and a mad Englishwoman whose companion was a "blue-caped little trained nurse" in spectacles who was having a trance in the corner, in which she saw Beethoven tied with pink and blue ribbons to the piano. The nurse, it seems, was helping Beethoven to free himself.

"Don't mind her," pleaded the Englishwoman. It was, after all, only a trance, such as anybody might have.

"Mabel did not mind," said Mrs. Draper. "She just sat there." She continued:

Arthur Acton, the gilt-edged "rag-and-bone man" of Florentine antiques . . . was, contradictorily enough, expatiating on the delights of a mechanical piano recently acquired . . . the approach of a comet was awaited — I forget which; there are not many. Ghostly manifestations in certain guest rooms of the villa were discussed, much to the discomfort of Janet Scudder.

Mabel sat on.

And this was not all, according to Mrs. Draper's amusing account. Mrs. Stanford White was there too, talking of ghosts and how to cope with them. D'Annunzio was expected but did not arrive, having, on his first airplane flight, been so violently sick that he had to go to bed afterward. After all this we are given a description of Tante Rose:

A gauntly sagging woman with sad grey hair and patient sallow cheeks walked into the room, her arms filled with roses and iris, and said to Mabel Dodge, in a frightened, flat, resigned American voice, "Mabel. I won't pick any more flowers unless you tell Pietro to shut up that white peacock. It is the third time he has attacked me today." And with slow, poignant determination she turned and walked out again.

Mabel did not move. She did not have to. She was everywhere. Mabel did not speak.

Words were too slow for Mabel, said Mrs. Draper. "She went quickly into where you lived and found you there, while you were still in the first throes of verbal communication. She was patient. She would wait for you. If you wanted to catch up another time, you would find her there, sitting."

If this sounds rather frightening, such was not the writer's intention. Mabel was a good friend to her through the years, often when she badly needed help. But Muriel was a wit above all, and could not be expected to forgo a chance to exhibit her chief talent.

Now here was that same Mabel, with her sphinxlike mien, transported to New York and bereft of the background she had so carefully constructed. She had brought with her the "yards and yards" of white Chinese silk shawls bought during her honeymoon; she had plans for them. After putting John into a suitable boarding school, she settled into an apartment at Fifth Avenue and Ninth Street and got to work. The white shawls were used in her bedroom as hangings at the windows and around the bed, their heavy silken fringes weighing down the bed curtains and trailing just enough on the floor. Mabel had a fancy to make everything white. Undeterred by the grime of New York, she directed that all the woodwork be painted the same pure hue, and then went to much trouble — but it was enjoyable nevertheless — to find furniture to match. The caretaker at the Villa Curonia back in Italy was commanded to pack up and send to her the polar bear rug that had graced the floor in the *gran'salone*. No doubt she felt virtuous and economical as she issued these orders, in the fashion of the rich. All the wallpaper in the new apartment was white, and she found a carved white marble mantelpiece for the reception room, where she used for curtains white embroidered linen from Italy. When it was all ready, she placed against this background various specimens of colored glass, which she had begun to collect. In the bedroom was a Venetian chandelier, delicately tinted. It was ready, as lovely in its way as the villa had been. But ready for what? What was she going to do?

At first, she tells us, she knew very few people in New York. In fact she knew more than a few, but Mabel wanted more and more. She needed lots of friends, enough to keep her in a happy whirl all the time, and in New York, after the excitement of the Curonia, she felt deserted. Mary Foote, the painter, lived close by, but Mary and her group were only one world, and Mabel was always greedy for several sets of people so that she could mix them up and act as a catalyzer. Without all this, she moped. Not so Edwin, who tried valiantly to enjoy the return to his own country. He missed Florence, too, but he didn't give in to repining. He took an office in the Architect's Building at 101 Park Avenue and went there every day. Mabel, who had never undergone the therapy of regular work, begrudged him his routine, envied it subconsciously, and was irritated by it, as she was irritated by practically everything he did.

And it is true that Edwin was often tactless. He committed one of his irreparable sins on the afternoon he came home to find his wife sitting disconsolate in the middle of her pretty new rooms, all dressed up in one of her Renaissance Villa Curonia costumes with nothing to do and looking extremely bad-tempered. Recalling a joke about Constance Fletcher, who always said it, Edwin unwisely quoted: " 'There was I all alone in a pink frock!' " and Edwin laughed. Laughed! Mabel ground her teeth, yet she did tell us about it where a vainer or more deceitful woman would have suppressed the story. To make matters worse, if that were possible, Edwin took John, home for a holiday weekend, to a football game at the Polo Grounds, though Mabel simply detested football. She hated, she said, to see the two males so cheerful, hated to see them set off for such an American afternoon. Football, of all things! She had refused scornfully to go with them. What, Mabel Dodge go into that crowd of gum-chewing men and boys in their derby hats? Smoldering, feeling deserted, she watched from the window as Edwin and John got on a bus and were whirled away.

How much longer, she must have asked herself, must she remain wedded to this clod? Yet she still shrank from the idea of cutting loose from him, however much she looked down on him. She simply had to have a husband, she thought; she could not envisage herself alone, coping with all the problems of life. Oh, it was complicated!

One evening she went out with Edwin, no doubt sulkily, to dine with an architect named Jack Oakman and his wife, who were friends of Edwin's rather than of hers. In their house she met a man who became very important to her; Carl Van Vechten. At that time Van Vechten, who was about a year younger than Mabel, was not yet well known, but he had made a start to what was to be a brilliantly successful career. He was then assistant music critic on the *New York Times*, but he soon branched out into other forms of journalism — perforce, as he left the *Times* for another paper, and even then soon lost the new job. Carl, or Carlo, was already the self so many people came to know and appreciate: genial, gregarious, and possessed of a mocking, lightly satirical sense of humor. Mabel liked him at once, and he her. When, at the first opportunity, she showed him her lovely new white apartment, he was suitably impressed. Soon they were intimate friends, having long, cozy gossips with each other every morning on the telephone. Van Vechten had been to Europe and even lived in Paris for a time with his first wife (he was now divorced), and Mabel felt that he was one American who really deserved her friendship. You would never find *him* going to football games!

Often he took her to rehearsals, not only of operas but of plays, for he was interested in the drama as well as music. Through him she met other people with whom she made friends, and she continued knowing Carl and holding him in great affection — though there were interruptions in their relationship, one at least continuing for years — even after he married the actress Fania Marinoff, with whom he was already in love when he first met Mabel. Mabel simply befriended Fania too. Carl Van Vechten was grateful to her.

"It was [Mabel] who introduced me to Gertrude Stein, to Jacques Émile Blanche . . . to John Reed, Hutchins Hapgood, Robert Edmond Jones, to Andrew Dasburg and Arthur Lee, to Leo Stein, Elizabeth Duncan, Edwin Arlington Robinson, Jo Davidson, Stieglitz and O'Keeffe, to the Honorable Dorothy Brett, Matisse, and assuredly the Indians," he wrote in his retrospective book *Fragments*, referring to acquaintances made over many years. "But I cannot begin to recall all the introductions for which she has been responsible. I think I owe more to her, on the whole, than I do to any other person." Such contacts, of course, were the breath of life to Van Vechten, who never got over the horror of his unwilling existence as a boy in his home town, Cedar Rapids, before he escaped and plunged into the brightness of New York and Europe. His appetite for gaiety and people — preferably people from anywhere but Iowa — never flagged through all his long life, and he did his best to immortalize Mabel as "Edith Dale" in his popular book *Peter Whiffle.*

"Mabel has her difficult moments, her difficult hours, her difficult days," he admitted in *Fragments;* "we have not constantly been friends." But, in sum, it was a long and hardy relationship.

Another important friend of Mabel's, especially in her early New York life, was Hutchins Hapgood. Unlike the butterfly Van Vechten, Hutch interested himself in economics and politics, most especially labor problems, whereas Carl, though liberal in his views, usually saw people less as cogs in the machine than as individuals, picturesque ones if possible. Hutch, too, came from the Middle West — Alton, Illinois — but his feelings about his home were nothing like Carl's blinding hatred of Iowa. His brother Norman was the editor of *Collier's* and he himself was a journalist, though according to Mabel he did not work at it regularly, having a certain amount of private income, thanks to his father. He met Mabel through another friend of Edwin's who became one of Mabel's, the sculptor Jo Davidson. Hutch's friendship with Mabel immediately struck root and flourished through the years.

"[Mabel] had just installed herself most attractively at Twenty-three Fifth Avenue," he wrote. "When I met her, she was completely innocent of the world of labor and of revolution in politics, art and history." At first he seems to have been shocked or charmed, perhaps both at once, by Mabel's ignorance, because, as he said, she lived completely in the conservative world and gave no thought to the subjects that absorbed him. Her "restless energy and enormous temperamental instinct," said Hutch, created frequent ructions around her in the only milieu she knew. There was no form, no mental form, to her "surging and changing inner existence," he said, and as he was connected with all the new movements, "all the isms and all the radical hopes and all the enthusiasms" of the city, she eagerly seized on him as her conductor to that world. He was more than willing to act as her guide and teacher, and they carried on an intense friendship, which was not quite an affair, for many years.

Hutchins Hapgood saw his new friend as "God-drunk." He explained the expression: "If at any time she became aware of something lying just out of reach, she was intensely restless until she had drawn it into her web. She was always talking about 'It'; and this was really why Mabel and I understood one another. I have been conscious since my childhood of the unseen cause of all seen things, which gives to all seen things their superlative beauty; and have been engaged in the hopeless quest of the Cause."

In explaining this passage, Hutchins Hapgood reminded his readers that he had, after all, studied philosophy as his chief subject when he was an undergraduate and, later on, as a graduate in Germany. He claimed to have been for a long time on the trail of the infinite, "and still the Infinite torments me," he admitted. Mabel, on the other hand, had had no mental training of the sort, had never studied metaphysics or logic, and knew nothing of physiological psychology or Plato or Spinoza or Schopenhauer. No doubt, thought Hapgood, these lacunae in her education explained why she was so eager on the subject of ghosts and the occult generally. It delighted Mabel that her new friend should have so much of a kindred nature at his fingertips.

"The fact that I could at least appear to recognize some of her cosmic emotions appealed to her greatly; so that for a very long time I saw her every day," he wrote. It was not always easy to do this, he admitted, since he lived with his wife and four children in a big old house in Dobbs Ferry, a long way from Manhattan, and had to commute. He had a job on the *Globe* — a now defunct paper — and sometimes he did his writing there in the office, at other times at the Harvard Club. But no matter where he was, Mabel found him, tracking him down by telephone or, sometimes, with the help of the chauffeur who drove her limousine and ran her errands. She was always asking Hutch to arrange an introduction to a person she thought might be interesting, or perhaps to find her a book or magazine necessary for her ongoing education in current affairs in the labor world, and Hutch was always ready to do her bidding. There can be no doubt that he was heavily involved with Mabel — in love with her, if you will — for a time.

When I first met Mabel, she was young and very pretty [he wrote]. Hers was an unconventional prettiness; she looked like no other woman who was pretty. It was one of her side attractions, but yet, in spite of the fact that some men fell in love with her, I don't think it was the characteristic or usual response in men's imagination. The normal way of a male is to fall in love with a woman who is like a plant, with roots in the ground and with a possibility of eternal flowering: a development from the physical into the conscious and the moral: the forming of the material of life . . .

But one of the most striking things about Mabel was that she seemed to lack this root-like quality.

Whatever this means (and I am not sure that I know), it meant something to Hutchins Hapgood. He carried out the thought by asking Lincoln Steffens once — he had introduced Steffens to Mabel — if he did not agree that she was like a cut flower, and Steffens seemed much struck by the figure of speech. It was her lack of roots, thought Hapgood, that accounted for Mabel's restless energy; she was, perhaps, always looking for the nourishment that came naturally to other people.

He listed elements in her personality condemned by many of her acquaintances: "her eager, sometimes graceless searchings, her terrific but formless needs, her occasional sharp unkindness, her extraordinary and otherwise incomprehensible jealousy, her inability to let go of anything even for a moment casually within her domain . . ."

In spite of this awesome list of faults, Hutch was in love with her. Among Mabel's private papers are love letters from Hutch, and in her book *Movers and Shakers* she published a poem she wrote to him, entitled "My Beloved." Hutch's wife, who wrote novels under the name of Neith Boyce, was cognizant of her husband's feelings — he never made any secret of them; anyway, his love for Mabel was kept within bounds by the lady herself. Neith and Mabel corresponded a good deal about Hutch without any ill feeling. There is no ill feeling, either, in Hutch's *Story of a Lover*, a careful analysis of his love for his wife and how he felt when she had affairs with other men.

In her memoir, Mabel spoke of the long conversations she and her friend used to have about herself. Hutch was always her confidant in New York, especially when she spoke of her perplexity about her marriage. She would talk and talk to him. Hutch wrote to her after one such session; "Dear Mabel — dear Unhappy One — I think I understand now, and if I do, I go back absolutely on what I said at first, about E. I now feel sure that for your sake and his it ought to end. And I think it would be incredibly foolish of you — and weak — not to do what is necessary."

This was advice very welcome to Mabel. She wrote warmly about how lovable Hutch was, the most sympathetic friend one could have. She spoke of his likeness to Francis Thompson's Hound of Heaven, being pursued by God and pursuing him as well, at the same time. He looked like a hound too, said Mabel, with full lips and "melancholy jowls." As for Neith, she let him think he was pursuing God, but she held the leash always, smiling secretly. She didn't take seriously his everlasting talk about his soul. Hutch was sympathetic, said Mabel, always ready to weep for one. When she talked to him about herself, tears came to his eyes and he passed his hand over her hair tenderly. Sometimes, she admitted, he was a little drunk.

He brought his friends to meet her, and she listed them — Lincoln Steffens, Emma Goldman, Alexander (Sasha) Berkman, the poet Jack Reed from Harvard, Walter Lippmann, Robert Edmond Jones, Bobby Rogers, Lee Simonson, all from Harvard as well. He brought Max Eastman and his wife Ida Rauh, Frances Perkins, Mary Heaton Vorse, Margaret Sanger and her husband, and a number of labor leaders, poets, journalists, editors, and actors.

But all Hutch's sympathy, and all his playmates, could not disperse the clouds that sometimes hung over Mabel's head when she began to brood about Edwin and his failings. She developed neurasthenia, sometimes lying awake for hours as she invited the occult to come and take possession of her mind. There were other symptoms, though whether they signified her personal breakdown or that of the surrounding world must be decided by the reader. She herself had no doubts. Once, for instance, while she and Carl Van Vechten were talking innocently on the telephone, they were interrupted by the most dreadful groan, fraught with pain and misery. Carl heard it too, of course. Time after time this happened. Then one night she woke up to see in the dark a column of smoldering flame which, though it had no mouth, *grinned* at her. Mabel knew that it was evil pure and simple, evil itself. Added to which, she got the most awful case of tonsillitis.

Finally she had recourse, not for the last time, to a psychiatrist. It was Dr. Bernard Sachs who, after listening to her troubles through several sessions, reacted just as she had hoped he would. Edwin was bad for her, he decided, and forthwith he spoke to Mr. Dodge himself, advising him to leave the white apartment and stay away until Mabel was stronger and, presumably, could bear his company. Naturally, Edwin left.

So there it was, with the wedge in at last. Edwin never came back to live with Mabel.

Mabel's objections to living alone were not, in the event, justified. Thanks to Carlo Van Vechten and Hutchins Hapgood and all their merry men, she managed quite well on her own, especially as she was not quite alone anyway: she employed a nurse-companion recommended by Dr. Sachs. As for the chorus of disapproval from Buffalo, she seems to have overrated the trouble it might cost her. We are not told how Sara reacted, though in Mabel's correspondence is at least one indignant letter from a champion of Edwin's, hinting that he had taken to drink and it was all her fault. We are not told what John had to say about it either, but according to his first wife, Alice, he took it hard. Edwin was the only father he had ever known, and he liked him. Besides, Edwin was presentable, a quality that matters a good deal to a boy at a snob school, and the same could not be said for some of his successors.

But Mabel did not waste time worrying about what people might be saying. During the quite long waiting time that intervened between Edwin's departure and the formal divorce, she did at last throw her bonnet over the windmill and go to bed with someone else — which was to be expected after all those years of unwilling fidelity. Even then, however, the short-lived affair was disappointing. She didn't enjoy it, and was awfully worried because she was not yet properly divorced when it happened. She was so worried that she told nobody about it but Hutch — because, she said, she told Hutch everything.

What really engrossed Mabel for a while, early in 1913, was the International Show of Modern Art, called the Armory Show because it was held in the unlikely venue of the Sixty-ninth Regiment Armory in Manhattan. The beginning of it all was in Alfred Stieglitz's famous Gallery 291, upstairs at 291 Fifth Avenue, a haven for young artists whose styles were too new and unconventional for public taste. Stieglitz gave wall space to such rebels as John Marin, Andrew Dasburg, and Marsden Hartley when no other gallery would consider them. Modern or old-fashioned, American painters and sculptors had a chip on their shoulders anyway. They alleged, with reason, that people wouldn't look at their work or take them seriously because all American eyes were turned toward Europe. Most rich people, they said, were snobbish about Europe, and neglected work that was often far superior to the stuff they bought merely because it was American in origin.

But when two American artists, Walt Kuhn and Arthur B. Davies, decided to take a look at what was going on in Europe, they found their horizons so much enlarged that they changed their minds about their grievances. In Paris they viewed works by Cézanne, Matisse, Picasso, Brancusi, Marcel Duchamp, Picabia, and others, and they were wildly excited. The New York exhibition, they decided, must be of a far larger dimension than they had originally planned; it would be a cross section of modern art from no matter where — never mind provenance. They arranged with these artists to borrow some of their works and came back rejoicing to prepare for what was now to be an international art show, to be held at the armory because it was the only building available that was big enough.

As a friend of the Steins, Mabel was keenly interested to think that all of Leo's funny pictures would at last be given the attention they merited. One day, talking to the show's public relations man, James Gregg, she told him about her experience with the Steins, and his attention was caught. Gertrude Stein's work had begun to be known for its oddity, but not many people in America knew much about it. Gregg suggested that Mabel write an article about Miss Stein to be printed in the magazine *Arts and Decoration*, which was featuring the Armory Show and many of the people in the background. Mabel, who was always giving away copies of the wallpaperbound "Portrait," was delighted by the idea, even though it frightened her too. She had never yet written for publication. But she got to work, astonishing herself with her own daring; she worked hard, and must have shown the piece as it developed to her most literate friends, Hapgood and Van Vechten, asking for advice. In March the magazine came out with her article, "Speculations, or Post-Impressions in Prose." In it Mabel said, in part, "In a large studio in Paris, hung with paintings by Renoir, Matisse and Picasso, Gertrude Stein is doing with words what Picasso is doing with paint. She is impelling language to induce new states of consciousness, and in doing so language becomes with her a creative art rather than a mirror of history." In the same publication, as a kind of accompaniment and illustration, appeared the "Portrait of Mabel Dodge."

When Gertrude Stein heard of Mabel's contribution she was rapturous. Letters published by Mabel show this; Miss Stein spoke of the article both before and after she saw it:

Your letter via Jo Davidson has just come, but not your article. Please send that, I want to see it, surely I will like it. Please send it quick.

* * *

I am completely delighted with your performance and busting to see the article, send it as soon as it is printed.

* * *

I have just gotten hold of your article and am delighted with it. Really it is awfully well done and I am as proud as punch. Do send me half a dozen copies of it. I want to show it to everybody. Hurrah for gloire.

Surely, one might think, a friendship based on such a warm exchange was good for years to come — but not so. Little by little, Gertrude grew cold toward Mabel until all correspondence ceased. Mabel, mystified, asked Leo Stein in later years why it had happened. He replied that in his sister's mind there had begun to be some doubt as to who was the bear and who was leading the bear.

No misgivings on this score, however, could spoil Mabel's pleasure in the International Show and all its peripheral excitements. She considered herself, though without ostensible reason, to be a part of it, no doubt because she had contributed five hundred dollars toward management expenses and often lent her car and chauffeur to help out by running errands. Certainly there was enough excitement to go around; people were discussing the works everywhere, with or without any understanding of what the artists were trying to do. Duchamp's *Nude Descending a Staircase* seemed to stir up the most passion. In the way people have, many of them took the picture as a kind of personal insult and had the darkest suspicions of its message. Anything so obscure was bound to be immoral, whether or not one could actually see the immorality. Mabel rejoiced in all the controversy. She felt as though the exhibition were her own, she recalled. It became, overnight, her own little revolution, and when people asked, as she reports that they did, "Well, who is Mabel Dodge?" she felt complimented. Though many of her readers scoffed at this and doubted that anybody had asked any such thing, I think that they did, especially when they saw the title of Gertrude Stein's "Portrait." It would have been natural.

In her apartment, Mabel found existence as an unattached lady far more pleasant than she had feared it would be. For the first time in her life she was on her own, and felt — so she says — that she must go through with it bravely and pitilessly. She did feel sorry for herself sometimes, but she suppressed it. She felt she was being awfully gallant, though she was a strange, lonely little figure. It was a pity no one knew how gallant she was . . .

There it is again, that saving trace of self-mockery.

Chapter Six

ONE OF MY friends who knew Mabel and didn't like her went to the trouble of having a button made, one of those plastic things with a pin, and sent it to me. The legend read: MABEL DODGE WAS ROUND AND SQUARE.

Literally this was the truth, though that was not really his meaning. Mabel admitted that she was rather square. At her slenderest she was never thinner than the tightly corseted debutante we see in the frontispiece of her first volume of reminiscences, and when we read her happy descriptions of the meals she enjoyed in France and Italy and New York we wonder that she was not fatter, especially as she detested spas and avoided them. With Edwin she drank lots of wine and learned a good deal about it. Eating and drinking were a not inconsiderable part of the pleasures of life at the Villa Curonia, and they continued to be in her New York existence. Mabel used these amenities to combat a neurotic fear that accompanied her everywhere. She did not know what it was but assumed it was insanity. Her pretty apartment, she said, was only a mask for the hideous reality that was hidden from others; only she knew the truth. She may have been romanticizing, but she may also quite reasonably have dreaded the thought of inheriting what she considered, reasonably enough, to have been mental disorder in her father.

Nevertheless, most of the time she enjoyed her freedom, and loved presiding at lunch in the flat, usually entertaining Carl and Hutch. Or she went out to lunch with some one of her new friends, though she felt it was much nicer at home. All through Mabel's life it was something of an effort for her to go out, but she made the effort constantly, restlessness battling with indolence. In New York just then she was full of aimless energy, as if every minute had to be filled. She was always on the telephone suggesting expeditions to someone, or giving errands to Miss Galvin, the nurse, or summoning her chauffeur and rushing off on some unimportant social errand. Probably, she mused as she arranged all this history for her analyst, it was a sign that her energies were not concentrated, that she was not embroiled in a love affair.

Still, she gave a very good imitation of enjoying a full life. Hutch helped a lot in this charade, for he had taken on the task of educating her politically. He did his best to bring her into touch with those people prominent in current affairs who formed the larger part of his acquaintance, and as he was immersed in the cause of labor, it was chiefly labor leaders Mabel met. Once he persuaded her to go with him to supper at Emma Goldman's. Miss Goldman was living in New York with Ben Reitman, and there too, at least on the evening Mabel dropped in, was her former lover Sasha Berkman, who had been in prison for attempted murder and had later written a book about prisons.

Mabel knew that these people were anarchists, and she felt a delicious thrill at the prospect of meeting them, of actually spending the evening with them. To her surprise she found Emma Goldman a very pleasant, warm, homey type intent on filling up the plates of her guests — "a homely, motherly sort of person." But Mabel was not so sure about Sasha Berkman, with his heavy jaw, veiled eyes, and thick lips. Hutch often said there was something very sweet in Berkman, but she could not see it, though she tried. Once he attempted to kiss her in a taxi and she was terrified. Though she had written approvingly to H. G. Wells about socialism, murder and anarchy were going too far. In the abstract, all this was all very well — even Emma Goldman seemed pleasant, and going to supper with anarchists was piquant and amusing — but being kissed, actually *kissed* by a convict who had been in jail for attempted murder — oh, no. She felt much more at home with her own kind, especially young men from good families, fresh from Harvard, who like herself were investigating the new and fascinating world of labor relations. She saw a good deal of one of them, Walter Lippmann, who often took her to lunch and gave her good advice on her personal life. Lippmann's worldly intellectuality — he was only twenty-five or so — amused her. They were to be lifelong friends.

It was Hutch, she wrote, who first thought of instituting her

"Evenings," as she called them — a kind of salon for which once a week the white apartment was thrown open to a large variety of people. It was bound to be an improvement, she thought, on the ordinary way she saw all these new acquaintances who were brought to her by Carl and Hutch and Lincoln Steffens. They all presented their friends to her, she said proudly; Carl brought Donald Evans, and Jack and Helen Westley, Fania, Justus Sheffield, the young music critic Pitts Sanborn, and Avery Hopwood the dramatist.

The first Evening was something of a catastrophe, for which Carl Van Vechten had to take the blame. He had fallen in love with the black race, which he had recently discovered in its own haunts uptown in Harlem, and he talked warmly to Mabel of the music and laughter of this nation, ignored at their own doorsteps. "How Carl loved the grotesque," sighed Mabel. He told her he was bringing two wonderful Negro entertainers to the apartment and said she must invite a number of people to see and hear them, so she did. She does not explain just what she expected, but we can be sure it was something arty, for she took care to invite only guests whose intellectual taste, she felt, could not be faulted. She was astonished, therefore, when the entertainers arrived. What Mabel described as an appalling Negress, in white stockings and black boots, danced to the music of a banjo played by a man who sang the words of a dirty song. Mabel could see Carlo rocking with laughter all the time, but the other whites were inclined to be sniffy. Mabel really took it hard. She felt that the blacks had let down the tone of the place, but she thought she was concealing her dismay until Hutch, over the heads of the others, telegraphed his sympathy. Still, these moments passed, and she was receptive again when Lincoln Steffens suggested a different type of salon for her.

Steffens, a radical journalist, had become well known for his articles in *McClure's Magazine*, a series of exposures of crooked city administrations later published as a book, *The Shame of the Cities*. From this he went on to produce more exposés, until Theodore Roosevelt lost his temper with this kind of journalism, and spoke scathingly of "the Man with the Muckrake." Steffens and Hapgood had met when the former was editor of the *Commercial Advertiser*, and they remained good friends. By the time Mabel met him, Steffens's most exciting work was behind him, but he was still a power among New York's radicals. Now he spoke seriously to Mabel about what he considered her "certain faculty." She attracted people, he said, and stimulated them; men talking to her felt that they could talk more fluently. If she had lived in Greece, he continued, she would have been called a hetaera. Why shouldn't she do something with her gift? She could organize all the unplanned activity around her and have intellectual Evenings — in other words, maintain a salon.

Naturally, Mabel was very flattered and gladly seized on the idea. Carl Van Vechten could no longer be trusted to shape the kind of party she wanted to preside at, but she knew a nucleus of people who would give the right flavor, people of all kinds. She knew Margaret Sanger, whose chief interest was, as Mabel put it, advocacy of the flesh — in other words, sex. Mrs. Sanger was to invent the term "birth control" and popularize the idea of it. Then there was John Rompapas, a serious, good-looking young Greek interested in just the sort of woolly philosophy she found attractive. She knew "Big Bill" Haywood of the IWW. She knew a number of artists she had met at Stieglitz's Gallery 291 — Andrew Dasburg, a beautiful young man, and Marsden Hartley, one of whose paintings she had bought at the Armory Show — and there were Emma Goldman and Berkman and any number of other people. She invited them to come on a certain evening of the week — Thursday it was, usually — and so her salon opened.

"I once went to one of Mabel Dodge's Evenings," the widow of a Yale president told me with the air of one making a confession. "I was just a young girl and my mother wasn't at all sure it was the right thing to do, but I had to. Simply everybody went, you know."

Mabel listed them: socialists, trade Unionists, anarchists, suffragists, poets, relations, lawyers, murderers, "old friends," psychoanalysts, IWWs, single-taxers, birth controlists, newspapermen, artists, modern artists, clubwomen, woman's-place-is-in-the-home-women, clergymen, and just plain men. This extraordinary mixture met, talked, and enjoyed themselves. Mabel tells us that she received people at the door dressed in her customary white, a long dress with perhaps a vivid scarf wrapped around her. She gave each guest her hand and smiled very briefly, so as to seem detached and impersonal. This was Mabel's favorite pose, though she did not really want to be detached; on the contrary, she loved mixing into other people's affairs. Still, it pleased her to seem remote and un-attainable even though she really felt proud and happily excited that so many people wanted to come to her salon. Later, when the first flush had faded, she suspected that a lot of the guests came only for that moment at midnight when her butler opened the door into the dining room to reveal the cold supper of turkey and ham, but at her most cynical she had to admit that a hard core of them loved the Evenings because they loved the talk. One could see how excited they got over the arguments. Mabel said it was a wonderful new game, her salon.

The hostess calls the tune, and it soon occurred to her that a lot of the talk, being undirected, did no *good*. She wanted a kind of forum, fruitful discussion, so she began to pick out her guests with special aims in mind. One evening, for example, Carl Hovey, edi-tor of the successful, slick *Metropolitan Magazine*, obligingly brought along his art editor to listen to the complaints of young free-lance artists who wanted to know why the magazine didn't buy more of their work at higher prices. They needed the money, as Mabel explained, so that they could afford to do pictures for the *Masses*, since Max Eastman and Floyd Dell, who ran it, couldn't pay them anything. Hovey and his art editor failed to see the co-gency of this argument, but it all made for lively talk. The hostess remained noncommittal, as always.

There was an evening arranged especially for the people Mabel laughingly called "dangerous characters": Bill Haywood, Emma Goldman, Sasha Berkman, Carlo Tresca, Elizabeth Gurley Flynn, and others. All had their say as to the most desirable way to bring about the revolution, and for one time at least the meeting was kept private, for Mabel had changed the usual date and invited only those people who could be trusted not to call the police. Some came in evening dress, and some did not. There were Hutch, Steff, Mary Austin, the Amos Pinchots, Helen Marot, Ida Rauh and Max Eastman, Gertrude Light, John Collier, Jo O'Brien, and a few oth-ers, but on the whole the hostess found this party disappointing. Bill Haywood didn't talk well that night, though Walter Lippmann did his best to draw him out, being kind but firm to no avail. Emma Goldman too was not at her best, but talked rather like a scolding schoolmarm. Hippolyte Havel, a famous village charac-ter, was scornful of the whole show, saying that they all talked like goddamn bourgeois — but then, Havel always called everybody bourgeois, it was his thing. "My little sister!" he said to Mabel, weeping alcoholic tears. "My little goddamn bourgeois capitalist sister!" The wonder was that this sort of thing wasn't said more often to Mabel.

On another evening Big Bill gave a tirade against artists as a class and mortally offended a number of them who happened to be present. Come the revolution, he said, they would have to accept the new concept of proletarian art and give up their jealously guarded position of being something rare and wonderful, for the state would see to it that everybody could be an artist. It was simply a matter of giving them enough leisure to draw or paint or model or write for themselves, he said. Glumly listening to this outburst were Andrew Dasburg, John Marin, Arthur Lee, Picabia — a whole lot of artists, including Mabel's old friend Janet Scudder. Only Janet took the trouble to reply.

"Do you realize that it takes twenty years to make an artist?" she demanded. Clearly, Big Bill did not, nor did he care.

The poets' Evening, too, did not go smoothly. George Sylvester Viereck read aloud some rather startling verses, at which Amy Lowell marched out majestically, and Edwin Arlington Robinson, Mabel's biggest literary lion, sat silent without contributing anything. Robinson often lunched with Mabel, whom he liked, but he was not a very social type; it was a feather in her cap that he had come at all, since what he preferred was drinking with one or two cronies.

Whether the Evening was devoted to poets, revolutionaries, or whatever, the person who probably enjoyed it most was Lincoln Steffens, who reveled in having a platform at 23 Fifth Avenue. He had been a kind of has-been for a long time, for people, it seems, can take just so much muckraking until they get tired of it. Now it was delightful to have an audience again — every week, too. He wrote, "I'm being listened to again, and in much the old way . . . I'm expected to be radical now, so I'm free of the incubus of caution." He did not have to depend only on Mabel's salon; he had a built-in audience among the young, particularly Harvard graduates. As a Harvard man himself, Steff kept an avuncular eye on the most promising recent graduates, of whom Walter Lippmann was one. John Reed, Class of 1910, was another: in Steffens's estimation he was the brightest of all. Reed came from Portland. Steffens was from Sacramento, and had met Jack's father at the Bohemian Club

in San Francisco, where both were members. The elder Reed had
asked Steff to look up his son in Cambridge, and when the boy
graduated and went to New York (after an American-style *Wanderjahr* — he worked his way over to Europe on a cattleboat), it was
Steff who helped him get a position on the *American Magazine*,
though Jack wrote for other periodicals as well. With three other
Harvard graduates he set up housekeeping in a famous old building
at 42 Washington Square, and he persuaded Steffens to take rooms
downstairs in the same building. It was an uproarious household
the young men had. They were always ready to put up visiting
friends. Steff sometimes lent his young protégé money, and it
was to him that Reed dedicated his rollicking poem *A Day in
Bohemia*:

> Steffens, I hope I am doing no wrong to you
> By dedicating this doggerel song to you;
> P'raps you'll resent
> The implied compliment,
> But light-hearted Liberty seems to belong to you.

Mabel loved above all one of the lines in the poem: "The short
and simple flannels of the poor." Within the poem Reed managed
to mention all of his friends; of Walter Lippmann he said,

> . . . calm, inscrutable,
> Thinking and writing clearly, soundly, well,
> All snarls of falseness quickly piercing through,
> His keen mind leaps like lightning to the
> True . . .

and of Alan Seeger,

> A timid footstep — enter then the eager
> Keats-Shelley-Swinburne-Medieval Seeger . . .

and

> The unkempt Harry Kemp now thumps our door;
> He who has girdled all the world and more.
> Free as a bird, no trammels him can bind,
> He rides a box-car as a hawk the wind.

Lighthearted verse like this was all very well and it had a large audience, but Reed had more serious ideas that drew him to Lincoln Steffens and, in the end, turned him against nonpolitical writing altogether. It was only a matter of time before he joined the *Masses,* which had recently been remade from a would-be popular periodical into an organ of socialist opinion. "Out of the middle-class revolt at the turn of the century, with its muckraking and its trust-busting, its progressive governors and its single-tax mayors, had come a great hope," wrote Granville Hicks in his biography *John Reed: The Making of a Revolutionary.* In 1912 Max Eastman asked Jack to become one of the contributing editors and he was glad to accept. He was at Bill Haywood's one evening when the talk was all about the strike of the silk mill workers in Paterson, New Jersey, in which Haywood was active. Mabel was there too, brought by the Hapgoods. Haywood told her that the strikers were trying, for the second time, to get an eight-hour day, but there seemed small chance of achieving their aim. It was a bad setup, he said, with the police on the side of the owners and plenty of violence that didn't get into the New York papers. The papers were involved in a conspiracy of silence, he said, and the public didn't realize that the police were no better than a troupe of organized gunmen who had shot and killed one of the strikers, Modestino Valentino.

Haywood said something about wishing he could show the general public a part of it, like Modestino's funeral. All the strikers followed the coffin on its way to the grave, he said; every single striker dropped a red carnation, real or artificial, into it, so that it looked like a mound of blood, and as they marched they sang the "Internationale." If only people could have seen it, the IWW could have raised badly needed money for the strikers' fund. They were running short of food. Mabel suddenly said, "Why don't you bring the strike to New York and show it to people? Hire a hall and put it on stage, the whole thing — the closed mills, the gunmen, Modestino's murder and the funeral, with Elizabeth Gurley Flynn and Carlo Tresca making speeches and all. You could have a pageant." As she spoke she remembered, still guiltily, that Florentine pageant that never came off, and Gordon Craig's bitter disappointment. Perhaps in this way she might expiate her sin.

Bill Haywood was favorably impressed, and Mabel was encouraged to enlarge on the idea. They ought to use Madison Square

Garden, she said. (It was still on Madison Square in those days, and seemed impressively large.) As for the pageant itself . . . Another guest suddenly spoke up, declaring that he would be responsible for that; he would write it. Mabel looked at the speaker and liked what she saw — a big young man with curly hair and an eager manner, John Reed. He moved over and told her that he would go to Paterson the next morning and see exactly what was going on, then come back to report.

As things turned out, Reed's report was rather late getting made because of what happened in Paterson. But it was very full when it appeared at last in the columns of the *Masses*, written in the magazine's characteristic style. Reed told how he had got there early, in time to see the pickets assembling for their usual stint outside the factory doors. They were quite peaceful, he insisted.

"All the violence is the work of one side — the Mine Owners," he declared.

Their servants, the police, club unresisting men and women and ride down law-abiding crowds on horseback. Their paid mercenaries, the armed detectives, shoot and kill militant people . . . Opposing them are about twenty-five thousand mill-workers, of whom perhaps ten thousand are active, and their weapon is the picket-line. Let me tell you what I saw in Paterson and then you will say which side of this struggle is "anarchistic" and "contrary to American ideals."

But to tell the truth, Reed saw little of the struggle on that day, since he was soon arrested for sassing a policeman. The policeman, he reported, tried to irritate him into saying something actionable: ". . . he god damned me harshly, loading me with abuse and obscenity, and threatened me with his night-stick, saying, 'You big ———— ———— ———— lug, I'd like to beat the hell out of you with this club.'

"I returned airy persiflage to his threats."

So Jack Reed was locked into the local jail. After an hour or so other people were put in too, until the place was crowded with strikers. In time, "I was taken before the court of Recorder Carroll," he wrote, continuing:

Mr. Carroll has the intelligent, cruel, merciless face of the ordinary police court magistrate . . . He sentences beggars to *six months* imprisonment in the county jail without a chance to answer back. He also sends little children there, where they mingle with dope fiends, and tramps, and men with running sores upon their bodies — to the county jail, where the air is foul and insufficient to breathe, and the food is full of dead vermin, and grown men become insane.

It was an age of innocence in American journalism.

Reed was given a sentence of twenty days, which he spent in the company of Bill Haywood and fourteen strikers — Italians, Lithuanians, Poles, Jews, one Frenchman, and one Englishman. Haywood was soon bailed out, but Reed did the full stretch and clearly had a wonderful time, making friends right and left. "And as I passed out through the front room," he wrote, "they crowded around me again, patting my sleeve and my hand, friendly, warmhearted, trusting, eloquent . . . 'You go out,' they said softly, 'Thass nice. Glad you go out. Pretty soon we go out. Then we go back to picket-line . . .'"

Jack came back a hero, no doubt about it. Very soon, more than ever steamed up about the pageant, he started working on it and went to see Mabel. The affair that resulted was so important in her annals that it was mentioned in her obituary in the *New York Times* on August 14, 1962: "One of Mrs. Dodge's more widely heralded emotional affairs occurred with Reed, the young revolutionary and journalist. It came to nothing, and Mrs. Dodge was married for a third time to Maurice Sterne . . ."

Came to nothing? That's not the way various people wrote it. At best it's an odd way to say that Mabel and Reed were never married. Otherwise it came to a great deal. One has only to read Hutchins Hapgood on the subject to know it. "It was at this meeting," he wrote in *A Victorian in the Modern World*, referring to the Haywood Evening,

that I saw Mabel look at Reed for the first time, but it was nothing to the look I saw in her face a few weeks later, when the rehearsal of the pageant was under way. As Reed was speaking, a look of concentrated passion that I had never seen equaled, came into Mabel's face. She was continually talking of "It," by which she meant some terrific power — she didn't call it God, for God implies a certain ethical slant in human conduct — but some sort of possession, unavoidable, possibly benevolent, possibly malevolent. When I saw that look on her face, I knew it was all over for Mabel, for the time being, and also probably all over for Reed.

Hutch's feelings about Reed, however, were mixed. He had met the younger man once with Lincoln Steffens, and was a little miffed by Reed's "Gargantuan gall" and general cockiness. They met for a second time after Jack got out of jail and made the Hapgoods and Mabel come to Paterson to look at the strike and witness him leading a mass meeting in song. Reed was good at that. Besides, it was by way of a rehearsal for the pageant, which was rapidly taking shape. Mabel was in raptures of pride and love.

"When his youthful, enthusiastic face looked out over the sea of humanity beneath him," wrote Hutch, "and that mass of humanity responded in rhythm, with deep, unconscious felicity and grace and love of love and love of life, it was to me a spectacle that I have never seen rivalled on the stage."

Granville Hicks, who was well able to conceal any lurking admiration he may have felt for Mabel, avoided giving her credit for thinking of the pageant. "At last, in the middle of May, the idea of the Paterson pageant was born," he says austerely. "Percy MacKaye, whose experience with pageants Reed respected, enthusiastically urged him to go ahead."

Everyone worked except her, said Mabel blithely; she thought herself fully occupied in inspiring Reed. The others slaved away to raise the money needed to rent Madison Square Garden, and though they did wonders in the two weeks they had at their disposal, the entire vast project had to be confined to only one night, at the end of May, which was all they could afford. Reed worked unremittingly, said Mabel, half the time in New York and the other half in Paterson, where he trained the strikers. He taught them new songs fitted to old tunes, like the one they sang to "Harvard, Old Harvard." Harvard was well represented on the working force, as Reed got Robert Edmond Jones, a classmate, to do the scenes — and there was no denying that the Jones boy had talent; he had to cope with two thousand people onstage at once, and he did it most effectively. There were eight divisions in the pageant, beginning with the mills at work and ending with a strikers' meeting at Helvetia Hall, complete with speeches. Mabel kept a fond eye on Reed, and when, on the last night, he had an attack of nerves, she recounted how she snapped him out of it by sending him on an errand — "Anything to get him moving again . . ." One can see how much she enjoyed the feeling of power that it gave her.

From a critical point of view the pageant was tremendously successful. Newspaper accounts on the following day were loud in its praise, and most of them mentioned the funeral procession, when the strikers tossed red carnations or sprigs of evergreen into the coffin. One report read:

Almost nothing happened at Madison Square Garden last night when about 2,000 silk mill strikers from Paterson, N.J., gave their Paterson Strike pageant on a stage one-third again as wide as the Hippodrome stage — nothing except that everybody was on his feet all the time, men and women were humming — if they didn't know the words — the "Marseillaise" when they weren't humming or singing the "Internationale," and the garden was packed, jammed, and Sheriff Julius Harburger was exhorting the reporters, and folks who had come to the pageant in limousines were gazing raptly at nothing at all while the tears ran down their cheeks.

It is customary to say that "the applause rattled around the hall like musketry firing." The applause last night didn't do any such thing. It was one chronic roar.

Notices like this were very pleasant, and Mabel hugged to her heart the coup by which the producers had managed to get the letters IWW in red lights up on each corner of the Garden, for all the town to see. She and Reed were still flushed and happy and congratulating each other when they sailed off for Europe the next day by prearrangement. Also with the party were Miss Galvin, Bobby Jones (who was, ultimately, going to work with the producer, Reinhardt), and Carl Van Vechten, all on their way to the Villa Curonia. Fortunately for their happy mood, they were not to know that the pageant didn't make money. The papers had printed dizzy guesses at how much they must have grossed for the benefit of the strikers; anything from ten thousand to fifteen thousand dollars was believed probable. Instead, as any organizer of charity benefits might have prophesied, they finished in the red, and by the time the press got wind of the figures their raptures had to some extent abated. One editorial observed, tardily, that the show had after all been produced "under the direction of a destructive organization opposed in spirit and antagonistic in action to all the forces which have upbuilded this republic," and that it furthered a spirit of anarchy. Obviously the strains of "The Marseillaise" had died out of the writer's heart, but by that time Reed had other things to think about.

According to Mabel, they did not become lovers until they reached Paris because before that she could not, for some reason, bring herself to do what she wanted. Aboard ship she argued that she didn't want people to see him going into or coming out of her cabin, but the reason, she confessed, was that she hated to "descend" from the heights into reality. It must have been tiresome for Reed when Bobby Jones, not knowing any of the details, talked happily of his friends' perfect love affair, and told Mabel that there was something wonderful and immortal about it. What Carl felt, or Miss Galvin thought, is not recorded. However, everything comes to an end, and in Paris Mabel's resistance gave way. "And now at last I learned what a honeymoon should be," said the woman who had, after all, been married only twice.

Having opened up the Villa Curonia, its mistress lost no time getting in touch with all her old friends. She found Blanche, the painter, and Arthur Acton, and all the crowd. She summoned the Drapers from their home in London, and they came for a week, bringing with them a number of friends including the pianist Artur Rubinstein. The party arrived late at night, and Muriel described what they found in *Music at Midnight:* everyone was a little cross at having to sit up late, she said. "Carl Van Vechten was there, playing *Scheherazade* a trifle sulkily on the piano. Robert Edmond Jones was there; indeed, he had wisely gone to bed. Jack Reed was there, pulling restless hands through curling hair in splendid impatience . . . and Mabel, of course, in the centre of it, sitting calmly." Muriel insisted on waking up Bobby, who was surprisingly good-tempered, sitting up in bed and saying, "I like your hat, and your earrings are perfect." Then he got up and brought out a basket of brocades and other fabrics, and they had a nice chat about clothes, costumes, colors, and rooms.

It was an interesting week, Muriel went on to admit, but not very comfortable. Almost everyone was in love or hate.

As the morning grew to noon, different members of the household would begin wandering through the many large and small rooms that honeycombed the Villa. Enemies of the night before would meet by assignation in what they had anticipated would be a deserted gallery and find themselves unwelcome intruders in a whispered conference. Mabel and I would always manage to exchange some signal of amity above the general traffic . . .

Bobby Jones so much admired one of Muriel's evening outfits that he begged her to wear it again the next day so that he might paint her. As she told it, she was wearing at the time a long lemon yellow dress with a bright blue bodice embroidered in scarlet and a turban decorated with a flaming osprey. It was — allowing for slight exaggerations — typical of Muriel Draper, her act, to wear such striking clothes, because she was such an odd-looking woman. Rubinstein described her face as that of a white Negress.

Coming to watch the sitting, Carl Van Vechten objected when he heard Bobby tell Muriel that her osprey should be at least six inches longer. He begged Bobby not to be ridiculous. Muriel, he said, was strange-looking enough as it was; she should always dress very simply in black with no headdress at all, no earrings, nothing but her own strange face. Hadn't Bobby any sense of dramatic values?

Jones said he wouldn't discuss it with Carl.

"But you will discuss it," Carl shrieked. "Your future depends on it."

They argued and argued at the tops of their voices while poor Muriel, hot and uncomfortable in evening clothes at that hour of the morning, just stood there, wishing she had stayed in bed. At last Reed appeared and shouted, "Carl, stop it, or you'll cry!" He led Muriel firmly to her room and said, "If you changed those clothes, perhaps, Muriel, you know . . . if you just changed those clothes." She changed.

Paul Draper and Artur Rubinstein, who had been practicing songs, were very late for lunch and continued arguing amiably about the music when they got to the table. To illustrate his point, Rubinstein insisted on singing very loud after everyone had sat down, at which point Mabel, who until then had been smilingly silent as usual, moved with "quick decision," ordered her car, and went off to Bologna for the day.

"If Muriel and I had been alone in the villa," wrote Artur Rubinstein in his memoirs, *My Young Years,*

it would have been heaven. In reality, it was hell.

Mabel Dodge was a young woman of around thirty with a pleasant face, a slightly too generous figure, and the fixed, absent smile of a Mona Lisa. She spoke in monosyllables, except when addressing the servants, and she answered any query with a short nod. Life at her Villa Curonia was a constant carousel. Our hostess showed a gift for gathering together the most incongruous combination of guests in the world.

He listed some of these guests: Gertrude Stein, "engaged in some interminable vocal battles with Van Vechten, Reed hating everything and everybody, Norman Douglas using with relish his most profane repertoire in swearing, and last but not least, myself, persistently jealous and irritable." As they took their leave, he added, "Mabel Dodge gave us another of her enigmatic smiles and a significant nod . . ."

Mabel naturally looked on that period from a different angle. She was madly in love, and took in very little of what happened except her moments with Reed. But she did remember, without pleasure, an occasion early in the summer, in Paris, before they started out for Florence, when a friend of Reed's, seeing him at the hotel, came in and greeted him and insisted on taking him out to lunch. Mabel heard the men's voices in the next room before they went out, and she said her heart began to break a little right then.

That afternoon, motoring south toward Italy, she was blank, in a vacuum as the men happily watched the passing scenery and discussed it. She was waiting for the night, and cared nothing for anything else. Everything interested Reed, she observed irritably. He always had to be carried away by people or things. She admitted that she hated to see him interested in things. She didn't want him to look at churches and forget her. Everything seemed to take him away from her. She could hold him, she said, only at night.

Now this, obviously, is insanity, an impossible way to carry on, and boded ill for the affair. No one can argue with Hutch's pronouncement: "Reed, emerging from the jail at Paterson, was put in jail by Mabel — a far more difficult prison to escape from."

However, for the time being there were wonderful moments. At the Curonia that silken ladder leading down from the upstairs bathroom was used at last as it was meant to be, night after night. No wonder Mabel by day seemed absent-minded.

Chapter Seven

IN THAT SUMMER of 1913 Mabel had her usual moments of terror that she was losing Reed, and when he contracted diphtheria she was actually relieved, for as long as he lay helpless in bed he could not go off half-cocked in admiration of an ancient building or a pretty girl. What woman, she asked her readers, would not welcome anything that rendered her lover helpless? But she grew bored at length with nursing and welcomed the coming of autumn, since it meant going back to New York.

There, Reed moved outright into the 23 Fifth Avenue apartment and lived with her openly. It was daring of Mabel to take this step, even though Miss Galvin too was there, but she was changing. She didn't care anymore for public opinion — and, to be sure, it made no difference in her life. Her friends accepted the situation, and that was all that mattered. One would have said that the scene was set for perfect happiness. Though she took up her life more or less as she had dropped it in the spring, though her salon reopened, she found herself more and more jealous of Reed, more clutchy in every way. Whenever he went to the *Masses* office or wandered out on an assignment she was upset, and she let him know about it. Why need he always be so excited, why did his zest for life spill over as it did with matters that she had no part in? When he said he had to go to the East Side for material for an article, Mabel didn't see why she shouldn't take him in the limousine, which would be much more comfortable; Reed did not seem to think this a good idea. Once he came home all steamed up over a chance encounter with a beautiful prostitute. They had had a long talk, he said, and through this woman he was able for the first time to appreciate all the mystery of the world. Not because it was such a corny statement but out of sharp jealousy Mabel had a fit, fell on the floor, and tried to faint.

After that experience Reed must have tried to control himself and keep quiet. But he was Jack Reed, always bubbling over; he could not change himself even for the sake of peace; he simply could not. Matters reached a turning point when Mabel tried to spoil a friendship that meant a good deal to him. The friend was F. Sumner Boyd, an English socialist only two years Reed's senior who had met him while working with the IWW on the Paterson strike. Reed admired Boyd intensely because, says Granville Hicks, the Englishman was the first thoroughly informed Marxist the poet had yet met. Boyd, for his part, liked Reed too. As soon as he heard that Mabel's party had returned, he hurried to pay his respects at 23 Fifth Avenue and passed the evening there. Mabel sat in sour silence as the men talked and talked; at last she gave up and went to bed but left her door open to overhear the conversation. When Boyd went away at last, she upbraided her lover, giving him her opinion of Boyd and keeping him awake for hours. It was too much. After a trip uptown the next day, she returned to the apartment to find Reed gone. He had left a note saying that he simply couldn't live with her because she crushed and smothered him.

Mabel was shattered. As always in moments of crisis she rushed to the Hapgoods in Dobbs Ferry, where she luxuriated in weeping hysteria, with Neith and Hutch helplessly trying to soothe her. All that night and all the next day she wept; she had not cried like that since her heart was broken in Buffalo, she commented. It did her good, so much so that on the morning of the third day she felt well enough to take Carl and the Hapgoods to lunch in Manhattan, and that night she went out to dinner.

The next morning Reed turned up. He had been too miserable, he told her, to stay away any longer. He had been to Cambridge, talked things over with his beloved Professor Copey, and here he was, ready to start all over again.

Mabel was of course delighted, but — at least, that is what she said in her memoirs — she knew that she would never again suffer quite so much over Reed. She was cried out. And Reed, too, evidently had reservations. His work no longer satisfied him; he seemed to be in a rut. So he was excited and pleased when Carl Hovey suggested that he go to Mexico and write a series of articles for the *Metropolitan* about the civil war raging between the government and Pancho Villa, the revolutionary leader. Certainly he would go, he told Hovey. Mabel did her best to dissuade him, but she hadn't a chance. Reed arranged to represent the daily newspaper the *World* as well as the magazine, and he took off.

But he was not allowed to enjoy liberty for long. It occurred to Mabel, after she had wiped her tears, that she could very well go along too, and she quickly arranged to meet him in Chicago, where he was to pause on the way. She herself paused on the way, in Buffalo, and saw her old friend Charlotte Becker, who was not pleased by what she considered an escapade on Mabel's part. She rebuked Mabel for wearing a bright orange sweater, which made her look like "a tuffy-wuff."

Undeterred, Mabel continued on this, her first trip to the West of her country. It was discouraging that Reed, when he saw her, did not seem as delighted as she thought he should be, and as they moved on together by train to El Paso, Texas, he neglected her, straying off time after time to the smoking car to talk with other men about Mexico. In El Paso things were even worse. Pleading the press of business, Reed rushed off and spent most of his time doing mysterious man things, leaving Mabel at the hotel — and she didn't like the hotel; it was ugly. Reed hardly ever showed up. When he did, it was to tell her repeatedly that she simply couldn't come into Mexico with him, until at last she was forced to agree.

What should she do, then? At first she thought she might just wait for him in El Paso; he would surely come back when the adventure palled. But what on earth does one do in El Paso? Mabel went shopping, a pastime that seldom failed to please. Looking for atmosphere, she bought whatever interesting goods she could find: opals, strange fruit, and a piece of embroidery. But when she brought these things home the hotel looked uglier than ever, and there was no one to whom to show her spoils. It was worse after Reed went into Mexico; she couldn't face staying there alone. At least they missed her in New York — she was always getting letters that said so — and in the end she went back, back to a place where she was appreciated.

Steff and Hutch had tried to carry on with the Evenings during her absence but gave it up. Things just weren't the same, they said, without her. But one good result came of this. At their first Evening Andrew Dasburg, a constant guest, had turned up, noticed that Mabel was missing, and asked indignantly where she was. When he was told that she was in El Paso he was disappointed and angry, and went straight home to paint a picture that he called *The Absence of Mabel Dodge.* The style of the picture marked a new departure for him. His colleague Marsden Hartley wrote about it to Reed:

To describe it is difficult. It is full of the lightning of disappointment. It is a pictured sensation of spiritual outrage — disappointment carried way beyond mediocre despair. It is a fiery lamentation of something lost in a moment — a moment of joy with the joy sucked out of it — leaving the flames of the sensation to consume themselves.

It was a completely new departure for Andrew, Hartley explained, which is why his friends were so delighted. Until this time his works had always been of a rather academic style. Mabel too was delighted, of course. She hung the picture on her wall and added, in time, the second one he made, *The Presence of Mabel Dodge,* next to it. From that time on until Reed returned she saw a lot of Andrew Dasburg, and she often wondered if she wouldn't have been better off if he, rather than Reed, had been her great love.

The *Metropolitan* featured Reed's first article, advertising it well in advance: "What Stephen Crane and Richard Harding Davis did for the Spanish-American war in 1898, John Reed, twenty-six years old, has done for Mexico." Reed had made contact with Villa, and the leader seemed to trust and like him. At least he kept him around, sending him into battle with the soldiers. In this way Reed met most of the leading generals of the insurrectionist troops, and he wrote vividly of the people he encountered, suspiciously well-rounded anecdotes that moved Hicks to say defensively, "He did not hesitate to re-arrange incidents to suit whatever pattern he desired, but he was rigorously faithful to the visual impression of each event. He was indifferent to the accuracy of the historian, but he had the integrity of a poet." In different words, Walter Lippmann said much the same thing: ". . . gradually what he saw mingled with what he hoped. Whenever his sympathies marched with the facts, Reed was superb."

Granville Hicks said that Mabel went again to Texas to meet Reed when he emerged, but she made no mention of a second trip. At any rate, she was delighted to welcome him back from the war; he was acclaimed on all sides and for a while she was very proud of her hero. But one can have too much of a good thing, and it soon seemed to her that people were fussing about him to extremes. One of her Evenings was held in his honor just the same — a John Reed Evening, it was called — and Mabel resented all the plaudits, and wondered in vexation why he looked so puffed up, literally, as if he had been pumped full of air. Certainly she begrudged him his place in the limelight, but it was not all tiresome. She was amused and tickled when the headmaster of the Morristown School for boys, where her son John was a boarder, wrote and asked Reed to come and talk to the school. Reed, she learned, had attended Morristown himself not so many years before. What a nice thing, thought Mabel, to get her two young men together! She ordered the limousine and took Reed, along with Lincoln Steffens, to the lecture, and they all had a delightful time. What John Evans had to say about it is not recorded, but he must have been pleased by the unusual experience — he didn't see all that much of his mother. When she went to Italy in the summer she had left him with the Hapgoods, whose son Boyce, being of his age, was a good friend; and now and then — but not often — he had a weekend with Mabel in New York. This was something extra.

So Mabel didn't mind this one occasion when Jack Reed was a lion. Otherwise, she soon tired of it. Young girls kept making up to her lover and she had to warn them off, but she could never be absolutely sure they would maintain the respectful distance she demanded. Now that he was a successful journalist he had new offers to go and report from far-off places. The most important of these excursions was one to Colorado, where there were labor demonstrations, and Reed was off for some months covering the movement. Ultimately Mabel stopped trying to keep him with her and made the best of it, which is how she happened to have her notorious peyote party.

It started when a cousin of Hutch Hapgood's, Raymond Harrington, came to town from Oklahoma, where as an anthropologist he had been working with Indians. While there he had learned that the Indians made much use of a part of the cactus called peyote, or peyotl, the button that grows on top of the plant. Chewed, it gave them a strange power: they passed into a new state of consciousness, a state which Raymond believed to be the true reality. Most people today know about peyote and the principle of hallucinatory drugs, but it was new to Mabel's group in 1914, and, given her passion for the occult, for godly goofiness in general, the subject was bound to attract her strongly. Throughout her account of the affair she insisted that she didn't realize peyote was a *drug*, but as she never defined what she considered a drug, this is not particularly enlightening.

When Raymond spoke of what a good effect peyote had on the Indians, she listened voraciously. Those who took it, he said, did much better beadwork than ordinarily, using patterns that harked back to the ancient ways and had long been lost. Such Indians, he said, became imbued with heightened nobility and were more fervently religious. Mabel was thrilled. When she discovered that Raymond had actually brought some of the stuff to New York with him, she insisted that they all try it. The one thing he didn't tell her, it seems, was that he himself had never taken peyote, but he laid down certain rules, saying that the experiment must be undertaken in a serious, anthropological spirit, with the ceremony as near as possible to the real thing. Mabel agreed to all this, and invited a number of friends to partake.

Raymond arranged her reception room with the props he said were necessary. He covered a naked electric light bulb on the floor with red silk to represent an Indian fire, and brought in a few eagle feathers and a drum he had obtained in Oklahoma. He told all the others — the Hapgoods and Mabel, Andrew Dasburg, Max Eastman and his wife, Bobby Edmond Jones, a man named Terry, and a girl named Genevieve — that they were to sit on the floor and sing along with him as he played the drum. He would keep drumming, and their chants were to continue without interruption, another carrying on when one paused, until morning. The peyote he put in a little heap of buttons on the floor in front of his crossed legs, and he told the guests to chew them, as many as they wished, but one by one. Then the lights were turned off, and Raymond began drumming softly and singing an Indian chant. Next to him, Hutch tried his best to imitate the sound, and the others joined in, each chewing away at a peyote button.

Each, that is, but Mabel. She tried a piece and didn't care for it because it was bitter. At least so she said later on, but her former daughter-in-law still thinks that she didn't try any. That was typical of Mabel, said Alice Rossin. Instead, she watched the antics of the others, laughing.

Hutch wrote his impressions of the evening long afterward. After chewing two buttons, he felt a strong reaction. "It didn't seem strange to me," he said, "when Raymond left his seat and ascended through the air to the ceiling, still continuing the monotonous music," and when he himself went to the bathroom to be sick, as he leaned over the toilet and saw flames darting out of his mouth he didn't find that strange, either. He lay down and felt himself turning into an Egyptian mummy. Well, he thought, why not? Later, when the party was long over and he compared notes with the others, he learned that Raymond (after coming down from the ceiling) had gone on a long voyage to wander for months and months in a tropical valley full of huge birds and animals of hitherto unknown colors. It was generally conceded, however, that Neith had had the best experience of all. Before finishing her first button she had felt so sleepy that she went to her room and lay down and slept, and had very nice dreams all night.

Mabel, when she had laughed her fill for several hours, got bored and decided to get away from the chanting circle. The Eastmans had already quietly left, as did Andrew and Hutch when they saw that their hostess was going. Each had a bed in the apartment, Dasburg's in a next-door flat which Mabel had added to her own. Only three remained singing around the little "fire": Terry, Raymond, and Genevieve.

In her room Mabel could still hear the singing, and it worried her. She began to pray, but the singing interfered, and as she tried to go to sleep she longed intensely for *something* to break it up. Suddenly she heard somebody walking fast and furiously into the reception room — Andrew, who was telling them all harshly to stop singing and shut up. She hurried to her door and saw him throwing open the windows, letting in the first rays of morning light. Raymond was expostulating with Andrew: "Stop, it's dangerous, it's terribly dangerous," but Andrew paid no attention. Genevieve rushed over to Mabel.

"Oh, Mabel!" she cried. "It's terrible!" And she ran out of the apartment. One of the men ran after her, but she had disappeared from the street.

This was serious, because Genevieve had just arrived in New York and didn't know her way around even when she was in her right mind. It was very cold outside, too cold for wandering about without a coat. Andrew lifted the telephone receiver and began to call the police, but Hutch made him stop. Wait, he said, and began picking up and hiding the remaining peyote. He wanted to call his doctor, but before he could do so the telephone rang. It was Max Eastman, telling them that he and Ida had heard Genevieve crying in the street and now had her safe — it was amazing luck. Then Hutch's doctor came over and gave them all some sort of treatment, and everybody was all right except for Genevieve. It took her years to recover. In Mabel's correspondence are letters and telegrams from her agitated father, who lived in Chicago and had to be summoned to look after his daughter. There are also strange messages and drawings from Genevieve to Mabel.

"She wasn't very stable to begin with," explains Alice Rossin. "Evidently the peyote pushed her right over the edge."

The doctor told Mabel that peyote *was* probably a drug, and she was horrified. She continued to be wary of the stuff for the rest of her life, even though she spent years among Indians who used it as a matter of course.

All of Mabel's correspondence, or nearly all, written before she left Italy was accidentally destroyed; otherwise, the collection of her letters and papers that is today in the Beinecke Library at Yale University would be even larger. As it is, the great mass of paper is testimony to the fact that she never threw anything away, and one can well understand the eagerness with which, a few years before her death, she seized on the idea of sending it all to New Haven and getting it out of the way. It is this correspondence that gives the lie, for one thing, to the impression she seemed to wish to convey of that period in New York, an impression of idle frivolity. Lovesick she may well have been, but idle, never. There is a great mound of letters accepting or politely regretting invitations to her salon. Upton Sinclair, it seems, addressed her as "Comrade"; so did Elizabeth Gurley Flynn. Zoë Akins would have liked to meet her, and in the meantime was sending the manuscript of a play on which she wanted Mabel's opinion. There are abusive anonymous letters and very many begging letters. Frequently one comes upon a friendly, informal note from Dr. Smith Ely Jelliffe, one of New York's very first psychoanalysts. (Mabel had Dr. A. A. Brill come in and talk at one of the Evenings, too.) Max Eastman telegraphed an invitation to Mabel to take over an entire issue of the *Masses* and edit it for either April or May 1914. There are several communications from the notorious Aleister Crowley: did she or did she not attend one of his parties? We do not know. Harriet Monroe hoped that Mabel would find the time to introduce a charming young English poet, Rupert Brooke, to her friends.

There are letters from Mabel herself, for she kept copies of those she thought merited saving for posterity. One letter alone takes up page after page; Mabel wrote it to her friend John Collier, at that time working for the People's Institute in New York. Mabel explained him as one who spent his life encouraging immigrants to hang on to their ethnicity. He was later very much involved in the movement to protect the Indians of the United States. In the letter she recounted in great detail one of those so-called psychic experiences she loved. She was staying with the Hapgoods, she said, when it happened; Reed was still in Colorado. What it all boils down to is that she had a sore throat and heard a lot of noise in the night of bumps and poundings. The following day Andrew Dasburg came out to Dobbs Ferry and they all experimented with automatic writing, with the apparent result that everybody slept badly afterward, if at all. In the morning Neith said to Mabel, half-seriously, "Now, don't you haunt *this* house, Mabel." At any rate, Mabel's throat hurt more and more, until finally she consulted a doctor and found that her tonsils were badly infected. They were duly removed.

When Reed returned, they went up to Provincetown in the spring. Many of Mabel's friends did that; someone had just discovered the delights of the little fishing village where one could rent a cottage and live the simple life. The Hapgoods took a house there and so did Mabel, though in her case life was not so simple — she had her servants, as usual. Now and then Reed invited friends to come and stay, and Mabel did not object even when one of the friends was Boyd. She had learned her lesson.

In Provincetown it was the fashion among the ladies to wear Peter Thompson dresses, two-piece costumes of middy blouse and long flannel skirt, usually of navy blue. Mabel had some of these Peter Toms, as they were called, and wore them most of the time because they were becoming, comfortable, and one didn't have to wear much lingerie under the heavy skirt. One day, strolling with Reed, she came upon an old dory at the beach and decided to take a row in it. They were a fairly long way out at sea before they noticed that the boat was leaking badly; there was no question of getting in before it sank. But Mabel could not swim, so at Reed's direction she kicked off her shoes, got into the water, and clung to the overturned boat. Reed, an accomplished swimmer, trod water in her vicinity and shouted for help, and soon they saw the reassuring sight of a couple of men launching a vessel and preparing to come to their aid. In the meantime, however, Mabel's heavy skirt, now sodden, began to drag her underwater.

"Take it off," said Reed.

Mabel protested that she couldn't. Under the garment she was wearing only a short shift. She would drown, she said, rather than remove her skirt, but Reed grabbed her belt, unbuttoned it, and tore off the garment just as the rescue mission finally arrived.

"Here you are," said one of the men jovially. "Give us your hands and we'll have you up in no time."

Mabel said that she didn't want to be pulled out, and Reed had to mutter an explanation to the Good Samaritans. They understood at once and were very tactful. Mabel was permitted to hang on to the stern of the boat, and they pulled her in that way. Once arrived in the shallows, they hurried away and left her to scutter up the sands to her cottage, where Reed was waiting with a blanket to shield her. So much for the emancipated woman.

Summer arrived, and in July Mabel took ship for Europe once again. With her went Neith Hapgood with two of her children, Boyce and Beatrix, also John Evans and Miss Galvin, but not Reed. Reed had been told by Carl Hovey that he ought to go to Europe and write about the troubled scene, so he went to Portland first to see his parents and say goodbye. It is hardly accurate to say that everyone expected war, but editors like Hovey and journalists like Reed could see that something was brewing. Mabel and Neith, however, seem not to have considered it at all. In Italy Mabel sent word to Carl Van Vechten, who was in Paris blissfully showing the town to Fania Marinoff, that he must come and stay at the Curonia as soon as Fania had departed.

She was gratified to find the villa in very good shape, with all the servants happily lined up to greet them. All seemed set fair for a lovely holiday, but suddenly Neith began to be difficult. Not for nothing had she spent so much time soothing Mabel in the bad patches, when Mabel had heard bumps or felt strange, inexplicable sensations as of some otherworldly warning. Neith now complained bitterly that there was a malign influence in the very air of the Villa Curonia, and it would not let her sleep. She declared that if it went on she would have to go away. It was her turn to be a nuisance, and she took every advantage of it. Mabel was vexed, but there seemed nothing she could do but give in, allow Neith's moods to dictate, and agree to leave the Curonia for at least a few

days. They could go up into the mountains, she said, to Vallombrosa, and see if Neith didn't feel better there. So it was arranged,
and they were in the act of packing and moving when Carl Van
Vechten arrived. He was not at all pleased by the prospect of a stay
in the Italian countryside — what he had looked forward to was
the gaiety of Florence. They were quarreling about it when news
arrived that made them forget all such considerations: war had
been declared in Europe. It was the first of August, 1914.

Carl and Neith were immediately frantic to get back to America
— Carl because of Fania, now halfway across the Atlantic, and
Neith because her husband and the other two children were at
home. Mabel, on the other hand, wanted to stay in Italy. It was
what she had meant to do, and she didn't see why a mere war
should make her change her mind. She grew far more determined
when she had a cable from Reed saying that he was on his way and
hoped she would meet his ship in Naples. It was quite clear to her
that she was bound to stay, and she looked with disapproval on her
friends for their pigheaded determination to leave her, but they
paid no attention to her protests. Carl, indeed, scarcely heard
them, he was so busy dashing around Florence from bank to travel
agency to consulate. Why wouldn't they be reasonable, Mabel
asked herself; why didn't they calm down? They could all repair
to Vallombrosa, find a cottage, and live quite well until the war
ended. But no, they did not listen.

The consul suggested that they were more likely to find a ship if
they went to Naples, and Mabel, who wanted to be there anyway
for Reed's arrival, consented to come with them. Sure enough,
Carl found a ship immediately and took passage for the whole
party with the exception of Mabel. She was sending John Evans
back, and even Miss Galvin. With Reed on the way she didn't
want to be bothered by them. But up until the last minute she
couldn't take it in that they were actually going, hardheartedly
leaving her in a war-torn country. How *could* they be so selfish?
Mabel and Carl had quite a severe quarrel about it, and did not
speak for some time afterward. But there it was — everybody
sailed away, leaving her alone in Naples.

Most women might not think it such a tragedy, but Mabel, as
she admitted, had been very much accompanied all her life, and
didn't know how to cope on her own. This, of course, was not
strictly true. She had been on her own in El Paso, for one thing,

but she chose to forget it. She filled the few days of waiting for Reed in Naples by buying a set of embroidery and stitching in her hotel window. Naples was very quiet, and nobody would have thought there was a war on except for the difficulty of cashing checks. On the day Reed's ship was due, Mabel dressed carefully in flowing white lace, with parasol to match, and went down to the dock to meet him. She said he was charmed to find her so calm, so unflurried. Yes, he said, he was expected in Paris, but in the meantime there was no tearing hurry and he had never seen Pompeii, so they hired a carriage and rolled off to spend a pleasant afternoon sight-seeing.

Reed went to Paris by way of Geneva, where he stopped for several days. Mabel is vague about this interval, but it seems that she followed direct to Paris and joined up with him again. It is amusing to read two contrasting accounts of the period, one by Granville Hicks and the other by Mabel. Hicks gives us a picture of a frenetic Reed, totally absorbed in reporting, rushing all over the place in his attempt to get to the front, scarcely aware that his mistress was with him; while Mabel in her version is only interested in her own moods, which, it goes without saying, were for the most part as black as pitch. With her lover out and about all the time, she stayed in bed most of the day in their "somewhat dreary apartment" on the Left Bank. She cried a lot, waking up thoroughly only when Reed was with her, and at night she wet his face with her tears. None of his professional activities interested her in the slightest. They went to London, and Boyd was there to take up even more of Reed's attention. Finally Mabel could bear it no longer, and she decided to go back to New York, where she could be miserable in comfort. She realized that Reed was relieved when she left; what she did not yet know was that he was embroiled with another woman in Paris. He was to make a funny story out of the situation, telling a friend in Berlin of his emotions "when the girl's husband was threatening to shoot him at the same time that Mabel Dodge was trying to commit suicide."

Not long after Mabel got home, she had a cable from Reed, saying that it was better for them to separate. "Forgive me," said the message in French. "I am in despair." The dialogue that followed is fascinating. Mabel retorted that he should take a grip on himself, adding, "Your true work is here. Hovey is not crazy about your latest article. I will always be your friend."

Reed's next message was: "I love X.L. Forgive me and be happy."

Mabel telegraphed X.L. direct: "I understand everything; come to me when the time arrives. I love you"; and to Reed she cabled: "All this will pass, but friendship endures."

The lovers chimed in together: "You are so noble, we are suffering horribly for you . . ."

It was a relief, mused Mabel, not to love Reed anymore. For a while she was immersed in the pleasant fuss of moving from her apartment to a larger one in the same house, just downstairs. When the flurry was over and she looked around for some other interest, she suddenly decided that what she needed was a child — a warm armful, somebody to keep her company, an investment in life. To be sure, she already had a child, but John didn't count. Owing to one thing and another, she had never really known him as a baby. She regretted it now, but it was too late to start all over again with him. No, what she wanted was another baby, and she set out to find and buy one. It must be an orphan, she decided, to avoid complications later. It took several visits to various orphanages before she had to admit that it was not so easy, after all, to find an infant; there were few really healthy unattached ones. Mrs. Rossin thinks that it was Neith Hapgood who found the child she got hold of in the end, but according to Mabel's account she picked up little Elizabeth herself in a charity home where, as usual, they had no young babies. Elizabeth was eight or nine when Mabel saw her, a pretty blond child sitting on the floor, playing with a doll. When the matron offered her, Mabel was indignant. She didn't want a great girl, she said; what she wanted was a baby.

"But we have no babies," said the matron. "We only have Elizabeth because the family that has kept her for a year doesn't want her: she's not good at school. She's a nice little thing. Why don't you take her home for the weekend and see?"

Not good at school? Mabel's heart went out to Elizabeth. She agreed to keep the child for a few days, on approval, and carried her off. On the way home they stopped at Wanamaker's and bought her some pretty clothes, and that was fun. So in the end Mabel capitulated and took Elizabeth — not, she tells us, through formal adoption, but just on agreement that she would be responsible for the child's keep and education until she was grown up. The hint about Elizabeth's limited intelligence was not false. She was always to be slow.

"Just blah," Alice Rossin recalled. "She was supposed to help me with the children, but she wasn't much use. She was dim, really. John was right when he once said to Mabel, 'Mother, you sure drew a blank with Elizabeth.' " Still, there she was, a pretty, sweet child, decorative enough.

The war was a long way off. Mabel's life filled itself with little arrangements, friends, and her own bursts of energy. Bobby Edmond Jones, back from Germany, was broke, so Mabel moved him into the little apartment where Andrew Dasburg had slept the night of the peyote party. It was pleasant to have such company because, as she said, little Elizabeth wasn't much use in that way.

But soon she had another cause to take up her attention. Isadora Duncan came to America with her troupe of young girls to give dance recitals. There was a bond between Mabel and Isadora. Mabel's aunt's house in the country had been the place where Isadora, as a young girl, first danced professionally. Since then Mabel had watched her perform many times and admired her. After losing her children so tragically when they drowned in the Seine, Isadora had become more and more interested in children generally, and she wanted very much to have a school somewhere in which she could teach dancing to infants. She had been in Russia, where the government's promises to give a great hall and a place to keep dozens of children had not materialized, at least not to a satisfactory degree. Now she wanted New York to provide premises for the same purpose. She planned to teach poor children from the East Side of the city without charge in return for a place large enough for her purposes. She had moved with her retinue into a loft, and Mabel tried to help her. Several places suggested themselves. The Harvard Stadium? The Yale Bowl? Too far off, Isadora thought. What about one of the city's armories?

Mabel sought out friends who might help with their influence and advice. She interested Walter Lippmann and persuaded him to become part of a committee to help Isadora start a school. Then she tackled John Collier, and he thought the best way to go about it was through the mayor, with whom he was acquainted. A date was made for Collier and the mayor to meet Mabel and Walter in Isadora's loft, which was decorated by the long blue curtains Isadora took everywhere with her, and furnished with a piano and with couches on which cushions had been scattered. A few dim lamps served for lighting. Isadora, surrounded by her brother Augustin and his wife, with four of the older dancing girls, was half seated, half lying on the largest couch, of course in a graceful attitude. Around them in the darkness, peering out from the blue curtains, were the small children who were going to dance for the mayor to show him what Isadora could do. It was all so hushed, so graceful, so otherworldly, that Mabel felt unusually short and square and earthy. Her gloves suddenly ceased to fit her hands, she confessed. Then Collier arrived with the mayor.

Mayor John P. Mitchel was a young Catholic. Even before anything was said he looked alarmed, and his alarm deepened when Isadora got up and approached him. Seductively she took him by the hand and tried to lead him over to her couch, but he pulled away and sat on the piano stool. Isadora took her place again, and the children ran out of the shadows and grouped themselves around her feet in a well-drilled manner. Then Isadora, who must certainly have been drinking, attacked the mayor. How long, she asked, was he going to keep "that woman" in jail? This was a reference to a woman convicted of murder whose case had been in all the papers. What use was it, asked Isadora, to keep anyone in jail? With some effort Collier managed to get her off the subject, and asked her to say something about her methods of teaching the dance. Oh, said Isadora breezily, the mayor wouldn't understand anything like that. Her children, she said, lived for *beauty.* They didn't have to go to school, or to church on Sunday to listen to stuffy old men telling them how to behave. They lived in beauty, listening to poets and musicians.

In some embarrassment, the mayor did his best. Couldn't they see the children dance, he asked, to which Isadora replied grandly that she didn't think the children felt like dancing that afternoon.

Poor Mitchel got away as fast as he could. Isadora then turned to her other guests as they sat in silent dismay to say that New York was a very strange place. Two policemen had dropped in on the loft, she said, one recent evening, when she and her sister-in-law were entertaining the German ambassador, all of them lying on the couch and drinking white wine. Isadora had given the policemen money and they went away. Wasn't that strange? As soon as the visitors were out of the loft, Walter formally dissociated himself from any committee that had anything to do with Isadora. He had been badly shocked. John Collier merely said that it was evidently impossible to do anything either for or with Isadora, and Mabel had to agree. After that she saw Isadora only when she was on the concert stage. But it was quite another thing with Isadora's sister Elizabeth. They became good friends.

Elizabeth had taught dancing all her life, traveling sometimes with Isadora but mainly keeping a stationary center for pupils. It was her ideas, Mabel said, that were put into practice by the larger, more beautiful, altogether splashier Isadora. Together the sisters had started a school in Darmstadt, funded by a grand duke who was one of Isadora's admirers, but it was Elizabeth who took care of the children and worked with them while Isadora wandered. The little pupils were brought up according to Duncan's ideas of Greece, art, and beauty, and they always wore blue tunics with blue capes and caps. Wherever it went, the school's director was Max Merz, whose ideas stirred much amusement in Mabel.

Once Rabindranath Tagore came to the Darmstadt school and talked to the children. At times Isadora would descend on the colony, usually bringing with her a companion, and then they had a feast of rejoicing at which Isadora danced with the children, corrected their work, and generally kept in touch. Then came a day when she arrived to ask if she might take all the older lot, six sixteen-year-old girls, to travel with her and work as her chorus. Elizabeth thought this reasonable and readily agreed, but Max Merz, Elizabeth's lover, was furious. However, the Duncans had their way. And after all, as Elizabeth said, they still had all the younger ones, the eight-to-twelve-year-olds who had been collected here and there. It was with these youngsters that Elizabeth hoped to start the new school in America.

This was not at all the same thing as Isadora's ménage, and Mabel threw herself into the project. She lent Elizabeth money and looked for a house for the school, finding it in Croton-on-Hudson, on top of a hill. She took for herself a four-room cottage on the flanks of the hill and moved in. There was a shack on the grounds for Bobby Jones. When Mabel went in for something, she always did it thoroughly, and the connection with Croton was the beginning of an important new phase in her life. She loved, she said, the feeling of being natural; she loved the country. And just down the hill lived Max Eastman, who sometimes dropped in on her until his wife heard about it and was hurt; but that sort of thing didn't interest her anymore, she said. She was wrapped up in Elizabeth Duncan's school. She telephoned or wrote to friends, asking them to contribute to its support, and for Elizabeth's sake she listened patiently to the long-winded maunderings of Max Merz.

She seems thoroughly to have enjoyed her new position as Queen of Croton. She persuaded the school to accept little Elizabeth as a pupil (though Elizabeth Duncan didn't think the child had any aptitude), and then she really went to extremes, taking John Evans out of Morristown — that stuffy boarding school as she called it — and handing him, too, over to Miss Duncan and Mr. Merz. As the only boy in the school, John had to wear blue shorts and tunic to match the girls' uniforms. Barefoot, with his bow and arrow, he was beautiful, said his fond mama. No doubt he was, but it must have been a traumatic experience for a fifteen-year-old boy.

At the end of the term the school was ready to give a dance recital, at which occasion Mabel first saw Maurice Sterne, who was to be her third husband.

Chapter Eight

MABEL WAS VERY NASTY about Maurice Sterne in her reminiscences. So nasty, in fact, that one wonders if she didn't denigrate him merely because he belonged to her, and so couldn't possibly be worth much. The same process can be seen when she discussed Edwin and the nearly forgotten Karl, but with Maurice she really outdid herself. Actually, he was one of America's most highly regarded artists, already on the way to success when they met, and most people seem to have been fond of him. He was an artist in the old tradition, which is to say he had had his phase of *la vie de Bohème* in Paris and all that. He was good-looking in what Mabel referred to as an Oriental way — which is to say he was Jewish — and he liked women, and women liked him. In his memoirs, *Shadow and Light*, published posthumously in 1965, his point of view, his version of various incidents in their life together, offer a contrast to her account, embodying wide discrepancies that are bound to startle anybody except, perhaps, a divorce court judge.

Sterne was born in Russia in 1878 and came to New York as a child with his family to get away from anti-Semitism. He grew up in poverty on the East Side. He wanted to be a painter and he worked hard, so that with scholarships, jobs on the side, and a few benevolent patrons, he attained his ambition. He lived and worked in Paris, wandered about the Continent, made friends, had love affairs, and went to Bali, in the romantic tradition, to forget his hopeless passion for a virtuous married woman. In Bali he was inspired to draw and paint fast and furiously, and when after two years he reemerged into the Western world, his work brought him his first taste of success. The war drove him back to New York in 1915, and there, still unhappy over the unresolved love affair, he met Mabel and found her in a similar emotional vacuum.

Reed had returned to America ready to pick up the threads of his life with Mabel, and out of pity — she says — she consented to a trial period of warmed-over love, but it didn't work. When he went away she forgot him immediately, so she felt free to notice the very good looking stranger staring at her with what she described as a dark brown look at the Duncan dance recital.

She had heard of Maurice Sterne; everyone was talking about his Balinese paintings. After they had been introduced and she had noted his foreign aspect, which attracted her, she went to New York to visit the gallery showing his work. She was always to insist that it disappointed her — his colors, she said, were muddy, and Sterne himself has admitted that in his Balinese period he tended to use dark tints, though the reproductions of the Bali pictures in his book rather belie the statement. However, Mabel thought that he could draw, and she bought one of his drawings then and there. Then she invited him to come and see her at Sharkey Cottage.

Years later, writing of his marriage to Mabel, Sterne still sounded perplexed if not stunned. He seems to have wondered all his life how it happened to come about. For one thing, Mabel was not his type. He talks of how she appeared to him — "robust, rather than tall and slender, without the fine bone structure in which I had always taken such pleasure. (I'm afraid Mabel's bone structure didn't show at all.) She was one of the first to bob her hair and wore it in a bang on her forehead. However," he added, "her most amazing feature was her eyes. They were cool, dark gray pools, shaded with long black lashes." But he didn't like the occasional flash of cruelty he saw in those eyes. In contrast, "her voice was like a viola, soft, caressing, mellow, with confidential overtones."

Sterne irritated Mabel from the beginning. From her experience with him she came to many conclusions about artists, the whole breed, speaking of them in the scornful, sneering tone of some deliberately philistine captain of industry, so that one seems to hear one of her banker grandfathers talking. Artists, said Mabel, never take any exercise; Maurice never walked when he could ride. She implied that artists are parasites; she believed that the reason Maurice first came to see her after she bought that drawing was that he hoped she might buy another. Yet in spite of her dislike of all these qualities she took over Maurice Sterne completely, using her money and assurance. He was startled but gratefully accepted it all. It was a new experience for him.

"I was amazed with Mabel," he admitted. "For the first time in my life I could relax, rest my will, and do what someone else decided was best. It was a period when my own self-confidence had shrunk to zero. I was tired and diffident, and I found relief in Mabel's super-confidence." It was a mistake, of course, but a natural one. Take the matter of Mabel's limousine, to regard one of the details. Maurice admitted that he liked the use of that limousine very much indeed. It made things so easy!

"Thus," he said, "we muddled into a misalliance for which I was as much to blame as anyone, though I was to suffer terribly and my masculine pride was to sustain a great blow."

It started out, of course, as an affair. Sterne *was* a womanizer, and Mabel was attracted, so they went to bed together. But she was not willing to stand up to the world's opinion as she had been with Reed, and when they went to Provincetown that summer she arranged things in seemly fashion, taking one of the fishermen's houses for herself and her other guests while relegating Maurice to a coast guard cottage on the beach. The cottage was later taken over by Eugene O'Neill, but at that time it was Mabel's, and she enjoyed doing it up. Of course Maurice later painted a portrait of her — all the artists who knew Mabel painted her portrait. In the meantime he made a lot of sketches with the finished painting in mind. But she continued to write as if she had had no liking at all for his work; throughout her story of Maurice and the marriage she was savage. Yet she did marry the man at last, and she went to immense lengths to keep him concentrated on her. She was violently jealous, which may in part explain her attitude, but she may also have wanted to rewrite history, running him down in retrospect so that one will forgive her later treatment of the hapless artist. There was, for example, the time that Maurice, Bobby, and John Evans went swimming near the coast guard cottage and were caught in an undertow. The lifeguards got them out, but Maurice had nearly drowned, and they had to work hard to bring him around. Mabel would have us believe that she was totally indifferent to Maurice's fate, and left the beach before it was sure that he would live. Yet shortly afterward, when she noticed him staring at a friend of hers, Hazel Albertson, in that same concentrated way she had first seen when he was projecting his dark brown gaze at her, she was furiously jealous, and for the first time she began to think of marrying him.

She had misgivings, of course. Her mother might not approve, and Mabel, though she never said much about it, was dependent financially on Sara; she often overspent from her own resources and had to apply for more. Then too, John Evans did not like Maurice — at least that was Mabel's theory. She said he had a "strange antipathy" for Maurice — though antipathy on her son's part for her lovers seems natural.

She got rid of Hazel easily enough, but soon she saw danger from another quarter; she suspected Maurice of exercising his mesmeric talents on Neith Hapgood. One bright day Neith came tripping over the dunes all dressed up in a becoming green mull dress and a shady hat, in search of Maurice. Mabel bristled. To be sure, Neith did not know that Maurice was Mabel's property, but that didn't change things. Mabel was having none of it, and she immediately picked a quarrel with the Hapgoods, something to do with their eating arrangements, which they had hitherto shared. Hutch and Neith took umbrage, and they had no more meals together. It was hard on John, as he was no longer permitted to play with his good friend Boyce, but that could not be helped. Mabel was inflexible.

Autumn arrived, and they packed up and left Provincetown. Mabel had decided to leave Sharkey Cottage and move into a bigger place at Croton called Finney Farm. Maurice came along, of course, and for a time she was busy rebuilding, redecorating, and stocking the house. She collected friends, too, to live there and relieve her of the necessity of being alone with her lover. Bobby Jones often visited them, as did Andrew Dasburg and Marsden Hartley. John Evans came for weekends from school, and after the quarrel with the Hapgoods was patched up Boyce usually came along to keep him company. In the guest house, called the Green House, back of the main building, lived Bayard Boyesen, an attractive, tragic-looking man whose father had been professor of Germanic languages at Columbia University. Bayard too had taught at Columbia, as an instructor in English literature, until he became disillusioned with teaching, feuded with President Butler, and left to become director of the anarchist Ferrer Association's Modern School. (This seems inconsistent in a man who had been a football star at Groton, and even less reasonable considering that his family was in the Social Register and he was proud of it.) Inevitably he had become disillusioned with anarchism too, and by the time Mabel added him to her household he preferred to stay indoors most of the day, ostensibly to write but really to drink Scotch. Maurice said that he polished off a bottle of Scotch every day. At one time or another Bayard seems to have been Mabel's lover, and she was still kind to him. She thought he was a wreck, but he was a romantic wreck, and John Evans liked him. So did Maurice.

It was an odd, variegated group at Finney Farm, noticeably male, as the only woman Mabel trusted around her at that time was Mary Foote, who lived nearby. Mary could not possibly offer a challenge because she was too old and plain to attract Maurice. Even Elizabeth Duncan was not welcome. Men were different, however. For a while Mabel thought of integrating Reed into the family because he was still buzzing around between trips and still talking of marrying Mabel. He had given her a ring; he had bought a plot of land on which he meant to build a house. Something had to be done about that, so Mabel asked Hutch to write to Reed, enclosing the ring and telling him about Maurice. When all this had been cleared away, she proposed that he join the household at Finney Farm. He actually did come, though he stayed only three days, saying that he couldn't bear it. (At least, so Mabel said.) Soon, however, she heard that he had a new girl living with him in Greenwich Village, Louise Bryant, whom he had met in Portland while visiting his parents. Mabel took the trouble to go to the apartment and look at the girl. She found out what she could, reporting airily that Louise had been married to a dentist in a small town in the West. She was clever, said Mabel, with "a certain Irish quickness," and very ambitious. Reed no doubt was a steppingstone to higher things. Thereafter Mabel kept a baleful eye on the couple.

They too visited Provincetown at times, and also lived now and then at Sharkey Cottage, for Reed had bought it. Mabel got a little tired of hearing about Louise, but after the lovers had married and gone to Russia together, "she wrote quite a good book," she admitted. She almost never mentioned Louise after that without an acid remark or two.

Because of Reed's early defection, Mabel had lost interest in the whole subject of Evenings at 23 Fifth Avenue. In time she gave up the apartment altogether, telling herself that she found all she needed at Finney Farm. What brought her to New York then was her growing interest in psychoanalysis. She saw a lot of Dr. Jelliffe, and three times a week she had a refreshing hour in the afternoon with Mrs. Emma Curtis Hopkins, an elderly lady who had been a Christian Scientist but didn't get on with Mrs. Eddy and now gave sessions along her own lines. Mabel sent most of her friends to Mrs. Hopkins. She also tried to get Maurice to see Dr. Jelliffe, but he wouldn't. A natural resistance, Jelliffe said benignly.

"I definitely did not belong in this astral sphere nor in [Mabel's] entourage," wrote Maurice.

Even from a professional point of view, it was strange that I, who loathed German transcendentalism and worshipped French realism in art, should have found myself in this atmosphere. I did not belong at all, in any sense, and all of them, including Mabel, looked upon me as an intruder. But Mabel felt she needed me for her "center," and was convinced that I needed her for my "center," which she considered physically alive but spiritually unformed. By virtue of contrast, since she believed I had very little other virtue, she thought we would both derive a great deal from an intimate association. Indeed, Mabel had always believed that if she had a physical relationship with a talented writer or artist, she would somehow absorb some of their power.

She really disliked intensely what I was, but she believed that, with effort, she might carve me into being nearer her heart's desire. She might have succeeded had she been content with enriching and cultivating me, but this was not her purpose. Mabel was bent on first destroying completely, and then creating a new, synthetic being — especially in her dealings with me.

Maurice irritated Mabel, and she certainly irritated him. He was impatient with what he called her false refinement, as when he was so much amused at discovering that one of the cats they had always thought female was, in fact, a tom. Mabel didn't think it funny at all, and refused to accept his word for it. But Maurice persisted — why didn't she *look?*

"Put down that cat," she said, in a fury.

"Why, Mabel, you're actually jealous of a cat, and an unmistakably male one, at that," said Maurice. "You disgust me," retorted Mabel, and she walked out of the room.

And there was another time when she wanted to experiment with the Ouija board, and she coerced Bobby and Bayard into helping Maurice and herself at a séance. They were all sitting there, waiting for the thing to move, when Maurice said solemnly, "I feel something . . . The table is trying to lift its hind leg. Evidently it takes *my* leg for a tree trunk." Again, Mabel didn't think him funny; she did not like any mockery of the mysterious occult.

"Had she not had so much money, she might have been a fortuneteller," Maurice concluded. "She looked like one, dressed like one, and had that kind of atmosphere."

Yet, in spite of these rough patches, Mabel and Maurice often discussed the possibility of getting married. In his book Maurice admitted that he thought it might be a good idea because he was so uneasy about his position. Unmarried, he felt like a kept man. Marriage might restore his *amour propre*, since people didn't laugh so much when poor men married rich women as when they simply hung around. As for Mabel, he thought she wanted it because she was basically a respectable bourgeoise, which is why she so often married her lovers. Through 1916 they talked about getting married; they talked and talked. They talked with other people too, among them Hutch, who told Maurice not to marry Mabel because, he said, she was a witch, who in order to remake him would destroy him first. Oh, she was certainly a witch, said Hutch.

"She might also be a reincarnation of Delilah," said Maurice lightly. Hutch was not amused. Mabel was insanely jealous, he said warningly; the only way she could be sure of a man was to castrate him.

But Mabel did have good qualities, said Maurice, looking back. She was admirable in many ways. Once a maid dropped a beautiful piece of glass that Mabel happened to be very fond of, and her only reaction was to kick the fragments aside and warn the girl to be careful to sweep up all the small bits.

Mabel said that Maurice, too, was insanely jealous and resented all her love affairs of the past. She told how she tried to show him that all that was behind her, and to prove it she brought out the many letters Reed had written her, a voluminous correspondence, which she burned then and there.

This, said Maurice in his book, was a barefaced distortion of the facts. She had never shown him Reed's letters or burned them; all she brought out was one letter from Andrew Dasburg, insisting that he read it. He did, and was horrified at her vanity and lack of delicacy because he was so embarrassed by Andrew's letter. "It was unbelievable that anyone but a craven exhibitionist could allow another person to read it at all . . . She should have destroyed this letter as soon as she had read it, but her vanity and exhibitionism made her treasure it, as proof of the depth of human suffering on the deprivation of MD [Mabel Dodge]." It was this letter, said Maurice, that he had advised Mabel to burn. (She never did, just the same. It is there among her papers at Yale.)

One Sunday, Dr. Jelliffe came to spend the day at Finney Farm. Of course Mabel had talked at length about her relations with Maurice, and she hoped the psychiatrist would be able to see for himself how crass and difficult her lover could be. They had a large party at lunch, and Mabel wanted to be sure Jelliffe saw absolutely everything.

Maurice was serving, and the maid was holding plates for him to fill. It seemed to Mabel that she could see him taking the chance to press against the girl's breast as he did so. She hoped Jelliffe could see it too; it would bear out everything she had told him about her lover. Apparently, however, he couldn't. Suddenly she pricked up her ears. Maurice was talking to one of the men in the voice she hated, a giggling voice, and when she looked at him she saw a spiteful expression on his face. He was saying, "I always think that cats are more a man's pet, don't you, Ralph? It seems as though women take to little dogs and men to cats. I think every spinster should have a little dog, don't you?"

The remark scandalized Mabel, who read all sorts of depravity in it. She blushed deeply. Again she looked at Jelliffe, hoping he too had heard it. They would talk it over the next day, she thought, but he was looking merely interested. There was no disgust in his face.

"That's enough, Maurice," said Mabel furiously.

Maurice looked completely bewildered, and so did everybody else. The next day Mabel got no satisfaction from Dr. Jelliffe, either, for he had seen nothing offensive in Maurice's remarks. Perhaps, he said, she was projecting her own interpretation into them? And Maurice was really upset. He didn't know what he was supposed to have done — he had only tried to take a reasonable part in the conversation — and he could no longer live with such antagonism in the atmosphere. He would leave the house, he said, and Mabel had quite a job persuading him to change his mind. For days afterward he was still trying to work it out. In the end Jelliffe suggested that perhaps they should separate for a while, and Maurice went to Pottsville (why Pottsville? There has been no explanation) until things settled down. Soon, however, they were writing lovingly to each other once again. They missed each other, and Maurice returned.

One of the ways Mabel was determined to reconstitute Sterne was to switch him off painting and turn him on to sculpture. We cannot be sure where she got this notion; she claimed that there was something "sculptural" in his painted work that showed he was on the wrong track with paint. Maurice may have given her the idea himself. Quite early in his career, in Paris, he had thought he would like to try his hand at sculpture, but naturally he wanted to take his own time getting around to it. Mabel was impatient and kept after him. She even bought a few hundred pounds of clay and set to work modeling it herself, hoping to stir him up, but it didn't work. Instead, she tried to paint. She never thought much of her efforts, but there is one painting by her at the Beinecke that is not half bad.

In search of rocks to paint, Maurice went up to the art colony at Ogunquit, Maine, where he enjoyed himself. Soon afterward, however, Mabel decided that it wasn't the right place for him — Ogunquit had been done over and over. Surely he could have found less hackneyed surroundings? Besides, the students made such a silly fuss over him; it couldn't be good for him. Mabel followed him up to Maine, looked around for a better background, and found it on Monhegan Island, where there were only a few cottages and a lighthouse — no young girl students at all. She took one of the summer places, Lodestar Cottage, and ensconced herself in it with Maurice. The only trouble was the neighbors next door, who insisted on being neighborly. Mabel was uneasy because they could see for themselves that she and Maurice were living together. To take off the curse, she imported young John and little Elizabeth. The presence of children, she felt, might lend innocence to the scene, a domestic complexion.

Nevertheless she was still unhappy, and soon she took the children and left Maurice to his own devices. She herself returned to New York and found a new analyst, A. A. Brill; she felt that she had reached the limit of Dr. Jelliffe, charming though he was. Until Maurice returned, she kept herself busy with this analysis.

Then she found a new interest: writing for the newspapers. For years Arthur Brisbane of Hearst Publications had been telling her that she could write, but she had seldom tried. (Brisbane was a friend from way back in Buffalo; he had married a Cary.) Once, it is true, Mabel had written an article and sent it to him — it was at the time America entered the war, and she started out with the phrase "We women" — but he didn't use it. Now she felt more serious about writing and Brisbane was receptive. She could do articles, he said, for the New York *Journal,* two or three a week, for which they would pay thirty dollars apiece. Mabel started in with enthusiasm. Brisbane gave her a lot of attention to begin with — editing the material, divulging valuable tips, making suggestions, and generally acting like the good editor he was. After she was launched, he turned his mind to other matters, while Mabel continued on her own quite successfully. The pieces were syndicated in all the Hearst papers, and she felt important and happy. It was an unusual experience for her to be earning money, and it was wonderful. She felt so well that she suggested to Dr. Brill that she no longer needed her analysis, but he was having none of that. She had hardly begun, he said; carry on!

So Mabel carried on, even though, without telling Brill, she continued to see Mrs. Hopkins as well at least once a week. Brill had no patience with what she called her mystic side; he wouldn't have let her go to Mrs. Hopkins. She never told Mrs. Hopkins about Brill, either, knowing *she* would not approve. Even Maurice was willing to see Dr. Brill, and went to him for several consultations.

Then one day, in the summer of 1917, a friend gave Mabel one of those little talks for her own good about Maurice. It was a pity, said the friend, that Mabel and Maurice, who were both such fine people and such an inspiration to all who knew them, should continue in their false position of nonmarriage, permitting themselves to be talked about in the most unpleasant way. Of course, anybody who knew them well would not join in the chorus, but there were others in the world outside . . . It was a great pity, that's all. It hurt to think . . . This drew blood. Mabel thought about it, and went on thinking.

In August Maurice's dealer asked him to come along with a few friends and take a holiday in Wyoming, on a ranch somewhere, and Maurice was delighted to accept. Mabel too thought it a good idea for him to go away — for once their two versions agree on this. She even suggested that the party look in on the Rumsey ranch, where John Evans was visiting this Buffalo family. One night at Finney Farm, shortly before Maurice was to leave, she was just saying goodnight to him in front of the party of guests, sending him out to the Green House in the rear as she always did for the sake of appearances, when she thought, This is ridiculous. The next morning she went out to the Green House and found Maurice placidly packing for his trip.

"Let's get married," she said.

She had never been so definite, and Maurice was quite pleased. He was even willing to change his arrangements for Wyoming, but Mabel didn't insist on that. They could be married that very day, she said, at Peekskill, and then he could go off to meet his friends in Wyoming just the same. A rather unusual honeymoon, to be sure, but why not?

So that is what they did. The guests served as witnesses, Maurice and Mabel were married, and the groom went to Wyoming. When he came back he found that Mabel had taken an apartment in New York for them; Finney Farm, she said, was for weekends only. She seemed a little surprised that Maurice still wanted a studio somewhere else in the city — why couldn't he do his painting right there? But he had his way. When it came to painting, Maurice knew what he wanted and insisted on getting it.

The news had repercussions, of course, but Sara did not, after all, cut her daughter off. Sara never did that sort of thing in spite of Mabel's worries; she was remarkably good-tempered about it all. Other people were not so forbearing. One feminist said she was deeply disappointed. Mabel, she said, had been an inspiration to many women, and now she had let them all down by marrying. Elizabeth Duncan was amused. "What did you do *that* for?" she asked. The person who took it most to heart, for some reason, was Hutchins Hapgood, who liked Maurice very much. Of course he liked Mabel too, but at that moment he happened to be very angry with her, and he has told why.

"On one occasion she heard that I was interested in a certain woman," he wrote.

Mabel had never been in love with me, although she was and is a great friend of mine but, nevertheless, she didn't want to have anybody else tend to draw me out of her circle. So, quite needlessly, she took a lot of trouble to break up this friendship. She wrote to Neith about it, wrote to my friend's husband, and took a trip of several hundred miles in order to persuade the lady to have nothing to do with me. She afterwards told me she did it for my good.

Hutch was still fuming, therefore, when he went into the Brevoort bar one night and ran into Maurice Sterne, who had only just been married, with Jo Davidson and they asked him to join them. Hutch drew a blank, as he often did, and had no recollection the next day of what happened, but Jo Davidson was able to fill in with the horrid truth. Thus Hutch learned to his horror that he had told Maurice he deeply sympathized with him for having married Mabel, adding that Maurice would regret it. At one point, evidently, Maurice tried to hit him. Hutch lost no time writing and apologizing, and Maurice was sweet about it, but . . .

Long afterward, in 1936, when *Movers and Shakers* appeared, with all its unpleasant attacks on Maurice, Hutch's drunken warning was bound to be remembered. Maurice Sterne thought of it, and so did Hutch himself, who wrote,

Unless one understood Mabel, one would think that what she wrote about Maurice Sterne was merely unkind, cruel, vindictive and deeply false. But when I wrote her after the book appeared, and told her what a remarkable production the book was, and how stupid the critics were about it, I also told her how badly she had acted, thought, and felt about Maurice. I said, "Mabel, it was all due to your insane jealousy."

In reply, Mabel admitted the truth of the statement, and she did not admit it in the spirit of confession, or of any false humility. She knew — and in some way she also conveyed to the reader, and thus mitigated, though it perhaps did not eliminate, the curse — that even while writing the book she was aware that the poison of jealousy was at work.

That is perfectly true. After all, how would we know of Mabel's faults if she didn't tell us herself? She was always remarkably objective, and should be given credit for it. Just the same, it was hard on Maurice Sterne, especially as he didn't get the last word in until after Mabel died.

It is a truism that marriage makes people change in their behavior toward each other, and the Sternes proved it yet again. Hardly were they moved into the New York apartment when Mabel was objecting to the smell of Maurice's after-dinner cigar. Maurice went out for his cigar after that, but he stayed away so long that

Mabel didn't like it. In the end she settled matters by giving him a box of the best Havanas, as recommended by Arthur Brisbane. It wasn't the smell of cigar smoke per se that she didn't like, she explained; it was just Maurice's cheap cigars. One up to Maurice, but he did not enjoy his triumph very long. Mabel hurt him deeply a week or so later by interrupting a rather sentimental speech he was making.

"I was telling Mabel that her hunch that we get married had been truly constructive," he wrote. "My feeling for her, which had formerly been centered on sexual attraction, had developed into love and affection, and a sense of well-being in her presence. This was far more than mere compensation for the loss of freedom which had at first interfered with our relationship." Upon which Mabel, whom such remarks made uneasy, snapped, "Don't fool yourself! The moment sex is over between us, all will be finished."

This speech horrified the gentle, sentimental Maurice. She couldn't mean it, he protested, but Mabel said she certainly did, and poor Maurice as a result was shocked into temporary impotence. He brooded and brooded about the situation. If he had known, he said, that all he could give her was the services of a bull, he would never have taken "that phony trip" to Peekskill. He began to think the marriage was a mistake. He couldn't work properly. He consulted Brill, who suggested temporary separation, and he also consulted his ordinary doctor.

"Why not go away?" asked this man. "I have friends in Santa Fe, New Mexico, and they say it's a wonderful place. Go out there and paint the Indians."

So Maurice went to Santa Fe.

Chapter Nine

MAURICE STERNE may have hit the nail on the head when he wrote,

Mabel was a very respectable bourgeoise, though like an impulsive adolescent in rebellion against custom mainly because of exhibitionism. However, when the initial impulse was spent, she always had middle-class scruples about her misdemeanors *against convention*. That is why her love affairs eventually had to be sanctified. She felt she had to pay her debt to society by marriage, like a good Buffalo Christian. Only when she had sexual gratification was she really alive, and since she was a Christian and not a pagan, she hated the sexual act for that very reason, and required a legal union.

Maurice exaggerated. Mabel didn't always sanctify her love affairs, but his statement carries enough truth to warrant consideration. She must have discussed these questions over and over with her psychoanalyst, and that is a pastime that runs into money. There is a story pertaining to this time in her life, when she was visiting her mother in Buffalo and, as was her custom, had brought with her a number of bills for Sara to pay. Sara was carefully going through them when she came upon one that startled her.

"Mabel, what is this?" she asked.

"What?" asked Mabel without interest.

"This bill from some doctor named Brill."

"That's right," said Mabel. "He's my doctor."

"But it really seems quite high," protested Sara. "Ten thousand dollars."

Mabel shrugged.

"You mean it has to be paid?" asked Sara.

"Yes."

"Well," said her mother in exasperation, "very well, I'll pay it. But so far as I can see *you haven't lost a single pound.*"

There were many doctor's bills during those weeks — not all of them for psychoanalysis, either. Whenever Mabel was prey to uncertainty she developed aches and pains, and about Maurice she was sadly uncertain. She missed him. On November 13, not long after he departed, she wrote to him disconsolately to say that it seemed "awfully queer" without him, but, she said, she loved him, and such love must be good in the end. A week later she complained in a letter to him that one of his friends, met by chance, had laughed in a horrid way while speaking to her, hinting that the actress Alla Nazimova, a former lover of Sterne's, was also going out west in the near future. To be sure, Nazimova's destination was Arizona, not New Mexico, but all the West was much the same to Mabel, and she was seriously disturbed.

In return Maurice wrote often to her, to protest his love and to talk about Indians and his experiences in this new world. He was enthusiastic about Indian dances but missed his wife, and soon he thought of an argument that was bound to fetch her out there. Why shouldn't she come, he wrote, and save the Indians? The suggestion worked. Mabel telegraphed that she was practically on her way. This was on November 27, but before she could move from New York she got a sore throat, and Brill said she mustn't try to move. However, her impatience won out, and on December 17, having telegraphed to Maurice and also arranged for John Evans to leave the ranch in Wyoming and meet her in Santa Fe, she set out, well primed with Indian stories collected from her friends.

It was fashionable to be interested in Indians just then. The seers and fortunetellers Mabel loved were prone to discover "controls" who were, allegedly, American redskins. Better still was a story she adored, about a white man who had been permitted to attend an Indian ceremony. His hosts, tribe unspecified, had insisted on blindfolding him at first, but not before he saw that he sat among the Indians on the floor of an underground chamber, a sort of roofless hole in the ground. The Indians around him chanted and chanted, until the white man felt shifting in the circle and a change of atmosphere. Wind blew against his cheeks, and he heard the loud humming of something like a helicopter roaring overhead. Yet when the ceremony was over and the Indians had stopped chanting and he was allowed to take off the blindfold, everything was just as it had been before. This story of magic thrilled Mabel. No doubt Indians held the key to all kinds of similar secrets, she reflected. Such miracles might explain the moving of the stones that constituted the Pyramids. They might even know the truth about Atlantis, Leo Stein agreed.

Then there was a dream in which Maurice's face was supplanted by a strange, beautiful countenance, the dark-skinned visage of an unknown man whose deep brown eyes met hers. The stranger was an Indian; he must be an Indian, thought Mabel.

But when she arrived in Santa Fe after the trials and weariness that necessarily accompanied a long train trip in 1917, everything was so new and strange that she forgot even Indians — for a few days. She was taken aback by the smallness and simplicity of Maurice's adobe house. There were hardly any motor cars around. Most people used horses and wagons, and Mabel felt a sharp, familiar spasm of jealousy when Maurice presented to her a good-looking young girl who drove a smart pony-trap and had, it seemed, offered a temporary home to young John because Maurice's house was too small for the three of them. This Sara Parsons was far too attractive, thought Mabel; Maurice *must* be in love with her. However, he assured her that he wasn't, and Mabel began to appreciate the better things of Santa Fe. The scent of burning piñon, for example, was delicious, and one smelled it everywhere. The air was marvelously clear and invigorating. Everything seemed new and delightfully simple. That night Maurice was overjoyed to find that his virility had come back. All in all, Mabel was in excellent spirits and thoroughly pleased with Santa Fe — except for the necessity of being nice to Maurice's friends. No doubt it was in an impish mood of mischief that she wrote, years later, of her first unfavorable impression of Alice Corbin Henderson, whose daughter John Evans was, after a few years, to marry. She and Mrs. Henderson met the very first day after Mabel arrived.

To begin with, Mabel resented it when Maurice insisted on taking her across the road for tea with his friends the Burlins. She never liked being a guest unless she was very sure of her hosts; she was far too fond of being master in her own house to relish casual, easy social mingling. But Maurice, it seemed, had made a firm date, and though she protested that she hadn't come west just to meet a lot of *people*, she went. It wasn't a big party, just the painter Paul Burlin and his wife Natalie Curtis, who collected Indian music, and a little Mrs. Henderson, who was knitting an army sweater. Mrs. Henderson immediately began to talk to Mabel of Harriet Monroe and her *Poetry Magazine*, which was published in Chicago and of which she, Alice Henderson, was a co-editor. She seemed confident that Mabel would be interested, but Mabel wasn't. She didn't care about poetry magazines, or poets like Alice Corbin Henderson, either. She was in a contrary mood, not liking anything much, and when she stood up to go, which she did very soon, and Mrs. Henderson invited her to come over to tea the next day, she was determined not to accept. She, Mabel Dodge Sterne, was certainly not about to start a round of insipid tea parties in Santa Fe, certainly not. To get out of it, she said the first thing that popped into her mind, that she and Maurice couldn't come to tea because they were motoring to a place called Taos.

She claimed in afteryears that she couldn't remember where she had heard the name "Taos." This is probably not true. Obviously she preferred to believe that she was mysteriously drawn to the town and that it was then an unknown, unexplored spot in the mountains, but Taos in fact was pretty well known among the artists of America. A number of them had come upon it and settled down there even before the art colony of Santa Fe was formed, living and painting near the pueblo. When the Burlins expressed surprise at Mabel's wish to go there, it must have been because they resented the possibility that anyone should prefer the smaller settlement to theirs. (There has always been rivalry between Taos and Santa Fe.)

Undeterred, on the next day Mabel set out with the unwilling Maurice, passengers in a hired Ford that was driven by the owner, along the long, difficult, but beautiful road to Taos. It took them half the day to reach the canyon of the Rio Grande. They paused for lunch at Embudo before entering the deepest gorge, and it was late when they emerged on the sandy plain that had to be crossed before reaching the big mountain, with Taos at its foot. It was dark by the time they arrived at the Taos hotel; nothing could be seen, but already Mabel was in love with the place. In spite of Maurice's protests — how could he tell if it was a good place, if he could work there, until he had seen it? — she insisted on setting things going, calling after dinner on the only person, according to the hotel people, who might help them to find a house. At best, those people at the hotel had been dubious about the prospect:

Taos residents, they said, lived in their own houses and so wouldn't be likely to rent them. But Mabel had had experience in persuading house owners to let her have what she wanted. She had done it, after all, at Finney Farm. It was merely a question of money.

The man recommended by the waitress was Dr. Martin, who lived near the edge of the town, not far from the hotel and the plaza. The Sternes walked down the road by the light of Maurice's flashlight, following directions. They could see very little, but Mabel was fascinated. In the dark two horses plodded by silently, their riders wrapped in white sheets. "Indians!" she whispered in thrilled tones to Maurice, and Maurice, who by this time had seen many Indians, assented.

Doc Martin was a hearty man whom Mabel liked, always, even though she didn't quite trust him. He was not very helpful at first, saying, like the people at the hotel, that Taos residents lived in their own houses. However, upon further thought he admitted that his next-door neighbor, Mr. Manby, had a lot of extra space in his house which he might be willing to rent to the Sternes. The fact that Maurice was a painter seemed to explain things to Doc Martin and reassure him; a lot of those fellows were to be found in the town, he said genially. He added that Manby was cranky as the devil, but one never knew. Mabel agreed to try him in the morning. It would have to be early morning, she knew, because their driver wanted to be on the road back.

Her mysterious love for Taos was slightly dampened after sunrise, when she looked around the plaza. It all seemed disappointingly ordinary. Was this all there was to it — the dusty road, the dreary-looking stores? If so, she could understand why people in Santa Fe had spoken disparagingly of Taos, but she was still confident that somehow her destiny awaited her here, so after breakfast they went to see the mysterious Manby, knocking on his door set in a high adobe wall. There was a metal sign to one side of it, she noted, advertising a land corporation. Manby did not look prepossessing when he opened the door, with his bloodshot eyes and unshaven face, but when he spoke the Sternes were startled and charmed, for he had a cultivated English voice and vocabulary. And his house was charming, though badly neglected and utterly filthy. Manby showed them the imposing extent of his land and spoke confidently of the development he planned to accomplish through his company, a prospect that was clearly far in the future. Though he seemed so eccentric as to be half mad, he and Mabel struck it off immediately. She knew how to talk to him. As Doc Martin had said, there was a considerable part of the house that wasn't being used and that was conveniently separated from Manby's living quarters. She was sure it would do for herself and Maurice. After a certain amount of persuasion Manby agreed to rent that part of the house to them for six months, and over her husband's objections Mabel told him that they would be back to take up residence on the first of the year. Then, at the outset of the return journey to Santa Fe, she asked their driver to take them the necessary mile out of the way to look at the pueblo.

The driver was impatient and gave them little time to look, but even one glimpse excited Mabel and Maurice. Taos Pueblo is well known now, but it came as a revelation to them — the heavy, simplified brown cubes that were piled up, as Mabel said, like children's building blocks in two distinct masses. As the visitors drove off, she looked back and saw two Indians in their white sheets standing on one of the roofs and looking after the car. She thought the place looked enviably self-contained and contented, and wished she belonged there. It was an echo of the emotion she had felt that first night when, in Florence, she looked out of her hotel window at the city's lights and vowed, "I will make you mine."

During the week that remained before the final move from Santa Fe, the Sternes went with the Burlins to see the Christmas dance at Santo Domingo Pueblo. Indifferent at first (because Maurice had arranged it), Mabel was soon in love with the landscape, beautiful and mysterious. In the hills nearby she saw a resemblance to Leonardo's landscapes, but the desert beyond them was new and breathtaking to a woman from her part of the world, and the mountains that edged it were purple against the sky. Here one might well realize life better than anywhere else, she thought, and she looked eagerly at the Indians who lounged in front of the pueblo's trading post. They had a "friendly aloofness" in their faces; their eyes were glowing and alive. She was charmed, too, with the Catholic church at Santo Domingo, its façade painted with two prancing horses, one red, one blue. When she heard singing and drumming farther on, she couldn't wait for her companions, but ran ahead of them to see what was happening. The sing-

J. LUDOVICI,   889 BROADWAY, N. Y.

Mabel Ganson as a baby.

Mabel Ganson, sixteen years old, 1895.

Mabel Ganson as a debutante, aged eighteen.

Mabel's father, Charles Ganson.

Mabel's mother, Sara Cook Ganson

Ganson, Kent, Porter, Dolbins and Howard
on Decoration Day, May 1895.

Mabel Ganson Evans, twenty-one years
old, 1900.

Mabel Ganson Evans with her dogs, 1900.

Mabel Ganson Evans and Karl Evans with their son, John Ganson Evans, 1902.

Karl Evans and his son, John Ganson Evans, 1901.

John Ganson Evans in Florence, Italy, 1905.

Mabel Ganson Evans Dodge, twenty-six years old, Edwin S. Dodge, and John Ganson Evans, 1905.

Mabel Ganson Dodge in her villa, Florence, Italy, May 1911. (Courtesy the Beinecke Library, Yale University)

The Dodges' villa, Florence, Italy. (Courtesy the Beinecke Library, Yale University)

Bedroom in the Dodge villa, Florence, Italy. (Courtesy the Beinecke Library, Yale University)

Mabel's third husband, the painter
Maurice Sterne. (Courtesy the Beinecke
Library, Yale University)

"The Big House" and environs, Taos, New Mexico. (Courtesy the Beinecke Library, Yale University)

Interior of the Taos house. (Courtesy Henriette Harris)

D. H. Lawrence reading at Taos, New Mexico. (Courtesy the Beinecke Library, Yale University)

Mabel, Frieda Lawrence and Dorothy Brett at Taos. (Courtesy Henriette Harris)

Mabel and Cady Wells on the veranda at Taos. (Courtesy, Henriette Harris)

Tony Luhan and John Ganson Evans, 1918. (Courtesy the Beinecke Library, Yale University)

Mabel Sterne in 1930. The inscription reads "For Henriette from Mabel. Tony's House. January, 1930." (Courtesy Henriette Harris)

Mabel Sterne, napping. Drawn by Witter Bynner, Taos, 1932.

Mabel Dodge Luhan and Tony Luhan at home in Taos. (Courtesy the Beinecke Library, Yale University)

Painting by Dorothy Brett of Mabel's funeral, now hanging in Emily Hahn's apartment. (Gregory Dawson)

Portrait of Tony Luhan. (Courtesy the Beinecke Library, Yale University)

ers were eighty or ninety old men standing about a great drum,
singing as a tribe, expressing what seemed to her the one unani-
mous expression of many. It seemed to Mabel that it was the first
time in her life she had heard anything like that, one voice speaking for a whole people. All of a sudden, after having lived in a
civilization where everyone strove for individuality and separate-
ness, she was brought up against this, the Tribe, in which lay an
instinct for wholeness, a virtue in togetherness. She was awed and
silenced.

It is, of course, not likely that Mabel really formulated all this
philosophical thought during her first experience with Indian dancing. That was to come later, when she was eager to understand
and accept Tony's way of looking at things. But it seems very
possible that at the beginning she was in that euphoric stage that
in many cases accompanies one's introduction to the high air of
northern New Mexico. It made her impatient to be told that it was
the altitude — "Oh, it's more than that!" she had snapped at the
driver in Taos when he ventured the suggestion. We don't like to
be told that our emotional excitements are due to physiological
causes, and that day at Santo Domingo she only knew that she
loved the dancing. She even felt a gush of appreciation and fellow
feeling for Maurice when he said, "It's wonderful, isn't it?" But
she was irritated by Natalie Curtis after the other woman led the
group to an Indian's house and asked him to give her a song. Natalie, it seemed to Mabel, didn't imitate the Indian properly when
he sang for her. She got the tones right, but the feeling was wrong;
she sang it sweetly, whereas when Geronimo sang it was strong,
full of life but impersonal. Mabel was suddenly depressed. A gulf
yawned between the Indians and the whites, she thought, and she
felt lonesome. But she was determined, sooner or later, to bridge
that gulf.

Then they moved to Taos. One wonders what Maurice's sensations were in those first days about his wife's sudden love affair
with New Mexico. He must have been gratified by the proof that
he had been right when he said that she was bound to like the
place and take to the Indians. He had long entertained a theory,
seldom expressed, that she had Indian blood. Such a thing was not
unheard of in old Buffalo families, he reflected, and Mabel certainly
resembled an Indian squaw, with her rather heavy build and fea-
tures. He thought that this supposed trace of Indian ancestry

might explain the way she immediately took to the Indians they encountered. At first he was indulgent about this taste of hers, but he could not share it. In his opinion Indians made splendid models, but socially they had little or nothing to offer, and Mabel's passion for Taos itself left him cold. His version of her choice of it as a place to live is interesting:

> Mabel had heard somewhere of a town in the hills of New Mexico called Taos, and insisted soon after she arrived that we drive up to see it. She was fascinated when we got to Taos and said that this was where we must settle down. I, on the other hand, did not like Taos from the moment I set foot there. I felt its void, a primeval space before concrete form began . . . There was a loneliness about the place under which I physically suffered. Our attitudes toward the Indians differed also . . .

One day, said Maurice, he and Mabel went out with a picnic lunch. To eat it they selected a spot with a magnificent view and brought out the lunch, a cold roast chicken. They had hardly unwrapped it before Indians began to turn up, though they had thought themselves quite alone. One after another, hungry redskins came on the scene, and Maurice suspected they had followed the Sternes from town. They accepted eagerly when Mabel invited them to join in the picnic, and in a very short time the chicken had disappeared, a fact that annoyed Maurice, for they had planned to eat what was left of the bird at a moonlight supper.

"I was disappointed but took it good-naturedly," he said, "believing that since the white man had taken their land away, it was only proper that we should feed them." However, when the food was gone the Indians simply walked off without so much as saying thanks, and Maurice thought this too much. It didn't help that Mabel defended them, arguing that Indians are too proud to say thank-you.

"Mabel hardly said anything those first few days at Taos, but I could see that she was deeply stirred," continued Maurice. "I was therefore not surprised when she announced, 'Here I belong, and here I want to stay.'" He remembered his Indian-blood theory and did not protest.

They settled down comfortably in their section of Manby's house; Mabel hired a local Mexican girl to cook for them, and turned with enthusiasm to a study of Taos, the background of the Mexican peasants (today called, with more tact and accuracy, Spanish Americans), and the history of the Indian pueblo so near to town. Young John Evans was still with them before going back east to school, and Mabel got him to drive the family to the pueblo. John was getting on better with Maurice these days, and one feels that Mabel didn't like the development: she loved to stir up trouble between her men. But she was happy and busy and didn't mind it as much as she would have in New York. She had brought with her on this expedition a bag of oranges, having been told that the Indians would appreciate the fruit. They drove up to the front of the great structure and parked near a group of houses that looked hospitable because its doors stood open, and a few children ran out to greet them. Then, said Mabel, a beautiful woman stepped to one of the open doors, a woman in Navajo dress with a tight, broad belt of red woven material and a full skirt and white embroidered petticoat. She smiled warmly at the strangers, and Mabel, immediately drawn to her — and not, of course, realizing that she was one day to take the woman's husband away — got out of the car and went toward her eagerly, the others following. She described her feelings as those of a hunter, cautiously ready to sprinkle salt on a bird's tail.

A sound of singing and soft drum-beating came to their ears, and Mabel halted in her tracks. But the woman smilingly beckoned the party inside, and they tiptoed through the door into a large, empty, whitewashed room, unfurnished save for mattresses rolled against the wall and covered with sheets. There was a fire, and before it a man was bent over a drum held between his knees. He softly beat it and sang in a low, resonant murmur. The fire perfumed the air, and bright sunlight came in through one window high on the wall. The woman signed to the visitors to sit down on the mattresses.

At length the singing stopped and the man lifted his head to reveal — as Mabel realized with a shock of recognition — that same brown face she had seen in her dream. He said, "I sing you a little song." And the dazzled Mabel handed him an orange.

That, she said later, was her meeting with Tony, her fate. To be sociable, Maurice asked Tony what the words might be of his song, but the Indian brushed him off rather coldly, saying that the song had no words.

"Thank you!" said Mabel. "I wish you'd come and see us down in Taos." To which Tony replied, "I seen you before, already," and gave her a swift, meaningful glance.

Was this exchange, as she fondly believed, Tony's avowal that he too had recognized something supernatural between them? It is unlikely that she ever pinned him down and questioned him closely enough to make certain; they were always to find verbal communication limited. Maurice, however, scoffed at this story of her first meeting with Tony and rewrote it completely in his book — it was not like that at all, he said. He first saw Tony Lujan at the Manby house, some time before the encounter at the pueblo: he was one of the Indians who turned up in increasing numbers every day, always at mealtimes. The others were the customary hungry creatures whom to his vexation Mabel was always inviting to stay and eat, but one day there came a different type who didn't look at all hungry — quite a magnificent man. To Maurice's surprise Mabel greeted this man familiarly, saying, "Come in, Tony." Where had she met him?

"She very seriously introduced us and he grunted something unintelligible while we shook hands," said Mabel's husband. "I did not like him even at this first meeting. He had an arrogance which, although it was not directed particularly at me, seemed to come from some deep inner feeling." Maurice thought of the line, "Oh, East is East, and West is West, and never the twain shall meet," and after Tony had left he said to Mabel that Kipling must have been referring to New York and New Mexico. The mild joke didn't seem to please Mabel, who was clearly not in the mood to be facetious.

"I am convinced," wrote Maurice, "that even then she was determined not only that they meet, but that they be fused."

The Sternes continued to entertain "dirty, smelly Indians" to lunch practically every day, he said with distaste, but Tony was different. "His white sheet was spotless, his long braids were beautifully arranged, intertwined with a white ribbon that made an exquisite pattern. He was well built, though on the portly side, and had an enormous chest. He stood out from the rest like a proud cock amongst a flock of meek chickens, strutting with his head thrown back, with the air of a conquering hero."

Curious as to how he had gotten that way, Maurice once asked another Indian if Tony wasn't a chief, but the man laughed scornfully and denied it. Tony, he said, was just a no-good show Indian, and Maurice accepted this remark with gleeful malice. It seemed that Tony's adaptability with white people and his general air of assurance owed themselves to a tour he had once made to Coney

Island with a Wild West show — a fact that Mabel never mentioned in her writings, which is understandable. As for that meeting that she so romantically described, when their eyes met in the
pueblo room and Tony said, "I seen you before," Maurice's story
was different. They had gone that day to visit Taos Pueblo, he
said, and as they approached a house, an Indian who had been
standing at the door rushed inside. Then a "handsome squaw"
came out to invite them in, and they entered to find the Indian
man squatting on the floor, beating a drum and singing as if ignorant of their presence, seemingly absorbed in some kind of mystical state, "until at last he slowly raised his head. It was, of course,
Tony." It should have been clear to anyone, said Maurice, that the
whole thing was a show put on to impress tourists. When Mabel
invited Tony to come and see them and he asked, "Where you
live?" Maurice was annoyed and nearly said, "You know damn
well where we live." After all, he had visited them once socially,
and Maurice had seen him several times snooping around the
house. Indeed, Manby, who took a very superior attitude toward
Indians, had warned Maurice that Tony had been seen "spying
around the place." Look out for him, said Manby, he was a no-
good Indian.

Then there was the dancing. Mabel and Maurice invited several
Indians in for a party they were giving, to dance for the company.
Tony was in charge, and that night he arrived with three other
inhabitants of the pueblo — of course at dinnertime, said Maurice
bitterly. After dinner Maurice, who had a slight headache, decided
to forgo the evening's drumming and excused himself to go to bed.
But before he left he talked to Tony in a corner and gave him
twenty-five dollars, explaining that ten dollars was for him and five
for the others. As far as he knew, the evening went without a
hitch. But a few days later, when he encountered one of the other
Indians in town, he was surprised that the man refused to return
his greeting and attempted to ride off without a word. What was
the matter? Maurice asked. The Indian burst out in angry explanation. He and his friends, he said, had played and danced for the
Sternes, but what had they received in return? Not a penny!

Maurice protested that he had given all the money to Tony.
Well, Tony, said the Indian, hadn't given them any of it. "Tony no
good," he declared, and Maurice felt bound to agree. He was very
indignant. It so happened that he ran into the offending Tony that

very day; when he got home he found Mabel preparing to go out riding with him. Maurice taxed him with the affair, but in vain. Tony, he said, was "arrogant." He simply got on his pony and rode off.

"That's right, you can go now, but you'd better not come back," shouted the infuriated Maurice.

Mabel had been standing by all the time and heard the interchange. "Her only reaction," said Sterne, "was to hurl a savage look at me and fling herself into the house." Only a stupid man wouldn't have found all this ominous, and Maurice Sterne was not stupid, but things did not yet come to a head.

The long winter months were whiled away. Maurice had at last decided that he was ready to try his hand at sculpture, and Mabel was pleased. She felt that she had gone through a lot to make a sculptor of him. Incorrigibly gregarious, she lost no time inviting friends to come and stay: two women from the East were the first to accept. All would have been well, she thought, if only they had had a decent cook; the Mexican girl was sadly inadequate. But Tony often came to eat with the ladies and sang for them, and they pronounced him charming. As soon as these guests had gone she invited Andrew Dasburg and Bobby Jones to come, and begged them to bring a decent cook with them. They turned up with a German man of awesome pedigree. He was an excellent cook, if extravagant, but Mabel found that she could not rebuke him in company. She did so once, and he fainted dead away.

Like other small communities, Taos was a hotbed of gossip. The worst offender, Mabel decided, was Doc Martin, who collected the news every morning and hurried out to disseminate it. It was too much to expect him to ignore the fascinatingly varied company installed at his next-door neighbor's, and he didn't. But Manby, as things turned out, was truly the worst offender. He grew suspicious of the heavily German atmosphere of the household. Andrew, who was born in Germany, loved to talk about the war with Maurice, who had at least visited there more than once. Like many other men in wartime, they kept a map and plotted the battles they heard of, talking far into the night about strategy. Sometimes the cook was in on these talks. For Mabel's part, she had taken to spending a lot of time at the pueblo, teaching the women how to knit (she had always been good at knitting and needlework). She concentrated on Tony's wife, because, as she said, she so loved that peaceful firelit room. During the daylight hours Andrew had taken enthusiastically to a new pastime, collecting santos, the crudely painted icons favored by the Mexicans. Some of them were remarkably beautiful and many were old. Andrew sent them to New York where a market for them sprang up.

One night Andrew and Maurice noticed what they had been aware of subconsciously for a long time, a kind of scratching on the roof. One of them said jokingly that somebody must be up there at the chimney, listening. It was not a joke. Soon afterward the household had a visit in the person of the law — at least, he was a retired mounted policeman who had been in contact with a genuine inspector and had brought him along. They demanded an explanation of the shenanigans in Manby's house which, they said, had been going on ever since Mabel arrived with her entourage. War games, a German cook, suspicious parcels and boxes arriving all the time, Andrew Dasburg and his wanderings from village to village . . .

The inspector told Mabel that she was suspected of pro-German activities. People said that big boxes of arms and ammunition were delivered regularly to her, that she was storing them in her house, and that at least one member of her household was going around to the Mexicans enlisting them in the German cause. Moreover, Mabel herself was inciting the Indians to rebel against the government.

But why? What were they trying to do? Mabel asked the inspector for details, and he replied that they were obviously making ready to take over for the enemy. The countryside around Taos, he said, was a natural gateway to Colorado and the West, a gate that could be used by Mexico. Struggling between wrath and amusement, Mabel delivered a broadside. The crates and boxes, she said, were full of groceries. The man who was visiting the Mexicans every day was collecting old paintings. As for herself and her suspect visits to the Indians, she was merely teaching them to knit. She added that her stepfather was Rear Admiral Reeder, that several members of her family were majors and colonels in the army, and that she demanded an apology for the whole ridiculous accusation.

Her indignant assurance had its effect. Mabel wrote to Washington, there was an investigation, and the dogs of war were called off — with red faces all round among her detractors. Mabel was always convinced that it was Manby's doing: it was he who had been sitting on the roof trying to hear what Maurice and Andrew were saying, perched up there with one ear to the chimney. He seemed unusually quiet for a while, but Mabel never accused him of having gone to the authorities. She understood this unattractive character, and knew that he was really an incurable romantic playing cowboys and Indians. Many years later Manby was the victim of a gruesome mystery that would have satisfied even his demands for melodrama, when he was found dead in his house, the head missing from the corpse. Later it turned up, however; his dogs had been chewing at it. Had they pulled the head from the body, or did it happen after someone got in and killed the old man? Rumor had always said that he was a miser and had a great fortune of gold hidden away. Someone might well have murdered him in the hopes of getting the treasure. Old-timers in Taos argued the question for years.

In spite of the spy scare, the odd little family at Manby's enjoyed that first winter. Mabel found an old-fashioned sleigh that had been forgotten in a livery stable, and she and Andrew, driving a sadly puzzled horse, went out over the snow in it, traveling for miles. Then the back of winter was broken and Easter loomed on the horizon, and she persuaded Maurice to come out on Good Friday night on a Penitente hunt, as the pastime was known locally. The Mexican Penitentes, like the Flagellantes of Spain, were a secret society. On that night they always selected a certain hill, which they called Calvary, and went through a somewhat grisly ceremony, pulling heavy crosses as they chanted, and pausing every so often to whip themselves. Naturally, they preferred to celebrate these rites in privacy. It was rumored that they had been forbidden by law to go through the crisis of the whole affair when a young man, selected as being the holiest in the village, was actually crucified. In any case the Penitentes, who had been excommunicated by the Church, tried to keep their ceremonies secret. But every year some of the Taos non-Catholics attempted to watch them, and Mabel was eager and curious. Maurice, predictably, did not share her feelings. Still, he went along with her and some of her friends on Good Friday night. Through the long, dark hours they waited, hiding behind clumps of weed and giggling and shivering. It was all very uncomfortable and unrewarding, and they had almost given up when they saw lights in the distance. After that, said Mabel, the ceremony was revealed to them. They saw and heard twenty or thirty men chanting and pausing now and then at representations of the Stations of the Cross, when she claimed she could hear the thump of cactus knouts descending on the naked flesh of backs and shoulders. Then suddenly, she claimed, she was ashamed of spying on such an intimate exhibition, and led her little company away.

Very different was Maurice's version. He said they saw nothing but the lights and were on their way home when they ran into the light-bearers they had pursued so long — a group of Anglo-American artists who lived in Taos and who had, like themselves, been chasing Penitentes all night. It is a typical divergence between the accounts of this married couple.

Chapter Ten

CANDELARIA WAS the name of Tony Lujan's wife. Her father, as Mabel said with a strangely misplaced pride, had been a remarkable man in his day. Manby had assured her of that, but by the time Mabel came on the scene the old fellow was dead. Candelaria and Tony had no children, and their house was always clean and uncluttered, unlike the one next door, where Tony's mother lived with her daughter and son-in-law, John Archuleta. There were many Archuleta children, and Tony was a fond uncle who visited them often, but Candelaria didn't get on with her in-laws. When Tony went next door, therefore, he went alone. His favorite Archuleta niece was a teen-ager, Paulita, who helped her mother with the children. Mabel got to know all these people and enjoyed their company so much that she went almost every weekday morning to the pueblo, coming home at lunchtime in a cheerful mood and even trying, she confessed, to look like an Indian. Indeed, the very evening she arrived to live in Taos she had persuaded her son to cut her hair short, and she wore it in a Dutch bob that was like an Indian's instead of her former style of puffs over the ears. The change annoyed Maurice, who preferred long-haired women, but Mabel was happy as she was. Usually she tied back her truncated locks with a length of ribbon, Alice in Wonderland style.

One Sunday morning, as she sat in the Lujan house knitting, Tony came in. He paused before her, wrapped in the Taos white sheet, staring down at the purple ribbon in her hair with peculiar intensity. Then he said, "Ni-i-ice color." So Tony liked purple, did he? As soon as Mabel could find one, she bought a shawl of the same purple and thereafter wore it every day, arranged in the fashion of Indian women.

The household at Manby's resented her frequent absences, and said so. John Evans, left to the devices of a tutor, asked her why she had to go to the pueblo so often. Was she sure, he said, that the Indians wanted her? Maurice told her that she was wasting her time trying to teach those people anything, and Andrew was plaintive because she no longer went hunting santos with him in the Mexican villages, but Mabel would shrug it all off, eat her lunch, wrap herself in the purple shawl, and lie down on a couch where she felt that she could wall off her critics. All her life she spent a good deal of time on couches.

Again one wonders: what had triggered her off? What sent her in this new direction? No doubt it seemed an adventure to her, and an enjoyable one. The Indian world in the handsome person of Tony Lujan — or Luhan, as she preferred to spell it — was unknown to her, and the unknown was always a challenge. Nobody in her group of friends had ever investigated the American Indian; people looked on the race with a sort of awe — at least the people of the eastern states did. Indians had been robbed of lands and power, but in the East they enjoyed a good press, witness Longfellow's *Hiawatha.* This classic was not so popular in the West; Mark Twain, for one, put into his *Adventures of Tom Sawyer* a "murderin' half-breed, Injun Joe." If Mabel had been a western girl she would no doubt have accepted her elders' opinion and thought of Indians as shiftless, dirty, and cruel, but she was an Easterner. None of her ancestors had been cattlemen or sheepherders; she had no vested interest in their outlook.

And Tony was a good-looking specimen, portly but tall and well built, and always fresh-looking, his braids smoothly plaited and oiled, Taos fashion, hanging over his shoulders, and his handsome blanket worn like a toga. He looked especially nice in colored blankets, but in hot weather he was handsome, too, in the ordinary white sheet. The Harvey guides, young women, liked to stop and exchange greetings with Tony, and introduce him to their tourists. He made a good impression. Tony liked the guides, too; he liked all women.

One morning Mabel went to the pueblo to find Tony and the Archuletas worried because Paulita was very ill, running a high fever and coughing. She had got her feet wet, said Tony, going out at night to the fields, which is what the Indians had to do to relieve the call of nature. Tony complained to Mabel that too many pueblo people had caught cold recently; it hadn't been like that in the old days. Mabel's version is that she saw that Paulita was really ill, so she insisted on calling Dr. J. J. Bergmans, the doctor employed by the government to take care of the Indians in that neighborhood — though, she said, Tony and the others did not seem to have much use for him. She bustled over to rout him out and insisted that he come immediately. Dr. Bergmans was not quick enough to suit her, but he did come at last, listened to Paulita's lungs, left some aspirin, and departed, after telling Mabel when she asked that the girl had double pneumonia. And that, said Mabel indignantly, was as far as his ministrations went. Paulita died that night without further attention from the white doctor.

The government archives contain a far more detailed account of this affair in an angry letter from Mabel to George Creel of the Bureau of Indian Affairs in Washington. She had already written to him about Taos in one way or another. Now she declared that Dr. Bergmans was an ignorant and inhumane man who owed his position to some kind of political pull. She had been asking around, and the facts, she said, were scarcely believable. The death rate was increasing under his care and she was told that he lost all the babies in the Indian pueblo. She described the case of Paulita (whom she called Pollita) in great detail. Paulita had had a cold on Sunday when she came to Mabel's house, and was later caught in the rain. Monday she came to see Mabel again, with a bad cough. Mabel sent her home in the car. On Tuesday when Mabel went to the pueblo she found Paulita very ill, and she sent Tony to the school to telephone Bergmans. As it happened, the doctor was there with the schoolmaster. He said he would be along, but it took him an hour. Bergmans took her temperature and said she had pneumonia. No, said Mabel, it was congestion of the lungs. He left her a good dose of cathartic and prescribed a tepid bath; he also left medicine to be taken every three hours, and a mustard plaster.

They arranged, said Mabel, that she would stay until bedtime, for Paulita's mother was confused and didn't understand the directions. Mabel gave Paulita the tepid sponge bath and dosed her, staying until nine o'clock. Leaving, she hoped the doctor would soon be back to give the girl a stimulant. But he didn't come, and at five the next morning Paulita died.

And another case, said Mabel, was that of an Indian hit on the head with a rock by another man. He went to see Dr. Bergmans and the doctor didn't clean the scalp wound. The Indian nearly died of infection.

A change was very much needed, said Mabel. She suggested that they put Dr. Martin back in the job, as the Indians had petitioned — at least she said they had petitioned for Doc Martin, though no record of this could be found. What is on record is an affidavit signed by Dr. Bergmans, as follows:

In reference to my attendance of Paulita Archuleta of the Pueblo of Taos, I beg to state that I was called to see her on April 9th, ultimo, at three o'clock in the afternoon, on my way to the Pueblo on one of my regular trips; that I responded to the call within 20 minutes, and found her suffering of congestion of the right lung, with high fever and prostration.

My diagnosis was made after thorough examination, after which I gave her the proper medicines myself by mouth, leaving her in the care of Mrs. Mabel Sterne, who volunteered her services, and who promised to carefully carry out my orders and give medicines according to my instructions.

I was in the Pueblo more than 3 hours, close to the patient and went over three times to attend to her, promising that I would at any time during the night come, upon being called.

When leaving I found her no worse, and expected a reaction during the night, aided by proper care and treatment, as I felt safe about the attendance.

I was not called during the night, and at 7 o'clock in the morning while getting ready to leave for the Pueblo, Mrs. Bolander, wife of the Teacher, notified me by telephone that Paulita had died at three o'clock.

Sometime later I was told by a close relative of the deceased that a blind Indian medicine man had "treated" the girl during the night, after Mrs. Sterne had left.

According to the description, which was given me, this so-called treatment was extremely injurious to her chances for improvement.

As for the Indian "hit on the head with a rock," Geronimo Sandoval, Dr. Bergmans stated that he had treated the man for two stab wounds that were made by a knife. He dressed these wounds every day for seventeen days, when the Indian was discharged as cured. "When the patient came to my office," said the doctor, "he was much intoxicated and almost uncontrollable, so much so that two persons had to hold him while I treated his wounds."

In the files of the Bureau of Indian Affairs is an interesting letter from the clerk who was put in charge of the resulting inquiry into

Mabel's complaint. This man, W. E. Robertson, made an appointment with Mabel and came to Taos to see her, but she put him off for some hours by simply not being at home. In the meantime, therefore, he met with the doctor, the schoolmaster, the schoolmaster's wife, Mrs. Bergmans, and Paulita's mother, Mrs. Archuleta. The point was made that Dr. Bergmans had been at the school that day expressly to examine the children, as he did regularly.

"Mrs. Sterne states that she followed out the doctor's orders with 'a good deal of apprehension,'" quoted Mr. Robertson, "but Paulita's mother says that she did not give Paulita any of the medicine that was left by the doctor, nor give her a sponge bath. The mother says Mrs. Sterne did not do anything . . . I am also submitting a statement made by the Governor and the President of the Council. From the latter mentioned statement it will be seen that the Indians are satisfied with the services rendered by Dr. Bergmans. Mrs. Sterne has evidently written an untruth, when she states that the Indians sent a petition to the doctor who was formerly their physician asking that he come back and take care of them. The Governor states that he has no knowledge of any such petition, as it was never brought before the Council."

At six-thirty that evening Mr. Robertson again tried to reach Mabel, and this time he found her at home. "She refused to make any statement in writing, and when asked for specific cases where the doctor had been negligent could not mention any," he wrote.

She also stated that it was her opinion, that the condition of the Indians would not be bettered by the removal of Dr. Bergmans and the appointment of someone else, if the new appointee was to be a contract doctor. She admitted that Dr. Bergmans was doing all and more than his contract called for.

I find that Mrs. Sterne has been in Taos since December, 1917. She can not, as she says, "have become friends with them and have had a good chance to see their life on the inside and to judge their situation," in the short time she has been there. The Indians at the Pueblo do not know her, and the only Indians she is acquainted with, are the few her husband has employed as models, and the ones employed around the house as servants, etc. . . .

She states "The death rate increases under his care and they tell me he is losing all the babies in the Indian Pueblo." This statement is not borne out by the records of this office. During the fiscal year ended June 30,

1917, our records show there were 8 deaths and 15 births; and during the fiscal year ended June 30, 1918, there were 10 deaths and 8 births. Of the deaths during the past year, only two were under the age of 20, one being 2½ years old and the other 19 years old, and six were above the age of 50, three of these being in the 70's. As to the doctor's losing all the Indian babies in the Pueblo, the Indians tell me that no white doctor has ever been present at the birth of an Indian child. It is their custom to not have any man at all present when a child is born, not even the father. The women of the village look after the bringing of the child into the world.

After a thorough investigation of the matters complained of by Mrs. Sterne, I find that her charges against Dr. Bergmans are entirely without foundation; that Dr. Bergmans not only lives up to his contract, but that he visits the Indians whenever he is called, whether day or night, (his contract calls for two visits to the school each week . . .); that the Indians are well pleased with the service rendered by Dr. Bergmans and that they do not desire a change, and that Mrs. Sterne has either willfully or ignorantly misstated facts in her letter to Hon. George Creel. I would therefore recommend that no further action be taken in the matter, and that any similar complaints filed by Mrs. Sterne in the future be disregarded.

Inevitably, Mabel got a black mark at the Bureau of Indian Affairs. Equally inevitably, she did not love them any the better for the result of their inquiries.

As for Paulita, Mabel attended as much of the burial ceremony as she was allowed to. The Indian women, wrapped in black shawls, wailed aloud as an old man made an oration to the dead girl, and the men, wrapped to the eyes in their blankets, squatted silent on the ground. Then Mabel had to go — "They have their own doin's," explained Tony's Uncle Joe — and watched the procession from outside as the body was carried to the pueblo graveyard.

Maurice, now well embarked on sculpture, was working on the head of a Taos Indian named Pete Marcus. He had built up an armature of plaster of paris and applied black modeling wax to it so slowly that Pete often fell asleep on the dais. Mabel was gratified that her husband was doing sculpture, but it didn't seem to matter as much as it had before they came to Taos. At least, however, they were not quarreling, and Maurice was amiably willing to come on an outing suggested by Tony, riding in the Indian's buggy to see the hot springs in the river canyon, where Manby had built a stone bathhouse. Pete Marcus and Tony rode in front of the buggy,

Maurice and Mabel behind. She wore her purple shawl pulled over her head, Indian fashion, and wished she were sitting with Tony — but Maurice did not know what was going on in that covered head.

It was a lovely day. The bathing place delighted Maurice and Mabel. She took her dip first while the men waited outside; then she came out and they took their turn. For lunch they cooked steaks on forked sticks at an open fire, and Tony washed the coffeepot afterward in the river. She watched him admiringly. He had an expressionless face when he wanted, she reflected, but it was always a very *kind* face.

After lunch they clambered over the rocks to look at an Indian carving that Tony interpreted for them. Then Mabel, for want of a couch, sat down on a sandy place near the edge of a little cliff, and Tony walked over and surreptitiously dropped into her open hand a small red bundle. Mabel was not expecting the move and was not quick enough to grasp the thing, which rolled over the edge and fell down to the level below. Maurice saw the incident, and picked up the red bundle. He studied it as if puzzled, and Mabel had time to see what it was — a small round bag of red silk, with something in it. Maurice, looking immensely surprised, stared at Mabel and glanced at Tony, who was busily, obliviously picking up blankets and things, and he finally put the little bag into his pocket. How Mabel hated Maurice for that! But nobody, of course, said a word about the incident.

As if nothing had occurred they drove back to Manby's, Tony now and then pointing out some item of interest on the landscape. When they arrived, Mabel waited at the door for Maurice to dig their various belongings out of the buggy. She watched Tony in the driver's seat. He stood up and stretched out his arms to rewrap his blanket, Indian fashion, about his body. Looking at her with a smile in his eyes, and unobserved by the stooping Maurice, he made a gesture as if enfolding her, too, inside the blanket. As she entered the door Mabel trembled. This was the sort of intrigue she loved.

She went to bed early, and as soon as Maurice had come in and was safely asleep she got up and rummaged out his clothes until she found the little red silk bag. It was a sort of sachet, she found, sweetly scented with a perfume she had noticed before when the breeze blew across Tony. She put it under her pillow and fell contentedly asleep. The next morning she sat up against the pillows, drinking coffee and watching Maurice as he hunted through his coat for the bag. At last he asked her if she had taken it, and she said she had.

"Is that a love token that Indian was giving you?" he demanded. Mabel laughed. What a word, she said jeeringly — love token! Maurice dropped the subject.

The love affair, said Mabel, evolved slowly and never came to its right and true consummation until she was free of Maurice, but Maurice contradicted her. She gave her account in great detail, lingering fondly over the development of the affair. She said that they spent a lot of time together, but Tony just talked, telling her about Indian attitudes. He didn't express himself very fluently in English, but Mabel managed to build tall edifices on what she imagined he was trying to say. Once she mentioned that she loved the empty white walls of the Lujans' room, and Tony rejoined that God had decreed that Indians should never own things. White people had things, but God gave the Indians just what grew on the mountain. Candelaria joined in and said something, which he translated for Mabel. "He say" — Tony never got his genders right — "he say God give white people things and Indians watch them go under them. You know. Wheel turning . . . So many things carry the wheel down, with the white people underneath. Pretty soon Indians come up again. Indians' turn next."

Mabel claims to have understood this immediately. From the very beginning, she said, she had had the power to see into his mind, see the pictures he was seeing. She saw the wheel slowly turning, carrying with it all the white man's civilization — machinery, sky-scrapers, motor cars, trains — all burying the white men under their weight, and on the other side the wheel emerging with the Indians uncluttered by things, their heads garlanded, their shoulders carrying corn and wheat, their people rising to take their turn.

This speech of Tony's was exceptionally long for him. Most of their communication, as Mabel said repeatedly, was terse; often he did not seem to feel the necessity of speech at all. On one occasion he took her two friends Julia (i.e., Alice Thursby) and Agnes for a drive to see a cave, and when the party returned to find Mabel waiting for them at the garden gate, Tony said nothing at all, but handed her a branch of spruce from higher up on the mountain. This was to show her where they had been, for spruce did not grow in the town. Mabel understood his signal, and hung the branch on her bedroom wall and treasured it. She did not have a chance to speak to him alone, and somewhat to her surprise he didn't try to manage it. She knew there was something happening between them. She knew that he was as conscious of it as she was, but he never tried to push matters along. He knew where he was going and she meekly followed his lead — she says. Probably, however, she was puzzled. Most decidedly, it was not the kind of extramarital courtship she was accustomed to.

Even at this point she was not quite indifferent to Maurice; the old habit of suspicious jealousy seems to have persisted. What was he doing, she wondered. The Burlins, for all their original scorn of Taos, seem to have overcome it to the extent of taking a house there and coming to live, at least for a period of time. They had a visitor, "a large, gray-eyed, rather solemn girl," who attracted Maurice's attention, so that, as Mabel spitefully said, he fixed his gaze on her and fascinated her. One night, it seems, he invited Mabel to join him and his friends at the town movie house, but as usual she refused, saying that she hadn't come to New Mexico just to know Americans. Then she did go anyway, alone, hoping to catch her husband out. She walked through the movie house, halfway up, to make sure he wasn't sitting there in the dark with "that girl." She wanted to know if he had lied to her. He had, she said cryptically.

Things were easier for Mabel — that is, it was easier to commune with Tony — when her friend Alice Thursby came to pay one of her frequent visits. Alice went out of her way to cultivate Tony, asking him to take her riding and inviting him to dinner at the Sternes'. Once when the two women were out riding with him, Alice obligingly dropped behind, giving Tony the chance to say to Mabel, "I saw you before you came. I dreamed you, but you had long hair."

Mabel declares that she answered, "Yes. John cut it off the first night I was here."

"Too bad," said Tony, evidently agreeing with Maurice in this matter at least. "You look nice with your hair, here on each side."

Mabel said, "I saw you in a dream, too, before I left New York. It made me come here."

Tony, without surprise, said simply, "Yes."

Did this conversation really take place? By the time she wrote her book, Mabel believed it did.

One afternoon she and McKenzie, John Evans's tutor, went out in the Ford with Tony, who wanted to learn to drive. Either because of something he did or just because the car was ready to break down, it stopped short a long way from town, and the Indian had to go to a nearby settlement to fetch horses. The car was finally towed back to Taos, but it was late, after dark, when Mabel got home. When Maurice met her at the entrance of the house he was so angry that he struck her across the face — so reads Mabel's version of the event. Mabel says that nobody else saw the incident. John was too far behind Maurice to have seen the blow. As for herself, she was habitually in such a tranced state that she thought little of it, and made no remark to anyone else. But in the morning there was a delayed reaction to the outrage: when she woke up she was too ill to get out of bed. She ached all over.

In the course of the day Alice went out, and so did Maurice. Mabel, left alone, lay there in misery, wishing for Tony — and then, late that afternoon, she heard him singing. She got up and looked out of the window, and there he was, sitting on the bench under the apple tree, softly singing. He stayed there for an hour before leaving, and Mabel lay in bed feeling better — so much better, in fact, that she was able to get up for dinner. For the first time, she said, she felt secure, safe. She came to the conclusion, which was borne out many times later on, that life among the Indians was always like that: they communicated with each other without words. Even singing was not necessary, said Mabel. Often Tony or another Indian would say that he wished So-and-so were there, and a few minutes later there came So-and-so, brightly smiling, though he had not been actually called. It was what we would call ESP, and Mabel firmly believed in it, and so, she said, did Tony, but whenever she asked him for an explanation he seemed to find it unnecessary to talk about it.

Tony's trip to New York grew out of an idea of Alice's. After talking to him and going around with him so much, and having conceived a great admiration and enthusiasm for the picturesque native, Alice was possessed by an urge to take him home and show him off to her friends in the East, especially to her brother. She talked it over with Mabel. If Tony went with her to Buffalo and New York, she said, he could then go on to Washington, D.C., and have an interview with the Great White Father, the President himself. She was so excited by the project that Mabel caught fire from her, and Tony, when they proposed it to him, was quite willing to try it. As Mabel explained, going to see the President was in the Indian tradition. They always hoped that the big boss would be able to help them, because once upon a time Abraham Lincoln actually had done them a favor. He had confirmed land grants they had received from the king of Spain, and at that time he presented all the pueblo governors with silver-headed canes. Tony might have hoped for some sort of coup like this.

The evening before they left he came to see Mabel and brought her two wild pink roses, the first of the season, he explained, which he had found miles from the village. Mabel was just thanking him when the Ford rolled up at the door, carrying John Evans and McKenzie home from some expedition, and she hurried to the garden gate to greet them, dropping the roses carelessly on the ground. Tony picked them up and, when John asked him to stay to dinner, he refused and walked away.

In the morning there was a great bustle getting the travelers off in the stagecoach. Tony's relations as well as Mabel's household were there to say goodbye. Tony, dressed in his best, with new ribbons on his braids, new moccasins, and a blanket of blue and purple stripes, never met Mabel's eyes. He embraced Candelaria by pressing her cheeks with his own, and he made the same gesture with the other members of his household, but when he shook hands with Mabel his grip was flabby, and again he didn't meet her eyes. The stage drove off, leaving Mabel desolate.

She felt lost, alone. Bitterly she reminded herself of the proverb from which she later took the title of her book: "He who loves with passion, lives on the edge of the desert!" A week or so afterward she got a letter from Tony, but it was a painful, almost indecipherable scrawl of misspelled words, phrases he had learned during his pitifully few days at school and was now trying to put together. She had no knowledge of how things were really going; it was Alice Thursby who told her about it all later. Everything had been wrong, said Alice, from the beginning. The minute the train pulled out of the station she knew that it was all a mistake. Tony looked strange to her. Where in Taos he seemed absolutely right, he now became just a brown-skinned man in a blanket. What was she doing? How had she got herself into such a fix? It seemed to her that everyone in the train was staring at the strange couple, whispering about them. What embarrassed Alice all the more was that in Taos, in an excess flow of admiration for her friend Mabel, she too had had her hair cut off, and at the time grown women simply didn't have bobbed hair.

Moreover, Tony too seemed unhappy. Once he came back from the washroom to say that there had been a cross man in there. He didn't, or couldn't, explain just what had happened, but we can make a guess. Throughout his life, as long as he traveled around with white people, Tony had trouble with washrooms. In his blanket and braids, and with his beardless face, he looked to white Americans like a woman. Men resented it when what they thought was an Indian squaw burst in on them in bathrooms. After she took to extensive motoring, Mabel had to get used to rows on this subject at filling stations.

By prearrangement, Alice's brother met her in Chicago, waiting for her on the platform. One look at his horrified if amused face was enough to send her into a frenzy of embarrassment, and she eagerly accepted his dictum that she must immediately buy Tony more conventional clothes. He took them by taxi to the nearest department store — probably Marshall Field's — and left it to Alice, who in turn left it to an attendant in the men's clothing department while she waited outside. She had never shopped for a man, so Tony was left to make his own selections. When he appeared once more, clad in a light green suit with blue shirt and what she described as a perfectly terrible hat, she didn't, for a minute, recognize him, but the braids were still there. Unhappily, Alice shouldered her burden once more and they resumed their eastward trek.

In Buffalo, the Carys laughed and laughed and laughed. In New York, Alice couldn't think of what to do with Tony. It was very hot and he was uncomfortable in the impure air, but there are certain things one does to entertain visitors in the city, and Alice tried. She took him to the Metropolitan Museum. This was an unfortunate choice; he hated the statues, pronouncing them dead. He hated New York altogether. He was homesick, and Alice gave in at last. Washington seemed out of the question, so she shipped him back to Taos by the next train.

The minute he arrived in the stagecoach, he hurried to pay his respects to Mabel. He asked her why he had ever left, what was the sense of it? Why did people live in places like New York? How could they bear it?

Because they didn't know any better, said Mabel happily, and for herself, she meant never to leave Taos again. She remembered that Tony had wanted her to buy a certain tract of land near the pueblo. She could build a studio on it, he said — didn't all Americans want studios? Now she said that she was going to get that land, and Tony looked gratified, but there was one matter he felt he must mention.

"You threw away the roses I bring you," he declared, and Mabel's heart was smitten with guilt.

In a long passage in *Edge of Taos Desert,* she tries to explain why this man, of all the men she had ever known, should have opened within her wells of emotion that she never knew were there. Tony and only Tony caused her to feel protective, and yet in turn protected. She had never known compassion and tenderness, but Tony evoked these. For the first time in her life she ceased being detached. Tony had somehow touched her innermost heart, where nobody had ever before been permitted to go. Sometimes in the future she was to deny the facts and tried to be cruel to him as she had been cruel to others, but her tenderness was never swamped. Though from time to time, being Mabel, she tried to escape and turn to other men, she was trapped, and for life. We will never know if Tony really meant to trap her, we know only that it happened.

Then, of course, she cried, "Oh, Tony, excuse me," and he gravely accepted her apology. At that moment and at many that followed she detected — and took, without complaint — an attitude in him that was slightly admonitory: the faint air, she called it, of a teacher's authority, and she liked it. What followed we cannot be quite sure of; it was one of her woolly ventures into the occult. She had a vision of what life with Tony was going to be. She saw that she must leave the world she knew and be with someone *real* at last, and Tony said, nodding his head, "I comin' with you."

Then they discussed that land she meant to buy, and the house she wanted to build on it. After Tony left, says Mabel, she went and told Maurice of her plans for the house. Maurice was surprised by the announcement and not at all pleased. It was June, he pointed out, and according to what he had planned he wasn't even going to be in New Mexico much longer. He would finish Pete's head, do another one of Pete's sister Albidia, and be ready to return to New York in August. So how could Mabel build a house in Taos? Perfectly well, said Mabel; he could go when he liked. She didn't care.

"You really wouldn't let me go without you?" he asked incredulously.

"Yes, I would," she said. That was all.

She did not mention in her book the awkward truth — awkward, at least, for Maurice — that he was dependent on her for every penny he spent, every mouthful he ate. The fact must have been uppermost in his thinking, but Mabel's mind did not work that way.

Her story is that she then hurried to the pueblo to tell Tony that everything was settled, and they started ordering the material for the house. At the time, one gathers, there was no hint of actual lovemaking between them. It would have been wrong, Mabel said, as long as she was still involved with Maurice. But of course she was impatient with her husband for working, as he did, with all deliberate speed. Having satisfied himself as to Pete's head, he then embarked on the bust of Albidia. In his hurry he did not try to make a plaster core as he had done with the first head, but began putting the black wax directly on the armature with a brush, layer by layer. Mabel wished he would hurry. Several times she mentioned that she would expect him to be gone by the first of August, but nothing hurried Maurice at his work; he was a deliberate craftsman. At some time during this period, she said, he moved up the mountain to Twining, a deserted mining town, and took possession of one of the deserted cabins. There, with Pete and Albidia to look after him, he went on modeling in black wax.

Down in the town, work proceeded on Mabel's house, with Tony in charge of the Indian builders. She exulted in the thought that she would soon have a true home of her own to make a life in. After all, she reflected, it was a first time. The Villa Curonia was Edwin's property, even though she had supplied the furniture and decoration. Finney Farm in Croton was rented, like her various apartments in New York. Never, until now, had Mabel actually bought and paid for a piece of land to live on. The earth she was buying was identified in her mind with Tony. At last, she felt, she *belonged* in the world, she had been accepted. Not that she thus became transformed into something other than what she had always been. She was what she was, a restless creature; people don't change, they only develop. The Mabel who was always putting out feelers, as she expressed it, continued to be the same woman, and she was not sorry. It was her character to be curious, and curiosity helped her in knowing and understanding people. People were her talent, she said. Andrew Dasburg painted and collected santos, and threw his whole being into these pastimes; well, she, Mabel, collected people with the same passion. That was the way she was, she said in a sudden little burst of self-defense, and she wouldn't have it any other way.

Probably we will never know just which little flurry in Taos brought on this particular declaration, but it is no secret that Mabel went on and on through the years, delicately manipulating people — creating fights and affairs, divorces and remarriages, love and hate — storm after storm of her own creating.

The land Tony had selected for her, just at the rim of pueblo territory, suited her more than any other site could have. It was bounded on one side by the main irrigation ditch, called the Acequia Madre, and at the beginning was bare of any building but a small, three-room adobe house which the former Mexican owners had occupied. At first Tony planned to add only one large room, which was to reach almost to the Acequia Madre, with enough space between ditch and house for a horse-and-wagon road. He arranged for a workforce of Indians and Mexicans together, and was himself the foreman of the crew. Every morning Mabel walked over to see how things were going, and Tony sometimes came to meet her halfway. They would walk together in companionable silence down the cottonwood tree avenue that had been planted by Manby. They didn't talk much, said Mabel, but they were glad to be together.

One morning as they strolled side by side, Mabel in the same kind of white dress she had been wearing ever since her Italian days and Tony in his white sheet, white leggings, and white moccasins, they met his Indian friend Antonio Martinez, who made a remark in the pueblo language to Tony. She asked Tony what it had been, and Tony answered, "He said, like a bride." Mabel's heart, she said, leaped and missed a beat. With Antonio they walked on to the building site, and she waited and watched and listened as the men discussed the work to be done.

Tony drew plans in the sandy soil and said to Mabel, "Here, I want a place big enough to put a big bed in."

Again his simple words had their effect. A flash of lightning struck through her, or so she said, because there seemed such portent in his simple instructions. She walked away from the men and sat down under a cottonwood to recover her aplomb.

In the following days she went sometimes to see how Maurice was getting on with his work. Slowly, very slowly. It was better to stay in Taos, watching the progress of the building. Every step in the process was fascinating — the choice of seasoned cedar logs for beams, the making of the adobe bricks, the carving — and all of it, she said, was done with loving care by the Indians. Nobody was hurried, everyone enjoyed himself in his work. One morning when she started out early to see what was happening, she found Tony sitting on a log some distance from the site. He didn't stand up when he saw her coming, but kept his face averted and his eyes veiled. She asked what the trouble was.

He said, "I was sittin' here this morning early. I don't know if I sleep or be awake, but I see you goin' by, goin' by, just like water."

Again Mabel understood immediately what he was trying to say — that she was too shallow for this new love to last. Indeed, she said, she always knew just what Tony wanted to say, though he had little English and it seemed to diminish as time went on. (This, she thought, was probably due to his desire to save himself from becoming too Europeanized. And yet at times he could be quite fluent. Was he, possibly, protecting himself against people he didn't like, didn't want to talk to?) Looking at him then, she felt misgivings about herself. Tony was in pain. What were they doing? Was this attraction between them a good thing, after all? She felt that she couldn't match him; he was deep and true, whereas she knew she was neither of these things.

Still, perhaps she could be. She tried to reassure him, but she may have needed a certain amount of reassurance herself. Again and again in her book about Tony she repeats that they didn't talk much. Most of the time they were together she didn't talk because she had nothing to say, and Tony seemed to accept her silence. For himself, she said, he didn't need speech to communicate: he could say many things without it. Not a day passed that Tony did not make her realize that she was rough and insensitive in comparison with him. Though we might not care for that sort of thing, Mabel loved it. He understood *everything*, she declared. When she behaved in a way Tony didn't care for, asserting herself and being bossy, he would manifest disapproval by his silence. But if she blundered and felt mortified, he was always there to comfort her.

Another thing. Unlike the men she had known, Tony never talked about love. He wasn't urgent or emotional, he just loved, and his love awakened love in her. She was, she said, in her eleventh hour when she met him, almost at the end of her rope. We don't know why she felt that way, but there is no doubt that she believed it herself.

However, nothing in this life is perfect, and Mabel was soon worried about one aberration, or set of aberrations, in her new love's behavior. In her account of the first time she saw Tony in the flesh, playing his drum by the fire in his pueblo house, he had acted in a manner that proved to be uncharacteristic, and he had been equally strange on the Sunday morning when he stared so at her hair ribbon and said it was a nice color. At the time she had noticed nothing out of the way; she didn't know Tony well enough to judge what he was like when he was normal. But now she did know him, or thought she did, until one Sunday when she went to call on Candelaria and Tony. She didn't often go on Sunday because, as she knew, life wasn't normal then. Some of the Indians would be at church, and she herself often used the free day to catch up on the little social duties of her other world. But on that Sunday she did go to the pueblo, and she was immediately puzzled by a kind of unfamiliarity over it all. Nobody was around, except for three or four Indians wrapped to the eyes in their thin sheets, squatting on the ground with their backs to one of the pueblo's many walls and looking at her without any sign of recognition. For her part, she couldn't have recognized them, wrapped up as they were. Most of the doors, including Candelaria's, were shut and blind. Mabel was bold enough to knock, but there was no reaction. The door stayed dumb and closed. Nobody called to her, and the drowsing Indians gave no helpful sign, but only gazed as she picked her way among them to leave. She arrived home puzzled and disappointed. It was a mystery, and as Mabel confessed to her readers, she could never leave mysteries alone; she was always asking Tony questions, probing, at the slightest opportunity. She couldn't understand, for instance, how he seemed able to summon his friends, yet when she asked for explanations he never answered in the downright way that would have satisfied her. And it wasn't only Tony who didn't give a straight answer to a straight question, said Mabel; it was all of them. It got on her nerves at first, she admitted, until at last she realized that it was unintentional; the question-and-answer mode of communicating was not a part of their system.

But she had not yet come to that conclusion, and because the incident of the closed door puzzled and worried her, she taxed Tony with it the next time she saw him, on Monday. The closed door, the silent Indians, her uneasiness — it had been *queer,* said Mabel.

"I asleep," said Tony.

Mabel persisted. Asleep, at eleven in the morning? After a pause, Tony seemed to make a decision. He said that he was going to trust her and speak of something most white people wouldn't understand. Then he brought out from the folds of his clothing a small packet, which he unwrapped, disclosing a withered round object — something Mabel immediately recognized, a kind of button. Peyote! She gasped, because she was shocked and frightened.

Tony tried to reassure her. Indians used it, he said, as part of their religion. They had taken the custom from their cousins, the Indians of Oklahoma; peyote was a god and a powerful one.

"He cure the people," said Tony. "He give us songs. He show us wonderful thing like colors we never see before. And some people see God. Once Enrique see Jesus."

He described the ceremony. The men, he said, bathed in the river, then dressed themselves in their best, while they fasted. Then they sat in a circle around a fire. One man sang and another played the drum, and the celebration went on all night. Sometimes they used peyote to cure sick people, but always, after a night of such ceremony, they felt lighthearted and refreshed.

Mabel declared that peyote wasn't all that good a thing; she couldn't help her opinion, but Tony was firm in his. She must have used it the wrong way at that New York party, he said, and that for the moment was that. A more agreeable topic of Indian custom was touched on when he suggested that she come with the Indians on their annual trip to the sacred Blue Lake up in the mountains. Every year at the right time, he said, when the snows were melted, the Taos Indians rode up to the lake and held a ceremony there. It would be in July. Happily she prepared for the trip, as did a number of the other Taos whites. It was a large party that started out, but Maurice stayed in Twining, working on Albidia's head.

Though it was only a twenty-two-mile ride to the lake, the party had to do it in three jumps. It rained so hard on the first day that they made camp on the way, and that night Mabel was very sick, going out into the woods time after time and feeling like death in the morning. The next night when she went to bed, Tony brought her a hot drink which he called medicine, and insisted that she take it. She did so because Tony told her to, but she was sure it was peyote, and she had misgivings. Never mind. The peyote cured her immediately, and its effects were so startlingly enjoyable that she went on and on about them for pages in her book. The remainder of the outing was uneventful.

When preparing for the journey, Mabel had bought a small tepee. As things turned out it was not used, but when she came back to Taos she asked Tony to put it up in her garden. She liked having it there, she explained; she liked to go out and lie on the cool grass inside it and be alone.

Chapter Eleven

Mabel's version:

With August scratching at the door, Maurice was still not ready to leave Taos, and, though naturally impatient to be rid of him, Mabel could not find it in her heart to push him out. It would have been brutal, she said, and she was too happy to want to be nasty, even to an outworn husband, so there was a tacit truce between them. In the end the solution was simple and easy. She went off on a protracted tour of the pueblos with Tony and other Indians, first to see a corn dance at Santo Domingo and then to drop in on other communities. Then the car broke down, as it so often did, so altogether it was a period of several weeks before she came back to the house, and when she got there she found that Maurice had gone.

At last! The next morning, she says, she went to meet Tony at the building site, and found him waiting for her under a tree. She dropped down beside him. "Maurice is gone," she said, and Tony nodded — but of course he didn't say anything about it. Instead they had a long, serious talk about peyote. It still frightened her to think of it, she said, and she told Tony that if they were to go on together — as they were, no doubt about it — it would be like crossing a great gulf to live with a man who used the stuff. In spite of the beneficial effect it had had on her, said Mabel, she didn't want peyote to be a part of her life. There could be no turning back once she had accepted it. Would Tony consider giving up the drug? Would he promise her? It is not very clear whether or not Tony promised, the account is so delicate and inconclusive, but he did say that everything would be all right, and with that she was reassured.

After this conversation they spent the day at the building site, watching the work. Mabel went back to Manby's at lunchtime as she always did, because as she said she had to make sure John was all right. Evidently he was, so she felt free to go back to the site, and that evening she and Tony strolled peacefully home and paused near the tepee in the garden.

Tony said, "I comin' here to this tepee tonight, when darkness here. That be right?"

"Yes, Tony," replied Mabel. "That will be right."

And, as she said at the end of her book, it was right.

Maurice's version:

Stuff and nonsense. Long before Maurice was out of Taos Mabel and Tony had had sexual relations. Vividly he recalled the occasion when he first realized it was going on. Very probably, one concludes, it was that same night when, according to Mabel, he struck his wife across the face. He said Mabel had gone out riding alone with Tony that afternoon, and Maurice had thought nothing of it until —

"When Mabel came home hours later I was appalled," he wrote. "Her eyes had the look about them that I myself had seen only after Mabel had been sexually gratified, when something would seem to come to life deep within her." He quoted scornfully those last lines from *Edge of Taos Desert* in which Tony proposes for the first time that he come to meet his mistress in the tepee. What nonsense! For fully two months before he himself left Taos, said Maurice, Mabel was hurrying out of the house every night to the tepee on the lawn, where she was meeting Tony.

"It could not have been that Tony kept coming for nightly tom-tom concerts," declared Maurice with heavy irony, "for the only sound that ever reached the house where I lay listening was the arrival and departure of a solitary horse and rider, and the creak of the house later when Mabel sneaked back to our bedroom."

Night after night the husband lay there in the dark fuming, futilely plotting vengeance, dreaming of murder. At one point he asked Manby to lend him a gun, and Manby obliged, handing him a revolver and saying, with an insinuating grin, "I hope you're fast on the draw." The thought that this old character knew the truth was overwhelmingly humiliating to Maurice. If Manby knew, he told himself, the whole town must be in on the shameful secret. Yes, of course, why hadn't he thought of that before? Everybody must be aware of that horse and rider, and the nightly visits to the tepee. Maurice never used the revolver, but kept it handy under the pillow where its presence carried a cold sort of comfort.

One night as he lay listening the horse didn't come, though Mabel had gone out to the tepee as usual. Maurice lay awake, balefully listening, but the minutes went by without their usual punctuation of hoofbeats. After about an hour of silence Mabel came softly back into the bedroom and crept under the bedclothes. For as long as he could, Maurice kept silence, but after Mabel had fallen asleep he laughed aloud, mockingly, and said, "Poor Mabel, poor, poor Mabel! Her lover doesn't show up, and she has to go to bed without her nightcap."

Mabel went into a rage, and ordered him to leave the bed. Maurice said, "This is my bed. You go back to your tent."

She attacked him physically, and they had an unseemly struggle which ended with Mabel being shoved out, falling with a bump to the floor. She got up in a fury and flounced out of the room, saying as she left, "Tomorrow you get out — do you hear me?"

And that, Maurice said, is the true story of why he went to Twining, the abandoned mining town, and there settled into a cabin with Pete and Albidia. Because, he said, no matter what, he could not yet leave Taos. He had to carry out his plan and finish work on the Indian woman's head as a companion piece to the one of Pete. In the cold light of morning, having faced these facts, he talked quietly to Mabel and proposed the move, and she too was calmer. She agreed to the program on the understanding that when he was satisfied he would leave the neighborhood of Taos altogether.

"Mabel was within her rights in ordering me out," admitted Maurice. "It was her house, her money, her food." He felt miserably low and humble about it, but those were the facts.

At last, satisfied with the bust, he went down the mountain to Taos and notified Mabel that he was ready to go. He would leave, he said, the next morning, and she nodded pleasantly.

"The change will be good for you," she said. "You will come back and everything will be all right again."

She repeated it when she kissed him goodbye: "You must not worry. Go east, and have a good time. Then come back and everything will again be as it was before."

She may have meant it at the moment, said Maurice, but he

didn't believe her. How could he? He knew that the marriage was finished.

But calamity was not yet through with him. He had put his two heads into crates and saw them safely loaded, he thought, on the same train as his. Alas, the grueling heat of the journey was too much for the waxen head of Albidia, which had no plaster core. The wax melted and ran, and when Maurice unpacked it in New York he found only a grotesque travesty of the beautiful thing. His trip to New Mexico had turned out to be a catastrophe in every way. Maurice seized a hatchet and hacked Albidia to pieces, but after years had intervened he found it possible to be philosophical about the whole adventure. In a discerning passage, he said,

> Part of the problem was that Mabel had always been enthralled by the mystical. She thought that she had finally found what she had been searching for in Tony and in the Indian mystique. As soon as she discovered the Pueblo Indians she was like someone under hypnosis. She sat entranced when they beat their tom-toms and chanted their weird music. Most of all, their silence fascinated her, and I must admit that practically the only words I heard them say myself were, "I'll have more chicken."

Moreover, in spite of all the pain he had felt at the time, he admitted that Mabel had been right to bring their marriage to a close, and he was wrong to try to hang on to it. The proof of the pudding is in the eating, and Mabel had continued to love Tony ever since. In the Indian, he concluded, "Mabel found the perfect rainbow . . . Tony was what she needed. Mabel had no vitality or creative power of her own. She was a dead battery who needed constantly to recharge with the juice of some man, though she might leave him 'dead' in the process."

He and Mabel, he recalled, often fought bitterly, after which he could go to his studio and immerse himself in work, forgetting all about the quarrel, while Mabel at home "chafed and fretted and resented my escape. When I returned, calm and happy, she was poisoned with envy and bitterness. This separate life I had, more than anything else in our relationship, aroused her fury."

This being so, Tony must have been for her like a rock in the desert, said Maurice. He was so foreign to her nature that she simply couldn't hurt him with her passionate outbursts of frustration, so she never even tried. Obviously Tony was what she needed — not a man who was akin to herself culturally, temperamentally or mentally, but the direct antithesis, "someone whose physical presence would liberate her from her inner prison." Maurice concluded, "What psychoanalysts, artists, and writers would not accomplish, this Indian medicine man did."

But this reasoning was accomplished long after the event, when all pain and passion had been spent. At the time there were various stages of readjustment to go through on both sides. Mabel had her share of hesitation and reluctance to let go, and even Maurice's departure did not, then, mean to her the absolute end of their relationship. It seems strange that she was not more than willing to wash her hands of Maurice, considering her obvious preference for Tony, and she gives no hint in her book of hesitation; but it is there, a matter of history. Perhaps she was not yet sure enough of Tony. She obviously tried for some months to maintain the fiction that Sterne had gone to New York for a temporary visit only. He quotes letters from her in which she speaks of the future, when he will return (so she implies) and resume the old life with her. Sometimes in writing to her Maurice complained that he was hearing gossip about Tony, but Mabel merely continued to write chattily about the new house and how it was coming along.

"You must have some curiosity about it," she wrote, as if to an unreasonable husband, "for probably we will pass our old age here together!" Not long afterward, when Maurice demanded a divorce and complained that her behavior was redounding to his discredit as well as hers, she struck a slightly indignant note. People always chatter, said Mabel: wasn't he exaggerating the case? But, she added on a graver note, "of course if you want a divorce it will mean a cessation of the maybe small but anyway partial income you have been getting. I am sorry for this for I hoped it would help to set you free to work."

This was written in March 1918. In the following August she was saying, as Maurice recalled,

I do not believe any irrevocable final separation is for us. We have meant and do mean a lot to each other spiritually. You know that. Of course I can send you $100 a month and probably more when you need it and I will do so — though not thro' lawyers . . . So long as you are loyal and do not dramatize our situation to others at my expense I will be loyal to you and as helpful as I can be. But if you continue to feel meanly towards me and talk so to others — it may make me feel like cutting away altogether.

She didn't carry out her threat. In the end she arranged through a lawyer to send the hundred dollars every month to Maurice, and he accepted it. Though, as he said, it humiliated him to do so, he had to. During their marriage Mabel had cut him off from all his friends and potential buyers. Besides, he had grown accustomed to depending on her money. He likened himself to an animal, once able to fend for itself but then domesticated by Mabel, after which it grows soft. Suddenly set free again, the animal perishes because it no longer knows how to struggle for survival. Not wishing to starve, therefore, Maurice swallowed his pride and took the money for two years, after which he had found his feet and was able to get along without it. It was a happy moment, he said, when he was able to cut loose and notify the bank that he no longer needed Mabel's money.

"I was too young to be pensioned," he said, "and in any case had not served 'in arms' long enough to be entitled to a pension."

Sterne's story had a happy ending. Soon after his return to New York, he moved out to Elizabeth Duncan's latest dancing school quarters, an estate at Tarrytown-on-the-Hudson, where she offered him a cottage. Maurice lived there for a while, teaching drawing to the girl students — the "Isadorables," as they were called. One of the girls was a slender blond nymph named Vera Segal, a younger sister of Vivienne Segal, a musical comedy star.

"Maurice and I met at the Duncan School, when I was 15," she said. "I was a very serious and precocious young girl, worked hard at my dancing, read Schopenhauer and Nietzsche, and had no use for boys my own age ... I fell in love almost at once with the magnetic older man who sketched us while we danced. My family was quite upset when they heard of my relationship with Maurice."

Perhaps it was as well, since Vera was so young, that they could not marry immediately because of Mabel. And Maurice was not eager to get married to anybody, considering what had happened to him so recently. Vera, too, was in no hurry.

"Mabel was at first very reluctant to divorce Maurice," she said. "I don't really know why, but I imagine that she wanted to protect herself from having to marry her Indian lover Tony, or perhaps she just was reluctant to give Maurice up entirely. Finally she did agree and she was granted a divorce for non-support."

At last Vera and Maurice were married in Vienna, and they went to live in the Italian hill village of Anticoli, where Maurice had spent happy months in the past. Theirs was an uneventful life and a peaceful one, but ill health eventually forced Maurice to give up painting and sculpture and turn instead to writing. Mabel's passages about him in her book hurt his feelings terribly, but as the years went on he stopped minding. Though he left Anticoli in 1934, the Italian townspeople remembered him fondly; in 1959, two years after his death, they notified his widow that they had named a street after him.

With Maurice out of the way, Mabel was free — though when had she not been? — to behave as she wished. Until that period, however, she had always avoided too obvious a defiance of convention. She often broke the rules of society, but it embarrassed her to do so in too public a manner. The record is clear, and according to her own candid account it is equally consistent. Let us look at the facts in summary. In youth she left her lover in Buffalo and went to Italy rather than bring scandal down on her head. In Italy, married for the second time, she knuckled down to her husband's notions of propriety to such an extent that she betrayed Bindo, a man she professed to love, by cutting him dead in public. In New York, though she wanted very much to be rid of her husband and persuaded him to move out, she did not dare live alone for fear of causing talk; she acquired a respectable companion who lived with her as chaperon. When she took Reed as a lover her sense of convention was shaken but not defeated for a long time, and though at last she brought herself to admit publicly to the liaison she was not easy in her mind about it. Later, living out of wedlock with Maurice Sterne, she was very uncomfortable; it made her unhappy to think that their neighbors in Maine must have known that they were lovers, and later, having moved to Croton, she insisted on pretending that Sterne was actually sleeping under another roof. Even then she was uneasy, and listened willingly to the suggestion made by a friend that she marry Maurice to make it all right in the eyes of the world. It is hardly the record of a brave, defiant character.

But Tony and her relations with him were of a different order. Tony was not just another man, she felt. He was a being so unlike his predecessors that she thought of him as the representative of another world, an alien creature with a set of quite foreign standards. *Marry* Tony? It is doubtful if she even thought of that at first. One might as well consider marrying a Martian — not that Mabel heard as much about Martians as we do.

She had been struck by lightning, that was all, and for a long time she was content to let matters drift. All of white Taos buzzed about the situation, which aroused in her a certain defiance, but nobody could touch or threaten her. She was, as she had always been, independent of the world in that she had money. The pueblo buzzed too, but pueblo life was so remote from hers, in spite of her attempts to get inside their daily existence, that it didn't impinge on her save that Tony was affected. Mabel used money to ease his path. Candelaria was in the way and had to be appeased. Quietly, tactfully, she was persuaded to remove herself. After all, there were no children of the marriage, and Candelaria's clan was willing to take the money. Tony paid a price and it must have hurt him, for he was no longer permitted to take his place in the Pueblo councils. But he was given his choice — Mabel or the pueblo — and he chose Mabel.

According to chitchat in Taos, the Indians had their own interpretation of these goings-on. Mabel, they believed, was *renting* Tony.

All this made little difference to Mabel's daily life. She had her many friends outside, and by this time she had collected as many as she desired in New Mexico, too. Probably her best friend was Alice Corbin Henderson, the "little woman" who had so irritated her when she first arrived in Santa Fe. Alice and her husband, the painter William Penhallow Henderson, thought they understood Mabel's feelings for Tony, and they supported her. Like most of the other writers and painters, they came from outside; they hadn't the prejudices of the old-time residents, to whom the affair was a great scandal. Mabel's love for Tony appeared to the anthropologists and archaeologists a fine, hopeful development. She would be able to help the Indians, they told each other, and she was in a splendid position to find things out about these interesting creatures. As for the old-time residents, let them condemn Mabel to their heart's content; it made no difference. (But somewhere in the middle of her she was aware of their feelings, and it hurt her.)

Because Mabel was like the European idea of most American women, restless and managing, she could not leave the pueblo alone. Conditions there, she felt, were unsatisfactory — as no doubt they were — and she had to work on this, writing to Washington, investigating the structure of government regarding American Indians generally, and talking to the pueblo people. Tony, of course, was her main source of information, but he had many relatives, and a lot of them readily made complaints when they realized that Mabel would listen. The matter of Paulita and Dr. Bergmans was not forgotten, either.

When Maurice made his jocular comment about feeding the Indians after depriving them of their land, he was expressing a sentiment fairly widespread in the United States. It would be an exaggeration to say that Indians were a tender spot in the American conscience, but there is something in it. Public opinion has never been easy on their score. Mabel was expressing this uneasiness when she mentioned more than once that the Carys in Buffalo probably had Indian blood: she found this possibility dangerous but romantic. There was also her fond memory of Karl Evans's passion for Indian artifacts. Mabel wanted to champion the rights of the Indians: she was chronically suspicious of the good will of the Bureau of Indian Affairs.

There is in the *Encyclopedia Americana,* published in 1949, an immensely long article about the development of the bureau. "In former years," it begins somewhat defensively, "an idea was prevalent that the national government had always striven to dispossess the Indians from the lands they occupied, or had sympathized with such efforts. This was the reverse of the truth." In fact, said the author, the bureau had to exist because of the record; Indians kept quarreling with each other and their white neighbors, and the government was always slow and reluctant to interfere. The government sympathized with the Indians and often had to take the part of some of them against its own citizens,

its commissioners usually reporting in their favor and even its generals in later days blaming the whites for the troubles: its courts deciding in their favor; attempting pacification amid local outcries against them, rebuffing appeals for aid and only using its armies to reduce the Indians and its administrative power to remove them when it was no longer politically possible to leave them in possession . . .

Even then, said the writer, the government has tried to deal righteously by the Indians, "but the complexity of the problem — one may say its insolubility till the country was very strong and the Indians very weak — along with the universal curse of 'spoils' in the administration — hindered success."

The history of the government's management of Indians is complicated. At first the idea was to put all of them together, regardless of tribe, on one vast reservation in the West. The plan very soon proved to be unfeasible; not all Indians *wanted* to get along with each other. Very well then, said the planners. We'll set up three huge reservations and divide the Indians according to kinship and friendship. This plan too was modified, perforce. A whole lot of smaller reservations seemed to be the answer, and in 1803 Jefferson formulated a plan to hand over to the redskins all the Louisiana Purchase territory north of the Arkansas, with no part of this land to be sold to the whites. In 1834, however, this design was modified. Indian territory was much reduced, and a superintendent of Indian affairs was appointed. As the law then stood, no white man could trade with the Indians or settle in their country without the permission of the superintendent or his agents.

In 1849 the management of Indian affairs, which hitherto had been under the War Department, was shifted to the recently formed Department of the Interior, where it acquired the name Bureau of Indian Affairs and a new title for the superintendent, who became commissioner of Indian Affairs. He had eight inspectors under him and "a large variety of subordinate officials and employees." Indian agents were appointed by the President, and they had considerable power — too much, if we are to believe the writer of the article, who said, "On their action depends often peace or war to great white populations, but in too many cases formerly they were the football of politics and sometimes scandalously unfit for their places." So much for the people in charge.

There was a kind of hierarchy among the Indians, bestowed on them arbitrarily by the whites. Some Indians were considered good, others not so good, this presumed virtue depending inversely on the size and power of the tribe. In theory each tribe was considered "a domestic dependent nation," though the customary appurtenances of nationhood were lacking, and everything in the way of intercourse had to go through special commissioners appointed by the President — until 1871, when Congress took over direct control. What the encyclopedia refers to as the fiction of Indian nations, however, remained. "The government recognizes its duty to protect Indians from predatory whites; Indian traders must have certificates of good character and may be licensed by the Indian commissioner, and the goods they sell are subject to regulation. No outsider can hunt, cut timber, or pasture cattle on Indian land without the agent's permission. Intoxicating liquors may not be sold to Indians." In short, the Indian bureau was and in many cases still is a very paternal form of government.

The article went into some detail about the education of Indians, which is carried on by various agencies: churches, missionary societies, and some private individuals, all actively encouraged by the government.

In February 1887, the government took a new step, passing an act through which "the system of tutelage and pauperization" might be swept away. "All reservations were to be surveyed," said the writer; "all Indians who wished to take up lands in severality to a certain amount might do so — and by the act become citizens."

Clearly, Tony Lujan of Taos was not one of those who chose to leave the reservation and acquire citizenship. Such small education as he had had been acquired in a Roman Catholic mission school, and his ambition had always been closely connected with the pueblo's good. He looked no further until Mabel came along, and even then it did not cross his mind that he might do better elsewhere. He was satisfied to be a member of Taos Pueblo. The larger and allegedly better advanced Indian tribes — the Five Nations of the Indian Territory — are the Cherokee, Chickasaw, Choctaw, Creeks, and Seminoles, who have governed themselves to a certain extent ever since the white man came to America, but the Pueblos have never been numerous or important enough to occupy such an exalted position.

Nevertheless they are exceptionally interesting in the eyes of archaeologists and anthropologists, two of whom have contributed to the encyclopedia an article on the subject. "The 'Pueblo' Indians, as they are called from their village life," says the piece, in part, "have risen in New Mexico and Arizona above the stage of savagery into a state of semi-civilization, representing the triumph of man over the adverse conditions of the desert and the inroads of fierce enemies of the lowest culture." That would be the various tribes of Plains Indians, who prefer riding and raiding and hunting to the less exciting work of tilling the land. They have always looked on the Pueblos as fair game, making forays on the peaceful farmers and robbing them of their domesticated animals and hard-won grain. It was a lucky accident that led Mabel to acquire a "civilized" Indian: her friends might have congratulated themselves that she didn't pick up a wild Navajo instead. As it was, the group she left behind in the East, at least many of them, were delighted. It was a fascinating thing Mabel had done, they thought, just the sort of thing one might expect of her; and some people, who would never have thought before of breaking their journeys between coasts, found excellent reasons now for getting off the train in New Mexico and making their way into the mountains to Taos to see how Mabel was getting on.

Chapter Twelve

THE WRITER Mary Austin, who was connected by birth and sentiment to the West, had known Mabel in New York and continued
the acquaintance after Mrs. Sterne moved to New Mexico. When
she herself decided to make her home in Santa Fe, they became
really good friends, often visiting back and forth. In her autobiography, *Earth Horizon*, she spoke of the Tony situation when it first
came to the community's attention: "Tony had a wife from whom
he was not divorced, and Mabel had a husband. The Pueblo and
the town were cut up about it . . . I began to get an inkling of how
the community felt. There was more than a little small-town opposition to Mabel and Tony's affair, and the beginning of a cabal
against them." A champion of Indian rights, Miss Austin did not
hesitate to take Mabel's side, even though she could not whole-
heartedly approve. "I advised Mabel to return temporarily to New
York," she added, "to make a beginning toward a divorce, and to
make an allowance to Tony's wife. Then I took pains to explain
[to the town's residents] just what it would mean to Taos financially, to drive her to abandon it. Things began to move forward
and to settle down."

Probably Mary Austin had less influence than she wished to believe on the protagonists of the drama, but things did, inevitably,
begin to settle down. However, at that stage of the affair Mabel
had no intention of marrying Tony, whatever the town and the
pueblo said of the association. Officially he was working for her as
a kind of major-domo and guide and, after he learned to drive,
chauffeur. Town and pueblo had to accept things as they found
them while Mabel serenely went her way, as was her habit in such
matters. After all, she had her money and her friends — she
couldn't be bullied. Though Alice Thursby continued to visit her

often, she did not have to depend on eastern allies; she had local friends too. Especially she saw a lot of Alice Corbin and Willy Henderson in Santa Fe, and probably as a result of this friendship John Evans and the Hendersons' daughter, commonly called "Little Alice," saw a lot of each other as well. The connection was interrupted but not ended when John went away to Yale.

When, in due course, Mabel went to New York for a visit, she took Tony with her. It is doubtful if he ever learned to love the city, but at least he was able to forget the unpleasantness of his first experience there. Naturally she arranged for John to come down from New Haven, and sometimes she made him meet Tony under the clock at the Biltmore in order to take him shopping. John did not care at all for this mission. People stared at the American youth and the portly braided Indian in his blanket, and, since the clock at the Biltmore was a favorite meetingplace for Yale students and their girls, John and his charge were naturally seen by some of his friends. He was in an agony of self-consciousness about this, but it was no use complaining to Mabel, who scoffed at such snobbery.

But it was in her day-to-day life in Taos, as she steadily added to her estate — as soon as the Big House was finished she began to build another one on Tony's Indian land allotment next door, and then she put up one house after another — that Mabel began to see herself as a woman with a cause, a duty to interpret the Southwest and its Pueblo Indians to the rest of the world. The concept in time became a vision of a colony, a utopia, an extension of her New York salon, where old and new friends might come and see for themselves what a wonderful place Taos was. It was from this impulse that she drew John Collier into her orbit once more. Collier has left a record of the way his life was altered in *The Indians of the Americas.* As we have seen, Mabel knew him in New York when he was with the People's Institute. The time of which he wrote here was 1919:

"I was thirty-five years old. I had organized and taught in the fields of social work and community development from New York to California ... Repeatedly, I had been solicited on behalf of America's Indian peoples; but always I had resisted and refused. It was too late, I believed; that golden age was done." That year he had been working in California and had become disillusioned with everything that had to do with community organization. He therefore took his wife, Lucy, their three young sons, and their dogs — the whole family — and set off in the car for Mexico, intending to camp in the Sonora Mountains for at least a year. They were on their way when they got a letter from Mabel repeating an invitation she had sent many times before, to come and look at Taos. On this occasion Collier was willing to listen, because, as she correctly pointed out, it wasn't much out of their way; "You can detour here, and go on to Sonora so easily," she urged. So they went, and they didn't see Mexico for another eleven years. They arrived just before Christmas, driving in a blinding snowstorm. They saw the procession into the pueblo church, "high along an avenue of fires to a vast chanting of pagan song," and then, two days later, the deer dance. Collier was enthralled:

Here was a reaching to the fire-fountain of life through a deliberate social action employing a complexity of many arts. Here was the psychical wonder-working we think we find in Greek drama as lived out in Athens four hundred years before Christ. And here was a whole community which entered into the experience and knew it as a fact. These were unsentimental men who lived by hard work, men who were told every day in all kinds of unsympathetic ways that all they believed and cared for had to die, and who never answered back. For these men were at one with their gods.

He was captured for what became twenty-five years. Tony trusted him, and Collier gained much of his knowledge through Tony and his associates. With Mabel's enthusiastic help he found a place in the Bureau of Indian Affairs, and became an important cog in the machine built up between government and Indians. In 1933 he became commissioner of Indian Affairs, a man to be reckoned with. He was already active in the cause by the time the matter of the Bursum bill cropped up in 1922, and it might be profitable to read what he had to say about it:

When Warren G. Harding became President, he made Albert B. Fall his Secretary of the Interior. Oil had been struck on the Navajo lands, which still remained tribal, and apart from the Doheny and Sinclair oil scandals, the Teapot Dome affair and other jockeying over oil, another oil scandal, though an impersonal one, developed over the Navajo homelands. Fall and the Indian Bureau concocted the so-called "Indian Omnibus Bill" which the House passed and which the Senate Committee on Indian Affairs reported favorably. Indian leaders drew up a petition and found a champion, Robert M. LaFollette, the elder, of Wisconsin, who succeeded at the eleventh hour in killing that bill on the Senate floor.

* * *

. . . Two-thirds of the Indian lands which still remained tribal were held by the Indians under Presidential decree, as distinguished from treaty. Oil was struck in the Navajo lands within the "Presidential decree" rather than the "Treaty" area of the tribe. Fall ruled that the oil belonged to the government, to dispose of as it might choose, and not to the tribe. The effect was to deny that the Indians owned some sixteen million acres of their own land, title to which had been confirmed in them by Executive Order. The Fall administration then set in motion an open drive, aimed principally at the Pueblo tribes, for the suppression of all the native Indian religions still existing. Finally, although first in order of time (I have held it back because it requires more lengthy discussion) Fall pressed the notorious Bursum bill with all the powers at his command, and the Senate enacted it. Then a storm broke. The Pueblos determined to battle with all their resources.

* * *

Fall's bill in the Congress, known as the Bursum bill, was simple enough. It transferred the Pueblo title from the Indian owners to the white squatters. For good measure, it brought the internal affairs of the city-states under the jurisdiction of the United States District Court. This last might not seem so bad from an outside point of view, but it actually meant the attempted establishment of a religious inquisition, for the internal affairs of the Pueblos are completely involved in their religions. Among the Rio Grande Pueblos, the rule of secrecy is inviolable. Under the Fall-Bursum bill, the Indian Bureau would have been able to keep the priests, governors and other principal men of these tribes in jail for contempt of court, or whatever, for most of their lives.

But no Pueblo Indian knew about the projected bill, which was carefully kept secret. The Indian superintendents knew, said Collier, but no one of them, though they had been hired expressly to protect Indian interests and were supposed to represent the Indians as a lawyer represents his client, wanted to leak information to them. Not a single Indian was aware of the bill.

As it happened, however, Collier was in Taos at the time, and Tony took him to a meeting at the pueblo, where he told them about it. Many meetings followed. The Fall-Bursum bill, said Collier, was read and explained and analyzed in English, Tanoan, Tewan, Keresian, and Zunian — all the Pueblo languages. The old men listened and understood and moaned, because they recognized it as a sentence of death. At Cochiti Pueblo the battle started when Alcario Montoya, one of their leading men, said, "We must unite as we did once before." He was referring, said Collier, to the ancient Pueblo rebellion of 1680, before the United States came into being, when the Pueblos rose up and drove every white man out of New Granada. He did not mean actual battle by force of arms; he meant to go to the law. There and then they organized the Council of All the New Mexico Pueblos, which met at Santo Domingo on November 22, 1922.

"All of New Mexico by that date was aflame over the Fall-Bursum bill; the artists and writers of Santa Fe and Taos joined in encouragement and deeds," wrote Collier. The Indians sent a delegation of seventeen men to the United States, all over the country, including the New York Stock Exchange. The governors of the tribes carried with them those honorable silver-headed canes that had been bestowed on them by the Spanish crown and Abraham Lincoln, and their impact was strong; it was a splendid job of public relations. At last, on a motion made by Senator Borah, the Senate recalled the Bursum bill. It was killed in March 1923; yet almost immediately thereafter the Senate's Indian Committee reported favorably on another Pueblo Lands bill only a little better than the Fall-Bursum bill. This too was killed after the pro-Indian forces were marshaled once more, but, as Collier said discontentedly, "*de facto* the white squatters and settlers remained on the Pueblo lands, and many Pueblos continued to starve." Fall's disgrace, indictment, trial, and imprisonment put an end to his particular crimes, "but the Indian Bureau moved automatically, implacably on," said Collier. Needless to say, so did he move implacably on, and in time he won. In the meanwhile, the bureau set out to destroy the Pueblo native religions, using lurid methods. They sent out inspectors who collected pornographic gossip about the tribes, "among whom," said Collier,

no pornography existed at all. Much of the gossip was unprintable. The Bureau submitted it for scrutiny to no Indian and to no ethnologist. The foul pages, numbering 193, were photostated and turned over to various emissaries under the seal of confidence, as well as to leading editors, churchmen and heads of women's organizations ... Then the Bureau struck publicly. These "agents of Moscow," the Pueblos and their friends, according to the Bureau's publicists, were likewise the emissaries of pagan religions unspeakably bloody and foul . . ."

Clearly, all this was a threat to Mabel and her household, but she did not yet realize it. She was busy trying to persuade one of the English literary world's brightest jewels, D. H. Lawrence, to come and visit. She had read some of his works and came to the conclusion that he was the only one in the world "who can really *see* this Taos country and the Indians, and who can describe it so that it is as much alive between the covers of a book as it is in relation."

The results of this experiment appeared a decade later in her first published book, *Lorenzo in Taos,* written as a letter to the poet Robinson Jeffers after Lawrence died. Mabel told Jeffers how she had written to Lawrence, though they had never met, and invited him to come and live in Taos. She wrote her persuasions at such length, she said, that she had to roll the letter up like a papyrus, along with a couple of fragrant dried herbs from the Indian country. For good measure she also sent Lawrence's wife, Frieda, an Indian necklace. This bauble could not be wrapped like the herbs in paper; it went in a package which was a long time arriving at its destination — if, indeed, it ever arrived at all. Lawrence's letters to Mabel often mentioned that he and Frieda were still waiting for it.

The papyrus went out late in the summer of 1921 and caught up with its recipient on November 5 in Taormina, Italy. It engaged the novelist's fancy. Lawrence, thirty-six years old, had developed an itch for travel that was never sufficiently scratched, and in several of his letters to other correspondents he mentioned that some rich American woman had invited himself and Frieda to visit, and that he was thinking of accepting. For a little while, if we can judge from his replies to Mabel, he was on the verge of setting out there and then for New Mexico. He asked a number of pertinent questions: how much would it cost two people to live in Taos, if they did all their own housework? "Because I loathe servants creeping around," he explained. "They poison the atmosphere." He mentioned having seen pictures of Taos in Leo Stein's house at Settignano, and we know from his published correspondence that he actually got in touch with Stein and asked him about Mabel. Stein replied, recommending her. Mabel, he said, was no lion hunter; she was quite a little lion herself. Lawrence also asked Mabel if she was related to Maurice Sterne, whose name he had heard in Italy, and no doubt she told him of the connection.

They would be leaving Taormina, said Lawrence, in January or February 1922, and would very likely come straight to Taos. His wife, Frieda, a German woman whose maiden name was von Richthofen and who shared with a large number of others in Germany the title of baroness, wrote an accompanying letter: "We are so keen on coming — both of us. The mountain lakes and the piazzas and Indians and I am very grateful to you for giving us the impetus for a *real* move and putting our noses onto the spot where I'm sure we want to go." Frieda had had to make many moves to keep up with her peripatetic husband, but what with the war and other complications the Lawrences had not yet stepped outside the confines of Britain and Europe.

All this seemed to make the Lawrences' visit fairly secure, and Mabel was excited and happy. She spurred on the builders to finish the Tony house, as this additon was always known to members of the family, and Lawrence continued to make encouraging noises by mail until suddenly there came different news in a letter from Frieda dated January 20. Lorenzo, it seemed, had decided to go to Ceylon, in the opposite direction to New Mexico, saying that he didn't feel strong enough yet to face America.

"Now we propose this," wrote Frieda. "Come and see us in *Ceylon,* and we will go with *you* to Taos from the other side — it might be very thrilling . . ."

It was not thrilling enough for Mabel Sterne, who had no intention of following anybody, not even the genius Lawrence, to his chosen terrain. Suspicion leaped in her. She became paranoid about the check to her plans. She felt that she knew what the trouble was: the Lawrences were scared. "Someone had 'warned' them," she wrote. "I was used to that. People were always warning other people about me. No matter if it was justified and I knew it was, still it always hurt my feelings and stiffened my backbone."

It should be possible, she felt, to use her famous will power and persuade him thus, by mysterious force, to come. Mabel concentrated on the job. "Before I went to sleep at night, I drew myself all in to the core of my being where there is a live, plangent force lying passive — waiting for direction," she said. "Becoming entirely that, moving with it, speaking with it, I leaped through space, joining myself to the central core of Lawrence, where he was in India, Australia . . . I became that action that brought him across the sea." She enlisted Tony in the effort, explaining to him that Lawrence would do the Indians immense good if he wrote about them. So Tony, though he seems to have had doubts that writing could help his people, joined in with his special brand of magic, and he too willed Lawrence to come until their combined efforts did at last have an effect. It took nearly a year, during which Lawrence and Frieda lived in Ceylon and Australia and Lawrence wrote a new novel, but at last, in September 1922, they disembarked in San Francisco and took the train to New Mexico.

Tony drove the car, and he and Mabel were there at the station in Lamy, twenty miles south of Santa Fe. Coming back something went wrong with the car, which made them too late, Mabel decided, to get to Taos that night. She took her guests, therefore, to sleep at the house of Witter Bynner, the poet who had settled in New Mexico and was living at that time with his secretary and lover Spud Johnson. She and Tony, she explained, could stay with other friends. Bynner was well pleased to welcome such a talent as Lawrence; as for Frieda, she summed up the situation at a glance.

"Un ménage, hein?" she asked Mabel when they were alone. "The young thin one seems rather nice." Before then, however, Lawrence had exploded at his wife in a burst of ill temper that startled everyone but delighted Mabel. She soon learned that it was characteristic.

They were delayed again the next day by a bad thunderstorm, but they got to Taos at last and dined in Mabel's Big House. Lawrence, or to give him the name most of his friends used, Lorenzo, was not nice about that house. Mabel had filled it with the furniture she had collected through all her various existences in France, Italy, and New York, including curios from India and China. She was very proud of the effect; after all, everybody knew that decoration was her forte. It was disconcerting, therefore, when Lorenzo giggled and said, "It's like one of those nasty little temples in India!" She did not know that he had taken a great dislike to Ceylon, as he usually did to any place where he had to stay any length of time, but she didn't like the remark. Life with Lorenzo, she discovered, was a bit like that all the time. He could be very crushing. But there is no doubt that much of what happened later was Mabel's fault too. Only a very innocent or foolish woman would have tried to interpose herself between D. H. Lawrence and Frieda, and that is what Mabel proposed to do from the first moment she saw the couple, if not before then.

After all, she had always reached out and taken what she wanted. Very little had ever stood in the way once Mabel made up her mind, and now she decided that what she wanted was Lorenzo. She ignored Tony in these plans because she had not yet realized that Tony actually counted and would not stand aside. As for Frieda, Mabel thought she knew the type — a pleasant, simple, booming kind of German woman; there would be no obstacle there. But she was soon to learn her mistake.

She was self-confident. She and Lawrence knew each other immediately, she said, as if they were of one blood, and they did in fact get on well those first few days, possibly because there was a chaperon in the house apart from Frieda, an old friend of Mabel's from Buffalo, Bessie Freeman, whose prematurely white hair gave Lawrence a feeling of safety. Besides, there was hardly time for trouble, since Mabel immediately shipped her illustrious guest to the Apache Fiesta, which meant driving for several days with Tony and Bessie. There wasn't room for everyone in the car, so Mabel decreed that she and Frieda should stay at home and get acquainted. It was vital, she said, for Lorenzo to see Indians as soon as possible, and the fiesta was an excellent opportunity. Tony didn't want to take Lawrence, said Mabel, but she made him.

"He is so good natured, Jeffers . . . and I am always *making* him do things that are nice for other people, but that leave him indifferent," she wrote. ". . . My need to bring Lawrence and the Indians together was like an impulse of the evolutionary will, apart from me, using me for its own purposes."

As soon as they were left alone, Mabel and Frieda had a long, confidential chat. Mabel thought the other woman a healthy creature, more interested in sex than anything else. "But one had to be careful all the time — to hide what one knew — to stay back with her," she added. "Any reference to the spirit, or even to consciousness, was antagonistic to her. The groping, suffering, tragic soul of man was so much filthiness . . . Offensive. I learned early to keep away from her any sight or sound of unhappiness that was not immediately caused by some mishap of the bed — for really she admitted no other." In the course of their talk, Frieda explained how difficult it was to live with Lawrence. Everybody thought he was wonderful, she complained, not realizing that she was something in herself, too. He couldn't get along without her, she said; when he was writing, she often had to help him. With *Sons and*

Lovers she had actually written quite a bit of it. And, she said, Lawrence had been unfaithful to her, not once but twice. At least he had tried to be, once with an American girl in Cornwall — though he admitted afterward that it had been a fiasco — and once with a young Cornish farmer.

"Was there really a *thing* between them?" asked Mabel eagerly.

"I think so," said Frieda. "I was dreadfully unhappy."

Lorenzo, returned, was not best pleased to find that the two women were friendly — at least so Mabel thought. However, he wasted no time on the matter. He had conceived an idea that he should work on a book with Mabel, a novel about her life. The suggestion delighted her. This was even better than being asked to sit for a portrait — after all, hadn't Gertrude Stein done something similar? But D. H. Lawrence was greater than Gertrude. Oh, yes, it was a wonderful idea, and they could start whenever he liked.

Before starting on the Mabel book, however, Lawrence tried to write his impressions of the Apache dance:

It is all rather like comic opera played with solemn intensity. All the wildness and woollyness and westernity and motor-cars and art and sage and savage are so mixed up, so incongruous, that it is a farce, and everybody knows it. But they refuse to play it as farce . . . But I arrive at a moment of crisis, I suppose every man always does, here. The crisis is a thing called the Bursum Bill, and it affects the Pueblo Indians. I wouldn't know a thing about it, if I needn't. But Bursum Bursum Bursum!! the Bill! the Bill! the Bill! Twitchell, Twitchell, Twitchell!! O Mr. Secretary Fall, Fall, Fall! Oh Mr. Secretary Fall! you bad man, you good man, you Fall, you Rise, you Fall!!! The Joy Survey, Oh Joy. No Joy, Once Joy, now Woe! Woe! Whoa! Whoa Bursum! Whoa Bill! Whoa-a-a!

Like a Lindsay Boom-Boom bellowing it goes on in my unwonted ears, till I *have* — to take heed . . .

Naturally enough, since it mocked a matter that was very serious to her, Mabel did not care for this article, and the morning after her genius's return was even more disappointing. He hurried over to the house, notebook at the ready, but when he saw what she had arranged for the interview his expression changed. Mabel greeted him on the roof outside her bedroom, and she was in negligee, or anyway in some loose flowing gown, with bare legs and moccasins. They sat in the sun in silence, which was sulky on Lawrence's part.

He said at last, "I don't know how Frieda's going to feel about this."

"Well, surely she will understand . . ."

No, said Lawrence, that was just it; she would not understand. Frieda had a German mind, indelicate and robust, not like the Latin mind that he himself so admired. Mabel was immediately on his side, she said. They were Latin together. In that hour, Mabel was convinced, he and she were psychically intimate. She knew they were the same kind of people. At least that is what she said in her book, but yet again one wonders. Is this self-mockery? It could very well be.

It was the first and last time Mabel and Lawrence ever had a protracted interview in private. Mabel seems to have thought it was Frieda who saw to it that Lorenzo was always chaperoned thereafter, but he must have been a party to the arrangement by which their interviews were always held in the Tony house, within earshot of Frieda as she bustled about the house. In these conditions the Mabel book never got a good start, and soon the project slipped into desuetude, though not before the genius gave it serious thought, as witness the list of questions he prepared for his subject. "Now I want," he wrote,

1. The meeting with Maurice
2. John, M. and You in Santa Fe
3. How you felt as you drove to Taos
4. What you *wanted* here before you came
5. First days at Taos
6. First sight of Pueblo
7. First words with Tony
8. Steps in developing intimacy with Tony
9. Expulsion of M.
10. Fight with Tony's wife
11. Moving into your house

One might notice that this outline is almost completely followed by Mabel herself in *Edge of Taos Desert*. The only thing left out is the item about Mabel's fight with Tony's wife, and this incident seems to have been completely hushed up. If Mabel wrote about it — and there is ample evidence that she wrote everything that came into her head — it was excised before publication.

She confessed that Frieda's opposition merely made her all the more determined to have her way with Lorenzo. She would save him from that woman or die in the attempt. She wrote:

Perhaps this is the time to tell you, Jeffers, what I think *I* wanted, and not to beat about the bush and cover it up with a maze of words. I wanted to seduce his spirit so that I could make him carry out certain things. I did not want him for myself in the usual way of men with women. I did not want, particularly, to touch him. There was no natural, physical pleasure in contact with him. He was, somehow, too dry, not sensuous enough, and really not attractive to me physically. But I actually awakened in myself, artificially, I suppose, a wish, a willful wish to feel him, and I persuaded my flesh and my nerves that I wanted him.

But she failed to get him. Sometimes she would be encouraged when he had one of his notorious bouts of rage with Frieda, but he always bounced back into harmony with her. Mabel let him tell her how to dress, though she had firm ideas before he arrived as to what suited her.

"Now I have always been, if not fat, well, square," she said.

Though longing to be like a willow, I have always resembled a pine-tree. Not the lofty kind, more the Christmas-tree variety. I tried to mask my solidity in so-called flowing lines, and all my clothes hung from the shoulders. I had recently had some new dresses made, of cotton crepe with wide, embroidered sleeves and round, embroidered necks ... The first time I put on the rose-colored one worked in turquoise-blue and pale yellow, I was obliged to go over and see Lawrence directly after breakfast. I felt so nice in this dress.

But Lawrence made a face and groaned, "Sancta Maria! These jibbahs! These Mother Hubbards!"

He explained, pointing to Frieda who was garbed in a full, striped peasant skirt with a bodice laced tight over her swelling bosom. That was the way women should dress, said Lorenzo, and Mabel promptly dropped her whole style and was soon swinging around in full skirts — and aprons too, because Lorenzo liked aprons like those his mother used to wear. She tried to scrub her kitchen floor. She tried to make bread. She tried to make herself over. There is no telling how long the effort would have lasted, but the Lawrences' visit was drawing to a close, though she was not aware of this.

John Evans, then twenty years old, was determined to leave Yale, come back to New Mexico, and marry Alice Henderson, though she was only fifteen and her parents naturally objected that she was too young. Mabel was inclined to agree with them, though she was never the conventional grabby mother, and *her* mother, Sara, was of her mind. Sara, in Youngstown, Ohio, carried on her mother's tradition of writing long letters full of gossip, advice, and triviality to her daughter. She said that she hoped the Henderson elders would not allow their child to marry so soon. In another letter she complained that John seemed to have no affection for her and her husband anymore, and in yet another missive she said that he ought to see reason about the thing. If Little Alice was willing to wait, he should do what the Hendersons wanted. She was quite out of patience with him, said Sara. After he had disappointed them all by leaving Yale, the least he could do was what they wanted about his marriage. But John did not oblige. He kept insisting that he and Alice wanted to marry then and there. Mabel gave way, and in turn reasoned with the Henderson parents until they too consented to the match.

The Lawrences were in on all this, partly because they were living with the family, and also because Mabel wanted to depend on Lorenzo, seeing him in the light of the man of the house. When Alice Corbin and her daughter came to visit, everyone had a lot of fun. Lorenzo turned everything into a party, Mabel thought fondly — and then ruined it all. She had written him what must have been a long, intimate letter, ostensibly to help him with the book, still presumably in the making, and she was horrified when he mentioned casually that he had passed it on to Frieda to read. How could he have done such a thing? The worst of it was that he seemed amused about the whole affair. Oh, he was impossible! And yet, just when she was on the verge of giving up, he would come to the house and complain about Frieda, and Mabel's heart would leap again with hope. Life with the Lawrences had become a habit, and she was much upset when they announced that they were moving on, though they weren't going far — only up into the mountain to stay at the Hawk ranch near John Evans's little property, the Flying Heart.

"Of course I did not feel any really fatal loss," she said, "because the rock bottom of my life was Tony, and I threw myself on the thought of him. But in the daily hours Tony was away from the house a great deal, and though other people came and went, no one took the place of Lorenzo. I missed our everyday rides and walks."

Alice and John were married before Christmas. It was decided that their real honeymoon trip would come later, when in the Ganson tradition they would spend a long time abroad. Mabel planned a family party with the Hendersons and the youthful couple at Christmas, and used it as an excuse when Lorenzo and Frieda wanted to come down from the mountain and stay for the holiday. This refusal on her part led to coldness; worse was to follow. When Mabel relented later and suggested that they all go to Mexico, Lawrence replied that he didn't want to go anywhere for a bit. "I don't feel angry," he added. "But just that I want to be alone — as much alone as I am — while I am here."

"Very well, we would be enemies now," Mabel decided.

To enforce my own feeling against him, I turned my tongue loose. I told funny stories about him and emphasized all the weak things in him. He was terribly easy to caricature . . . And not only he and I said these mean things about each other; Frieda, too, glad of the breach, very glad, did her share of slandering and slamming me and my people . . . John did quite a lot of this. He had felt Lawrence's antagonism to him — and he had hated my concentration upon him. Tony, too, went round saying Lorenzo was a snake and poison and a sick man, which last is almost the worst he could say!

At the same time, various people were telling me the things Lawrence was occupied in saying about me!

"He said you tried to make him fall in love with you. He said you tried to take him up on your roof and make him make love to you. He said you have an evil, destructive, dominating will and that will be the end of you . . ."

This hurt. That it was the truth made it worse. Small wonder that Mabel had a fit. According to her story, she simply passed out for twenty-four hours, "having a vacation from it all, lying on the bed with a smile on my face while doctors worked round, giving me all kinds of medicine, and Tony sat on the floor praying."

Soon afterward the Lawrences went to Mexico after all, and spent some months there with Hal Bynner and Spud Johnson, a journey that produced Lawrence's new novel, *The Plumed Serpent.* Mabel observed resentfully that he put into the book all the material about Indians and drums that he had gathered from Tony. "He simply transposed Taos and took it down there to Old Mexico," she said; and there is justification for the claim.

She threw herself back into the struggle for the Indians, whom she had neglected during Lorenzo's stay. The battle against the

Bursum bill was waxing hot just then, and Collier was making it hotter. According to Mabel, it was the Department of Justice that forced her hand. Some department inspectors came out to Taos to investigate the business, and decided that she and her house were the center of the trouble. Without Mabel, they thought, things would go more smoothly, and they had the wherewithal to get rid of her. Wasn't she corrupting a ward of the government by living with him without benefit of clergy? Mabel Sterne would have to move.

It must have been John Collier who carried the warning to her, though in her book she is not specific about it. She wrote several troubled letters on the matter, however, to Alice Henderson. Obviously she could confound their knavish tricks by marrying Tony, but she was, as always, worried about her mother, who held the pursestrings. What on earth would Sara do if Mabel were to marry an Indian? Mabel counted the money she would have to live on if Sara should decide to cut off supplies — four or five hundred a month, it would be. She wondered if she could manage. How about setting up a guest house on the property? Tony would be a great attraction, and if she had to, that is what she would do.

But there was one important thing that had to be settled — Tony's divorce. The application for it had gone down to Santa Fe, to one Judge Kiker, in whose power it was to grant or refuse it — for Tony, as Mabel had occasion to remember, *was* a ward of the United States of America. Judge Kiker did not like the situation any better than most of the other whites of the state, and so he tabled the application and might have forgotten it forever if a friend of Mabel's, a lawyer named Wilson, had not remonstrated with him on the delay.

"It's terrible for those kids," he said, referring to the young Evanses. The judge relented and granted the divorce; Tony's precious papers were deposited with Alice Henderson for safekeeping, and preparations continued.

"Mabel wanted my parents to help," Alice Rossin said, "and they probably would have done anyway, but she went a little too far, they thought. She told them that after all, she had helped John and me get married when there was a lot of feeling against it, and so she thought they ought to help her be reinstated with the public when she and Tony were married. It made them angry. But, of course, they did help, because they thought they should."

So Mabel and Tony were quietly married at last. "Nothing could make me give him up," wrote Mabel of Tony, "nothing will ever make me give him up." Sara, at least, did not try; she went on sending money to her daughter just as she had before.

"Mabel had built a spacious house on the edge of the Pueblo allotment, and half a dozen guest-houses on the adjoining field," wrote Mary Austin. "I went there often, for while there is practically no likeness between Mabel and me, very little consenting approval, there is a groundwork of an intelligent approach to problems of reality, and a genuine affection. There is about Tony a warm stability of temperament which makes him an acceptable third to all our intercourse . . ."

So far so good. But in London, where Alice and John Evans were on their honeymoon, when word of the marriage reached them, John took to his bed for two days; and Edwin Dodge is alleged to have said, when he heard the news, "Lo, the poor Indian!"

Chapter Thirteen ⊶⊨━━━━━━━━━

GOOD WISHES were sent by old friends and acquaintances in the East. Many were sincere, but some, no doubt, were framed to conceal amusement or even shock. Mabel particularly resented a comment made by Lawrence on a postcard sent to a friend in Taos: "I hear Mabel married Tony. Why?" They were not on such terms that she could have explained — not at that time, though they became friends again.

There was something on her mind that she was unable to discuss even with her friends: she had contracted syphilis from Tony. It is not surprising; many Indians were victims of venereal disease. But Mabel was a romantic, and romantics do not think in those terms. It was even worse for her then than it would be today; though people knew about such things, they never permitted themselves to mention or even think of them until, like Mabel, they had to face the facts. She was probably frantic at first. What was she to do about it? She could not rush off to the local doctor; Doc Martin was notoriously indiscreet. Nor could she very well take Tony to New York for a course of treatment. There was no telling how long it would take in those days, when less was known about venereal disease and the proper medicines had not yet been developed. Nobody in Taos could be trusted with the secret, Mabel reflected; even Santa Fe was too small a community. In the end she repaired with Tony to Albuquerque, where she found a trustworthy consultant. For years thereafter she carried on a surreptitious correspondence with the Albuquerque laboratory, dispatching samples and receiving reports of tests.

In spite of all her precautions, however, word ultimately got out. It was probably Mabel's own fault. She was incorrigibly indiscreet even where it would have been better to keep quiet. Like Midas's servant, she had to tell someone, and rather than go out as he did to whisper the secret to the grass, she confided in Carl Van Vechten. There seems no doubt that he kept quiet about it, but what is not so sure is that she confined herself to telling him. Someone else found out, somehow — there was a rumor, a whisper in the air.

In *Lorenzo in Taos* she does not, naturally, mention this matter at all. After the marriage she decided that she was growing tired of Taos somehow — one supposes that because she now had full possession of Tony, it was not necessary to live there all the time to keep an eye on him; she could take him with her. As usual, she had collected a houseful of friends, among whom was a young man she referred to as Clarence, though it was not his name. Clarence was a fixture of the family for some time. When John Collier and his wife, Lucy, urged her to take a vacation from New Mexico's mountains and try the heights of California for a change, Mabel agreed. She chose to live in Mill Valley on Mount Tamalpais, near San Francisco and the Colliers, and she moved there with Tony, Clarence, and two more of the Pueblo Indians, Tony's nephew Trinidad and her own maid, Albidia. For this number of people one house would not suffice, so Mabel blithely took two.

"We were a funny collection of people," she wrote with patent satisfaction. "Clarence so fashionable and fastidious in his modish clothes, Tony and Trinidad in blankets and with their long braided hair, and little Albidia like a Persian miniature with her black hair and long, dark eyes." She did not add that she herself must have looked somewhat out-of-the-way, having reverted to her old style of loose, flowing, embroidered dresses. Even in San Francisco, where people were accustomed to the unconventional, they stared at members of Mabel's party in the streets.

But something was missing; she could not feel right about life as long as she was on bad terms with Lawrence. Though she eagerly snapped up news about him from other people and thus kept tabs on him, she had not heard from him directly since they had parted on bad terms and he had gone to Mexico. She knew that he had quarreled with Frieda and permitted her to go on to England alone. She heard, and could scarcely believe, that he had actually visited Buffalo to see Bessie Freeman, and had taken some trouble to meet Sara. Then, according to Bessie, he had gone back to Old Mexico — "in company with one of those Danes," said Mabel resentfully.

She had hated the Danes, two young artists, and been jealous of them ever since Lawrence and Frieda struck up a friendship with them after leaving her, and asked them to come and live at John's ranch near Taos.

"When I could bear it no more," admitted Mabel, "I wrote him a letter . . . I told him he had hurt me, but that I had to have his friendship."

He replied immediately, on October 17, 1923. It was a friendly letter, though of course he lectured her; Lawrence could never resist the chance to lecture. She ought to give up trying to have her way in everything, he felt. "You have striven so hard, and so long, to *compel* life," he observed. "Can't you now slowly change, and let life slowly drift into you . . . People tell me you are divorcing Tony, and there is another young man, and so on. Probably it's not true. I hope it's not. I don't think it is. Tony always has my respect and affection . . ."

Of course it was not true. The other young man Lawrence mentioned was probably Clarence, and even Mabel would never have considered trying to make the flibbertigibbet Clarence over into a husband. The correspondence continued, as did the lecture. Shortly before Lawrence departed for England he wrote at length from Guadalajara: "Don't trouble about the Indians. You can't 'save' them; and politics, no matter *what* politics, will only destroy them. I have said many times that you would destroy the Indians." And the same went for Collier, he added shrewdly:

It is his saviour's will to set the claws of his own white egoistic *benevolent* volition into them . . . I tell you, leave the Indians to their own dark destiny . . . One day I will come and take your submission: when you are ready. Life made you what you are: I understood so much when I was in Buffalo and saw your mother . . . I was your enemy. But even saying things against you — and I only said, with emphasis and in many ways, that your will was evil masquerading as good, and I should still say that of your will: even as an enemy I never really forsook you.

In spite of the severity of parts of this letter, Mabel's heart was lightened. Even scoldings from Lorenzo were welcome just as long as they remained in touch. She began to write poems and short stories in California, most of them with Lawrence in mind:

> Bear with my weakness, my failure, my pain,
> Grant me this only, this darkness I need.

I sicken from sunlight, but give me the rain,
   for I am but seed.

She wrote a lot of poems, though the one she was probably proudest of was "The Ballad of a Bad Girl"; later she had it printed. Now she had something new to think about, menopause, the first symptoms of which were making themselves known. She wrote a long poem called "Change":

1. Transition

Languidly dying month by month,
Recedence of life in every cell
And along the nerves,
Gradual fading of the pigment
and departure! Departure everywhere!
Absence.

O God! Nobody home.

Motor-power growing fainter,
Yet, cruelly, enough to keep life
In this body,
But not love-life and the love-juices.

And what is a body
Without love to go on?
A misery, a doubt, a panic fear.

It went on for several pages, ending on a more cheerful note:

Blessed change!
You see, my own, how the heart opens
   To the new occupation?

The magnanimous mountain of the heart
Breaks open to embrace this influx,
Offering freely its eternal fire.
Here in this place, my own,
You receive at last
The power of the virgin.
This is the happy time.

She remained in touch with Lawrence. He wrote testily but with a kind of warmth from England, where he had rejoined Frieda. One of his letters was written in the old style of high rage because Mabel had asked him his opinion of Gurdjieff, the Russian mystical philosopher who had a large following and had set up a colony at Fontainebleau. Uncharitable people might say that Lawrence hated Gurdjieff because the Russian had succeeded in maintaining a colony, or utopia, whereas Lawrence himself had never achieved this goal, dear to his heart. But Lorenzo had a better cause for wrath; his valued friend Katherine Mansfield had died of tuberculosis at Fontainebleau due to what he considered malpractice and gross negligence. Gurdjieff's treatment, or part of it, consisted of making the patient sleep on a gallery above a cow byre. His theory was that cow's breath carried health to diseased lungs, but Katherine died all the same.

"I have heard enough about that place . . . to know it is a rotten, false, self-conscious place of people playing a sickly stunt," stormed Lawrence to Mabel. His strictures on Gurdjieff did not have any lasting effect on her, but for the time being she paid more attention to another portion of his letter, in which he repeated an earlier message to the effect that he wanted to come back to America. England was dead and hopeless, he said; the only chance was in the New World, and he planned to return with a small party of the faithful: Frieda, of course, but also Katherine Mansfield's widower John Middleton Murry and a woman he called the Honorable Dorothy Brett. This was exciting news, and Mabel hurried to invite the whole party to stay with her. In the end, for reasons of his own, Murry did not come, but the others did, arriving just six months from the time Lawrence had spurned the dust of Taos from his feet on his tempestuous way to Mexico. They got there a day before Mabel and Tony arrived from California.

Mabel's first impression of Dorothy Brett, whom everyone called simply "Brett," was unfavorable. She saw a tall, oldish girl (Brett was forty) with pretty, pink round cheeks and a childish expression. Mabel wrote, "Her long, thin shanks ended in large feet that turned out abruptly like the kind that children draw. She was an amusing and an attractive grotesque . . ." As she slowly approached, Mabel thought of her as "curious, arrogant, and English." But the probable truth is that Mabel was already jealous of this third member of the party. It was bad enough having Frieda there to stand between Lawrence and herself; now she must put up with yet another adoring woman, and the competition angered her. Characteristically, endearingly, she admitted it. She spoke of Brett's ear trumpet, which its owner called Toby, as an eavesdropper, a spy; the flat, dipper end of it, she said, seemed always to suck conversation out of the air, forever between Lawrence and the world.

"Good heavens! It was worse than Frieda's restraining presence!" she stormed. "It seemed to me that I never saw Lorenzo alone any more or had him undividedly," she added later. "I simply detested the kind of group life that had any more elements in it than Lorenzo and me or, at a pinch, Lorenzo and me and Tony and Frieda. The addition of Brett made it richer for Lorenzo, but poorer for me, it seemed. She paid all her attention to him, just as I did, and this is not the way to live a group life." Sometimes Mabel went out riding with Lawrence as they had done in earlier days, but it was not the same, somehow. She does not seem to have blamed her menopause for her new, more timid approach to riding, preferring to explain it by her "new, strange submissiveness" to him, but the fact remained that she didn't control her horse well anymore. Brett watched them enviously as they started out because she had never learned to ride, and soon Lorenzo took her on as a pupil.

"He taught her to have an imaginative relationship with the horse, to feel she was sympathetically en rapport with it, to feel 'the flow' between the horse and herself; but he never did teach her to ride well or to know how to *manage* the animal," said Mabel somewhat peevishly. "She was always afraid of it." But she added with good common sense — Mabel had been a horsewoman since she was a child — "It has been my experience that to the best horseman a horse is a horse, first and last, with no unusual, human traits. It takes a lively imagination to see in a horse what Lawrence saw in St. Mawr, for instance, and imagination interferes with horsemanship."

Living as they did in a small town, the members of this little colony often did things for themselves that city people won't bother with. For example, Mabel trimmed Lawrence's beard when he permitted it, and she loved it. Then came a day when her hair needed cutting. Hoping that Lorenzo would return the earlier compliment and offer to do the job himself, she spoke at length of how she hated the only available barber. Unfortunately he did not take the hint, but Brett did. Eagerly she said that she would do the job; she knew how, she declared, because she had often cut Katherine Mansfield's hair when necessary. (Like Mabel, Katherine had early espoused the fashion of bobbing.) There seemed no tactful way out of it, so Mabel sat down and let Brett cut, while Lawrence stood by and advised her. Suddenly Brett's scissors cut off the end of one of Mabel's ears. There was general consternation, and lots of blood.

"Why, you cut my ear off!" exclaimed Mabel, so interested, she later said, that she forgot to be indignant. Brett hated her, she knew, but surely this was going rather far? Indeed, as time passed, Brett seemed to occupy Mabel's thoughts more and more to the exclusion of Frieda, who had once been her only real source of grievance. As the summer went on, she admitted, her early soft feelings of submission abated, and she was full of impatience and irritation. "Brett annoyed me beyond words," she admitted. "She sometimes had a paranoiac glare in her eyes, directed upon me, whom she quite plainly detested . . ." She and Frieda would get together to complain about the deaf woman, who as she said sat in the doorway of life with her mouth slightly open, like a paralyzed rabbit, dreaming. The really irritating thing about her was probably not her half-open mouth but the fact that her gaze was always and forever directed at Lawrence — and Lawrence liked it.

"He did not seem to mind her sitting at her studio door watching him. Now, why should he like *her* attention and dislike mine?" asked Mabel. "Every time I showed any particular emotion towards him, he drove it back into me, and this was making me feel rather weak and ill at times." At least once she asked him outright what it was about Brett that he liked, and he said that she had a sort of touchstone about her that showed things up. Mabel was enraged. They were riding together at the time. A moment later she forgot her fury, because "with an intense blue look in his eyes, he rode his horse alongside me until his thin leg and thigh brushed against me . . . I knew he would never do that with [Brett], that he would never, with sudden forgetfulness, unconscious of himself, need, like Icarus, to reach out and replenish himself from her life." Icarus? Antaeus, surely. "Lorenzo seemed to have these involuntary impulses once in a while," she added. He would look at Frieda sometimes and sing softly,

Aupres de ma blonde,
Comme il fait bon, fait bon, fait bon!

evidently unconsciously. Just as he would hum at Mabel when she was in an aggressive mood, "Malbrouk s'en va t'en guerre!" But it wasn't all struggle or quarreling. Lawrence had a great talent for making a party go, and they used to play charades, imitating each other, mocking each other, and doubling over with laughter.

Inevitably, however, restlessness overtook Lawrence, as it always did. If he had ever really expected that it would be possible to create Jerusalem right there on Mabel's doorstep, he finally realized that it wouldn't do; he was temperamentally unable to settle down with her, even though she was trying hard to be submissive. He and Frieda thought nostalgically of the countryside, where they had taken refuge before on the Hawk ranch: now, of course, they were on better terms with Mabel, and they wondered if it wouldn't be feasible to live on John Evans's ranch, which Lawrence had renamed Lobo. This time there was no struggle, no ill feeling. Mabel was sorry to see Lawrence go, but he promised that they would come down often to visit her, and in a rush of self-abnegation she actually insisted on handing the property over to the Lawrences, first taking the precaution of buying it back from John — "for a buffalo-hide overcoat and a small sum of money," as she put it. Lorenzo would have hesitated to accept such a magnificent present, so Mabel gave it to Frieda, and Frieda paid her for it with the handwritten manuscript of *Sons and Lovers.* This gesture offended Mabel. She was fully conscious of the value of the manuscript, but she felt that Frieda was ungraciously refusing to accept her gift. Later she handed the manuscript over to Brill, the analyst, in payment for his work with one of her friends. This was typical of her — a grand but wrong-headed gesture. In another way too it went sour. Tony was angry that Mabel had given away the ranch because he had got into the habit of using it for his horses, and many of the other Pueblo Indians liked to hunt there. Mabel soothed him as best she could, assuring him that Lorenzo had consented to keep the horses there and would surely not object to the Indians' visits.

Besides, Mabel agreed with Lorenzo that she and Tony might keep visiting rights. There were two cottages and a small hut on the property. One of the cottages, they agreed, would be kept available for Mabel and Tony's convenience if they should want to come up the mountain; the other, of course, was for Lawrence and Frieda, and the hut was allotted to Brett. As all the buildings were in need of repair, a number of Indians were invited to come up and help with the work, camping at night on the hill behind the ranch. Various Mexicans were employed as well, to make adobe and do carpentry. What with the Indian encampment and Tony's horses, the place began to have quite a populated look, and Lorenzo was in his element bustling around, painting and building and cooking and making lists of things to be brought up from town by anyone coming their way — Mabel or the Indians or Spud Johnson. (In time, Spud transferred himself from Bynner's employ to Mabel's, and he remained in Taos for the rest of his life. Hal Bynner always blamed Mabel for this, and disliked her all the more.)

Lawrence's notes to Mabel often mentioned her ill health — she was undergoing a spell of it. "Every time he slipped away," she explained, "I had a queer relapse into psychic emptiness, as though the bottom had fallen out, and the queerest feeling of dispersal . . . It made one feel weak and inadequate for a few days."

Clarence, who had not returned from California with the others, now reappeared in Taos to stay at Mabel's. Of course he was anxious to meet the great man, of whom he had heard so much from his hostess, and Mabel decided that it was time to go and visit the Lawrences, try out the house, and introduce Clarence. They prepared happily for the journey, loading the car with food and blankets. Tony also brought his gun, and as they drove toward the ranch in high spirits, he explained to Mabel and Clarence that he intended to shoot porcupines because they did a lot of harm to the pine trees, girdling and killing them. Porcupines were on his mind; as soon as the car was unloaded and Mabel had started putting things away in the cottage, he took the gun and went down the hill into the forest. They hadn't yet really talked to Lawrence, whose reception left a lot to be desired: at the sight of the party when it arrived he had merely scowled and disappeared into his house. He emerged quickly, however, when a shot rang out from the trees. Mabel saw him crane his neck in its direction, and her heart sank at the sight of his angry frown. Then Tony appeared, smiling triumphantly and carrying a large dead porcupine.

"Shot a porcupine," he said jauntily.

"But I don't want any shooting here," Lawrence scolded him. "I like the porcupines."

This offended Tony. "They going to kill all the trees if you don't keep 'em down," he retorted. Then he walked off up the hill, still carrying his gun and the corpse, to join the Indians in their camp. Clarence went along with him. Together they put up a tent and arranged to spend the night there. This meant that Mabel would have to stay all alone in the cottage, a situation that didn't appeal to her. It was much pleasanter up there with the Indians. "The fire made a bright, warm neighborhood, and the happy Indians chatted and sang in their joyous ease, while down below, one felt a constriction and a gloom," she wrote.

True, that was the effect Lawrence often had. Thinking matters over, Mabel tried hard to see both sides of the question. She was naturally inclined to defend Tony; on the other hand, she was also inclined to make excuses for her adored Lorenzo. Naturally he was proud of his property, she told herself. For somebody simply to walk in and shoot an animal was an invasion of his rights. And yet Tony had always felt free to shoot there. They were Lawrence's trees, Mabel told herself: he hadn't asked Tony to come and protect them. Certainly it was a ticklish situation, and there they were, Lorenzo and Tony, both of them gravely offended.

Mabel went on thinking about these matters until she fell asleep, and when she woke in the morning her mind was made up. Lorenzo was at fault, of course he was. Feeling full of beans, she walked jauntily out of the ranch's limits and up the hill to the Indian encampment, where she had breakfast with Tony and Clarence and the other Indians. Then, fortified by her friends, she felt ready to take up arms. This matter must be settled, she thought, so she told Clarence to go down the hill and ask Lawrence to come and see her. Unwillingly, Clarence carried the message and came back to report: Lawrence had said that if she wished to see him, let her come down in person. This was a predictable reaction, but it infuriated the lady. She stormed downhill, marched into the Lawrences' cottage where they sat with Brett, and swept the master of the house off to her own premises.

She had planned to give him a piece of her mind. Instead, she said, "How *can* you treat me like that?" and burst into tears. It was submission with a vengeance.

"Well," said Lawrence, "I can't stand a certain way you walk. As you went by my window this morning . . . ."

It was true: she had to admit it. She had flounced her skirts in a sassy way. Of course he resented it! Mabel cried some more, and then they had a long talk and made up.

"We drove home to Taos, and that was the first and last time we stayed in the cottage," she wrote.

But, though everyone tacitly agreed that it was safer not to stay the night, she and Tony still went up for the day now and then; even so, in spite of all precautions, the sparks were apt to fly. It was not so much Lorenzo's behavior that caused trouble, however, as Brett's. She was always there. She got in the way. She presumed. Once Mabel admired a small painting that Lawrence had made and he gave it to her. Brett promptly stole it and took it away to hide in the house. When Mabel discovered her loss — as she did almost immediately — she rushed into the house and sought for it, turning things over, pushing them around, even knocking them down before she found the prize. Brett snatched it away again and ran out of the house, Mabel in hot pursuit. They ran around the cottage until Mabel overtook the quarry and got her painting back once more. All this time Lawrence, faintly embarrassed, could only protest rather feebly.

Brett or no Brett, Mabel couldn't stay away. They had a good life up there, she said. Lawrence did the chores every morning, with Brett helping, while Frieda sewed or followed some other sedentary pursuit. Then Lawrence would go down to a favorite pine tree, to sit under it and write. In the afternoon he would work with the Indians around the place.

"Brett worked with them too," Mabel said. "That is, she did what she could. When there was nothing else to do, she handed things . . . They had fun together and I envied them, because they liked to *do* things!"

One of the things they liked to do was paint. On one occasion all three of them, Lawrence and Frieda and Brett, collaborated on a large picture of the ranch with the desert below. Stung to emulation, Mabel too began to paint. But it was not in her nature to keep the relationship on an even keel, and soon she was offended by something Clarence reported Lawrence as saying. Clarence, she observed jealously, was getting really intimate with Lawrence, and he often brought back gossip about what the genius had said of her.

"He says your will is on him," Clarence told her. "He says when he is up at the ranch, he can feel you sitting down here *willing* him!"

After such a conversation, Mabel went to her desk and wrote a long letter to Lawrence. Ignoring the fact that Frieda would be reading the letter, she reproached him for being disloyal to their friendship. While she was at it, she spoke her mind about Brett and her "ludicrous" attitude toward him. "We have to have our Bretts and Clarences, but we need not take them too seriously," she said.

Lawrence's long reply was not calculated to soothe her: "I wish to heaven you would be quiet and let the hours slip by," he said in part. "But you say it's not your nature . . . That wearies me . . . But in you, even your affection is a subordinate part of your ever-lasting will, that which is strong in you . . ." Which left Mabel with a lingering resentment. For some time she stayed away from the ranch, and by the time the Lawrences came down for a visit her feelings were somewhat soothed.

What happened thereafter is rather hard to understand. It seems clear that Clarence and his tittle-tattle exacerbated the trouble, but why should Mabel and Lawrence have been so seriously taken in? Probably it was because neither Mabel nor Lawrence had enough of that particular humor that helps to deal with such characters. They took people too seriously. Of course it was Lawrence's business to do so: he was a novelist. One might suppose Mabel, however, to have had more common sense.

She happened to be entertaining on the evening they arrived, and as her guests they were invited to attend the dinner party. But it was a rather formal affair, and Mabel was more occupied with the other guests, old friends from the East, than with the Lawrences. There was a lot of talk about mutual friends in New York, people the Lawrences didn't know, and if Lorenzo seemed sullen and un-sociable Mabel put it down to that. He was touchy about these social matters. Later in the evening, though, when he and Clar-ence went off to the edge of the porch and talked for what seemed like hours, she realized there must be something more in the wind. It was a relief when Frieda announced that she was going to break it up. They had been talking long enough, she said, and she went over and interrupted them. After the Lawrences had gone back up the mountain, Mabel, curious as ever, made Clarence tell her what the two of them had been up to. After fencing unavailingly, Clar-ence confessed: he and Lawrence, he said, were planning to ride off into the desert and get away from it all. They would never be seen in Taos again.

"Now, of course I felt that it was my duty to tell Frieda about this," said Mabel. "Just as one would if a child confided he was going to run away with another child. Would one promise to keep his secret and let them run? Hardly." The passage gives an interesting sidelight on her methods with children, but we are never told what Frieda did about it after Mabel told her — something effective, no doubt.

A short time afterward the Lawrences happened to come down to Taos again to stay overnight. When, after supper, Lawrence and Clarence slipped away, Mabel was about to raise the alarm, but she need not have worried. They soon reappeared, carrying with them a bottle of bootleg liquor. Everybody had a drink or two, even Lorenzo, who scarcely ever touched hard liquor, and when the Victrola was cranked up, Mabel actually persuaded him to dance with her. Lawrence had always refused to dance, calling it tail-wagging. This time, however, he allowed himself to be dragged out on the floor, and when Frieda stepped out with Clarence, Lawrence's energy redoubled. Frieda, said Mabel, looked very nice that night, glowing and self-confident, and she and Clarence danced well together, a fact that enraged Lorenzo. He pushed Mabel around vigorously and used her as a battering ram whenever they met Clarence and Frieda on the floor, round and round and round, bumping hard. Brett circled the two couples with her ear trumpet, following wherever Mabel and Lawrence went, trying to bump Mabel and yet leave Lawrence unscathed.

"Lorenzo kicked Frieda whenever he could," said Mabel.

The music stopped at last, and Frieda and Clarence disappeared through the door into the dark. Mabel was highly indignant. Such a thing simply was not done in her group, she explained; whatever they did was done all together. She tried to stir up Lawrence about it, but he only said sarcastically, "Ah, youth and middle age!" and laughed nastily. If Tony had not insisted that it was bedtime, she would have waited around until the suspect couple returned, but Tony did insist, and they went home and to bed. They lay in their hammocks in the upper porch, and though Tony quickly fell asleep Mabel could not. She lay awake until she heard Frieda and Clarence come back, and as she heard their voices going on and on, easily heard in the stillness of the night, she was overcome with a passion to know what they were saying. She got up and had managed to get downstairs, out of doors, and halfway across the yard before she heard Tony calling, in a "terrible voice," "Come back here!"

No, she could not go back, not until she heard what was going on. By the time she reached her goal, however, she found that Frieda had retired and Clarence in his room was also going to bed. She called him out. What, she demanded, was going on?

Clarence said that Frieda had told him many things: Lawrence was determined to destroy Mabel, she had said, and she was scared of him. Mabel gasped most satisfyingly, but in the middle of the talk she heard an ominous sound, and she saw Tony's car disappearing down the drive, aiming for the pueblo. She was horrified. She wrote:

Nothing mattered to me now but the fundamental reality of my life: Tony. And he had gone away. I knew he was not one to play and pretend, to make a threatening gesture and to revoke it. No. He had awaked to see me creeping away in the night, and when he had summoned me back from a flight that must have appeared to him in one light and one only, I had disobeyed him and gone on. I knew then, as I should have known when my compulsion was carrying me over beyond the boundaries of custom, that he would not stand for it.

She sent Clarence after him to say that he must come back. Clarence obeyed, and returned with the news that Tony had gone to his mother's house and would be back in the morning. And that was that; though when the Lawrences wanted Clarence to take them back to the ranch that day, there was a confrontation.

"You devil! I know you now!" cried Clarence to Lawrence, who replied, "And I know *you* now, to my chagrin."

Tony, not Clarence, drove the Lawrences back.

Mabel was aggrieved when she heard, in the customary roundabout way that one heard things in Taos, that Lawrence was blaming her for all that had occurred. In several of his notes he mentioned, clearly in response to things she had said, that he wasn't mad at anybody, not even because Tony had sent up and taken away two of the horses that they were accustomed to riding. ("I think we done enough for those Lawrences. I'm going to send for my mare. Better my nephew use her," Tony had said, and when he sent one of the Indians up to get her, the man had taken another horse along as well, for good measure.) There were a lot of letters back and forth at this time, because the Lawrences were planning to go to Mexico again, and some of their luggage was still at Mabel's.

"Thank you for sending the things," wrote Lawrence. "Would you like to hear all Clarence said to me? Pfui: you have some admirable young men ... And you know quite well there is no need for either Clarence or Tony to be 'mad.' It's pure bunk. But you always bring these things about."

Yes, she did. Here, for once, Mabel's detached attitude seems to have failed her; she really did feel she was being unjustly used.

Chapter Fourteen

THE PRESENCE of Lawrence, though she believed in his formidable qualities as a genius, never inhibited Mabel in her own writing. Even before he left Taos she was working away at her memoirs, the pages, quickly filled with Mabel's large, swooping handwriting, piling up steadily. Alice Rossin has said that nineteen volumes were finished, and she knows what she is talking about, for it was Mabel's habit to summon her daughter-in-law and make her read the work aloud whenever a group of guests assembled in the studio. This was almost every evening.

"Anybody who was staying there would sit in on it," reported Mrs. Rossin. "There would be Spud, of course — he typed it as Mabel wrote it — and perhaps Ida Rauh and Mary Austin and Clarence, but, most important, there were Lawrence and Frieda and Brett. I had to read everything out loud, and it was a nightmare. Once Mabel asked Lawrence what she should do with the manuscript, and he said, 'Take a boat out to the middle of the Atlantic and sink it.' Lawrence was *very* unfair."

Later he relented. In April 1926, he wrote to Mabel at length about her work, saying, "Collect your MSS and keep them all in a safe. Don't show them to anybody else, just now. Labour and wait ... Then, after a few years, take out your MSS again, and do what you wish with them. But not now. For the moment, let them lie still." He criticized the writing carefully, too. He liked the portion (now included in *European Experiences*) about the chauffeur in Florence, as well he might, since it could have been a story of his own. He added, "The only real touch of real love in your book was for Violette in Paris, and that was deathly. With your men, you only want to resist them, fight them, and overthrow them."

Mabel wrote shoals of letters to Lorenzo in Europe, enclosing manuscript pages, and he was conscientious in replying. From his repeated mention of his *bête noire* Gurdjieff, we know that Mabel never gave up her efforts to tempt her genius into the fold, but she did not succeed; Lorenzo remained aloof till the end. However, he made an attempt to do something about Mabel's work, after all. Richard Aldington was pulled into the affair when Lawrence gave him some pages of the manuscript to read. Aldington suggested that Mabel present the work to the Académie Française, where the pages would be safe and private and sure to be published at some future time. But this plan proved sterile, as a professor consulted by Lawrence replied that there wasn't the slightest chance of interesting the Académie, which cared only for historical French material.

In Lawrence's letters to Mabel there is often some mention made of Brett, who had dutifully returned to the ranch to look after it while its owners were away. Everyone in the circle spoke as if Lawrence's absence was only temporary; in the meantime, the arrangement worked out comfortably. Brett and Mabel, without the irritating presence of their beloved, discovered that they liked each other, though there were reservations on both sides. Between them they kept the Lawrences up to date on Taos. Brett announced to them when Mabel began driving her own car, but it was Mabel who told them when Tony's mother died. On one occasion she seems to have proposed bringing Tony to Europe, but Lawrence advised against it: it would be cruel, he said. He was probably remembering the occasions when Mabel brought her husband to New York. Tony was always ill at ease there, at a loss for something to do while his wife was rushing about on her own affairs. When the Luhans went to parties or entertained at their hotel, Tony would squat on the floor in the corner, softly tapping his drum and singing to himself. Mabel found this perfectly natural, but most New Yorkers did not. And people outside were not yet blasé enough to ignore the sight of a tall Indian with headband and plaits and a blanket wrapped around him. They would stare and even follow him about.

Certainly Lawrence, during those last few years, did not neglect his would-be patroness. He wrote often, and in a manner noticeably more friendly than before, but letters were not enough to fill her restless life, and she was discontented. She had her friends, and Tony, and the houses she was always tinkering with — but was it enough? She was forty-seven now, and impatient. Of course there were John and his wife and small children; that seemed to be working out all right. Mabel had never resented Little Alice, and sometimes she actually liked her. In 1926 the young couple went to live for a time in Buffalo, where John had developed a desire, inexplicable to his mother, to see more of his grandmother and birthplace. Once there he found a job as a bank clerk, where he earned something less than twenty dollars a week. Mabel, en route from New York, came to visit them in a suspicious mood. Whatever possessed her son to do such a thing, after all her careful lessons and attempts to give him a sense of beauty? Buffalo, of all places! She had intended him to do a course of analysis with Brill, but her first sight of the house where they were living astonished and delighted her. Alice had furnished it wonderfully — the child really did understand decorating — and Mabel sat down and cried with relief.

She had to undergo a serious operation in New York that year, to undo what the surgeon in Florence had done to her, stitching her uterus to her bladder. It was a comfort to have "the children," as she referred to John and Alice, so close at hand.

"We got on well enough," said Alice Rossin. "She had a very strong will, but it didn't usually rub me the wrong way, and I would forgive her anything for what she did about Mother that time. Mother had TB, you know, which is why Daddy brought us out to Santa Fe in the first place. Once she was really terribly sick. I was sure she was dying, and so was her doctor, but Mabel marched in and packed her up and took her out to California, to a specialist she knew there, and made her take things easy. Mother never looked back: she lived for years afterward. Mabel did more good in five minutes than the Santa Fe doctor had in years."

But no matter how much appreciation Mabel found, she was depressed. She missed the old days when Lorenzo had kept everyone laughing, and in an attempt to reproduce them she invited other people, artists and writers and dancers, to come and live in Mabeltown. Here and there, young beginners like Jean Stafford were startled and pleased to receive an invitation from Mabel, always with a sprig of fragrant desert plant, to come and stay for a time. Some accepted, and found themselves bracketed with successful people like Thornton Wilder, who came more than once to Taos accompanied by his sister Isabel, or the poet Robinson Jeffers and his family. Una and Robinson Jeffers coincided at least once with the Wilders, who witnessed a dramatic occurrence when Una made an attempt to commit suicide because her husband was paying too much attention to a lovely young pianist who was one of Mabel's protégés.

"I think Mabel was encouraging that affair," Isabel Wilder said, thinking back. "She was an incorrigible meddler, you know."

At about the same time Mabel divulged a new project she was considering, to make of her estate a guest house, or dude ranch. She had entertained this possibility once before. Now, though Sara had not stopped supplies, Mabel felt poor, and so revived the old idea. It was to be a deluxe guest house, luxurious yet western, with Tony for a built-in extra attraction. There were already lots of rooms in the various houses scattered over the grounds, and if the thing turned out to be popular, they could always build more. Mabel proposed to Isabel Wilder that she be the manager, but Isabel felt that she had enough to do looking after her brother Thornton, and she begged off. So Mabel invited Erna Fergusson of Santa Fe to come and take on the job instead. Erna, a member of an old New Mexico family, had what Mabel considered the proper attitude toward Taos and its Indians. She had always been interested in Indians and had written books on the subject.

Yes, said Erna when Mabel asked her; she would like to manage the guest house. So she came to Taos and moved into one of the houses, and Mabel embarked on an orgy of shopping. She bought textiles for furniture and curtains, and bed linen, and rugs, furniture, choice blankets of native manufacture — everything needed for a guest house. It was fun until, some months later, the estate's owner had second thoughts. Did she really want to hand over her lovely houses to any Tom, Dick, or Harry who felt like coming? John Evans and many trusted friends were sure she didn't until, as suddenly as she had embraced the idea, she turned against it. Of course she didn't want a guest house, said Mabel. Erna Fergusson had to be paid off, and John complained bitterly of what the whole thing had cost.

"But it was just as well," said Mrs. Rossin. "Can you imagine how she would have treated paying guests? Why, she often couldn't bear the sight of her regular guests, who were friends. She would spend the whole day locked away from them."

In 1930 word came that Lawrence, after increasingly ill health, had died in Vence, France. The sorrow Mabel felt at the news did not hold her back from getting to work immediately on a book about him. Various other women had the same idea, but Mabel was the first to cross the tape, publishing *Lorenzo in Taos* in 1932. While waiting for the book's appearance, she passed the time by interfering in John Evans's matrimonial affairs. He and Alice were not getting on, so Mabel took him on a trip to Mexico to relieve the pressure, Alice remaining behind with the children. In Mexico John met the novelist Claire Spencer, the daughter of one of Mabel's friends. Soon he was asking Alice for a divorce so that he might marry Claire.

"And Mabel helped him," said Alice Rossin. "I've never held it against her too much. It was Mabel, that's all — she dabbled. She always had this insane desire to break people up. We got a legal separation in 1931. Grandma was on my side and tried to bring us together again by cutting down on John's allowance, but his mind was made up. He and Mabel were awful about my money — I don't know what I would have done without Grandma." Alice and John were divorced in 1933.

Deprived of her guest house, Mabel thought of a new use for the estate. In spite of Lorenzo she had retained her interest in the teaching of Gurdjieff, and now she made the acquaintance of one of the Russian mystic's leaders, the poet Jean Toomer. Toomer, a charming man, had collected around himself a number of followers, and Mabel thought of turning her place over to them. She wrote to Toomer telling him that, apart from everything else, she needed Gurdjieff's teachings, and Toomer himself, to make her life complete. She and Tony were perfectly happy, she said, but they didn't have enough in common; they couldn't talk about things, and he spent a lot of time out of doors with his farm and animals. Gurdjieff and Jean Toomer between them would supply her spirit with the nourishment it craved, in return for which she would be happy to provide accommodation.

Toomer, who had grave doubts, wrote to the editor Orage in England (Orage handled the practical details of the movement), and asked his advice. The offer was indeed generous, he said, but there were drawbacks: the lady's temperament might create difficulties. Orage evidently agreed, and the move to Taos was never made. After Toomer married, Mabel lost interest in Gurdjieff, though she may have kept in touch with Jean for a time. It was probably his visit to Taos when he explored its possibilities that started the rumor that Mabel Luhan was thinking of ditching Tony and marrying a black man. (Toomer was a mulatto.)

All these pastimes — the talk about schools of philosophy and guest houses, the imminent divorce of John and Alice, and the rest of it — were thrown into insignificance when *Lorenzo in Taos* was published. It was Mabel's first book to see the light, though she had written it most recently. It attracted an immense amount of attention — comments varying widely from warm praise to the chilliest horror. Fanny Butcher of the Chicago *Tribune* did not exactly commit herself: ". . . primarily an intimate portrait of D. H. Lawrence done in sharp, clear, brilliant lines by one who knew him in that strange, tense way that human beings do sometimes know one another," she said. Lewis Gannett went into more detail:

If you are one of those who hate and despise Lawrence, you will find here material to feed your conviction that he was a superman, a John the Baptist . . . Hate and love ran side by side in all (Lawrence's and Frieda's) channels of communication, and Mabel Luhan tells the story with an intense, pained honesty that gives the reader a shocked sense that he has intruded on privacies never meant for print. But Lawrence himself believed in honesty rather than privacy . . . It is always a moving book, at times a revolting book, at other times almost a very great book.

The critic William Soskin in the New York *Evening Post* was more severe. "It is not a pretty book," he declared. "To any one who has deep regard for 'Sons and Lovers,' 'Women in Love,' and 'Aaron's Rod,' the picture of Lawrence as a sadistic, violent, arrogant, hypersensitive man must be considerably repulsive. Since Mrs. Luhan has no literary record of importance to justify her part in the drama, many readers will regard her quite unfavorably." However, he felt that her courage and vitality deserved admiration, and he relented enough to end his diatribe: "Mrs. Luhan's book seems to me the most valuable of the personal biographical stories about Lawrence . . ."

Joseph Wood Krutch, discussing *Lorenzo* in *The Nation*, quoted Matthew Arnold on the Shelley group: "What a Set, what a Set!"

Many reviewers were violently anti-Mabel. One in the *Southwest Review* referred to her as "this unhappy, rootless, inert, but wilful female." A columnist in the Chicago *Herald-Examiner* described her in detail: "She is short and stocky, wears her black hair cut with bangs, low over the eyebrows, and has the manner of a woman who is used to much attention."

In London Peter Quennell referred to the book as "that naive yet somehow rather engaging essay in self-revelation," and a letter from Brett in the *New English Weekly* of London did its bit to brighten the literary scene:

[W]hen I first read "Lorenzo in Taos" I was flabbergasted [she wrote]. I had never realized the extent, the width, depth and height, so to speak, of Mabel Luhan's dislike of me. It loomed up large as I read, and, strange to say, preposterous. I was taken aback; anyone would be after six years of close friendship. Could, I pondered, an intimate, warm friendship spring out of such a beginning, which was genuine, the beginning or the end? Which is the ultimate truth? Life in Taos is not easy; the luxuries are limited . . . Mabel and I, since 1926, have weathered through all the ups and downs, the encroachments on friendship, that difficult living creates. We have ridden together, driven together, pulling each other out of mud-holes, talked, and read murder stories through long, cold winter days, and as she says, we continue to click. There is tolerance and understanding, and above and beyond the wear and tear of everyday life, an enduring click. That is my answer to "Lorenzo in Taos."

As was to be expected, opinion among Mabel's other friends, even those not so intimately connected with the book, varied widely. Ida Rauh hated it. She had been very fond of Lawrence, and in a letter to Mabel she likened her to a venomous spider, casting her web over her prey. Clarence said the book depressed him for days. Carl Van Vechten thought it fine. Bobby Edmond Jones said frankly that he didn't recognize the Mabel of the book and didn't like her at all; indeed, he begged off coming to see her until he could get over his impressions. Hutch thought it gave brilliant portraits of Lawrence and Tony but not such a good representation of herself. Jean Toomer called it a brilliant, revealing work. Ivy Litvinov and Naomi Mitchison in Russia liked it very much and wrote at length to say so. (Mabel later sent a copy of some of her other writing to Naomi Mitchison, who said it was a pity it couldn't be published, but that of course it couldn't.)

In 1933 the American world was presented with not one, but two new books from Mabel's stable: a novel by John Evans entitled *Andrew's Harvest* and the first of Mrs. Luhan's series of *Intimate Memories*, called *Background*, the account of her life from 1879, when she was born, to 1897, the year of her debut. John Evans's book was well received by the critics. It was *Background,* coming close as it did on the heels of *Lorenzo,* that really started the critics buzzing. "If Mrs. Luhan keeps up the horrid vitality of 'Lorenzo in Taos,' " said Lewis Gannett on March 3, in advance of its appearance, in the *Herald Tribune,* "that will be another great book." In the same paper, after publication, another reviewer commented, "[The book] sheds a new light on Buffalo and is well calculated to startle the iron deer out of the ancestral shrubbery . . . It's very different from the home life of the late dear Queen; and though we ourself were raised on the old 'Police Gazette,' it gives us a moment's pause."

Mabel had evidently told somebody that the rest of her memoirs were to be kept under lock and key for another fifty-nine years, until all the people involved were dead. But the New York *World-Telegram* announced, on March 17, "Well, the latest is that Mabel has repented. She has rewritten Volume Two and it is being offered to magazines for serial publication." Since it was to be about New York's literary life, the article continued, certain people were to have their hideaways ready. The most enthusiastic reviewer was Elizabeth Shepley Sergeant, in the Sunday *Herald Tribune* of March 9. Admittedly, she said, the book might shock Mabel's relatives — if any remained in Buffalo — "but its uncompromising and unforgettable portraiture of well-known social and family figures, swimming in a juice as rich and highly colored as that which sustains the character of a Bronte novel," would seem to a modern reader naïve. In a perceptive passage, Mrs. Sergeant continued,

In the center of the picture, of course, we see Mabel Ganson herself, a lonely, explosive, powerful, adventurous, coldly observant but enchantingly fluid and adaptable child, sealed to love and feeling by her parents' mutual attitude of hatred and silence and their inexpressiveness to herself, but all the more open to sensuous experience, esthetic experience . . . It was as if, dwelling in a house where life was not, she was forced forever to search for the living spring in other people's houses, minds and hearts and, so vicariously merged with their secret essence, claim the latter for herself.

The book, said Mrs. Sergeant, certainly established Mabel's place as an artist.

A week later, Herbert Gorman in the *Times* chimed in with

equal praise: "It is an important document and a genuine addition to the history of *moeurs* in America. It may not have taken courage to write, but it certainly took intelligence." A fine book, he concluded, and one that would prime the reader for what followed.

Not surprisingly, the reviewer on the Buffalo *News-Courier* implied that Mabel was "wilful." But on the whole the consensus was excellent, and Mabel's publisher was happy.

Early that summer Mabel's mother, who had said very little about the book, died, leaving her daughter a prey to remorse. Mabel wrote to her friends asking their opinion: did they think she had had anything to do with Sara's death? Mary Austin, for one, was prompt with reassurance. People always hated it when their relatives wrote about them, she said, but it was doubtful if any of them died of it. Mary herself had brought down a lot of family criticism on her head when she published her autobiography. Mabel wasn't to give it another thought, said Mary. A Buffalo friend was not so kind. Of course Sara had hated the book, she said; how could Mabel not have expected it? She herself had been physically sick when she first tried to read it, but she had conquered her weakness. But opinions from other Buffalo residents were more soothing than that, and Mabel, in the end, was comforted.

Sara's death, however, led to other complications. All through Mabel's adult life she had never had to worry about overdrafts, knowing that Sara, in the last analysis, would come up with the necessary sum. Now Sara was not there, and her daughter soon found herself in debt and nowhere to turn to.

A good manager would have done very well on her income, but Mabel had never learned to be a good manager, and evidently it was too late to begin. Still, she tried. She knew that she had spent lots of money on her furniture — why not sell some of it? She kept the possibility in mind, but for a time did nothing more. Life went on as usual, which is to say that Mabel brought out another book.

This time is was not a section of her reminiscences, but a pleasing little account of one day in the life of a woman who has married a Taos Indian and settled down in his country. On a winter morning (the book is called *Winter in Taos*) Mabel wakes up in her cold bedroom, realizes that the chimney needs cleaning, and sneezes. She has a cold coming on; she had better stay in bed all day. Her thoughts wander, as she has breakfast on a tray, to a stray kitten that used to share the meal, begging for the milk. Nothing makes a room so contented as a cat, mused Mabel: "But they drive the birds away . . . Really, to watch one's own dear cat slink out on a branch of the great cottonwood tree, wrap itself flat around it, and then try to dip the baby orioles out of their bag with a long paw shaped like a lemonade spoon, is just about enough to turn one on the whole race of them forever."

Mabel tells about the pigeons, living in "a Mexican village" reared on high, thick posts that lean every which way. They didn't eat the pigeons, she explained; they just had them. They loved to watch them. There were wild birds to watch, too — bluebirds, canaries, wind birds, orioles, wrens, a mockingbird, and sometimes a magpie. Then there were "the coarser birds" — rooks and ravens and crows. Mabel talked about all her dogs, in the past and present. While the servant Max was cleaning the chimney, she took refuge in Tony's room. And what was he going to do today?

Over to Arroyo Seco, said Tony, to trade oats for beans. Which made Mabel think of the oatfields and all the other farming done by the Indians. She approved of the way they threshed grain in the old days when she first came to Taos: horses tramped in a circle on the threshing ground, then the women cleaned it by hand. But the government came along and sold the Indians a threshing machine. Most of them didn't like it, and somebody burned it one night; the old way was best, they thought. However, the modern-minded Indians got another, and another, and another, until it was exceptional to see horses used on the threshing ground.

"When they planted and harvested and ground their grains all by hand, there was no cost and no waste — all pure gain for the labor they put into it," lamented Mabel.

But in those days they planted less and they lived off their corn and wheat, with wild vegetables and wild game. They worked so constantly in the fields that they burned up the starch that poisons sedentary people . . . That kind of life is changing very fast. They got so much more grain by the use of the machines that they began to trade it to the merchants in greater bulk than they were accustomed to do.

Formerly, they only needed a few things from the stores; coffee, sugar, salt, calicos and silks — not much more; but with the coming of machines they began to trade wheat and corn for canned foods.

Her thoughts moved on to Tony's horses, which he fed with some of his oats. Most of these animals they just had, like the pigeons; Mabel had "only two or three," but Tony had a whole herd, which he called "the family."

There was an odd little incident when Tony, ready to leave, leaned over and kissed Mabel on the cheek, and she said sharply, pulling back, "Look out! If I have a cold you'll catch it."

Tony looked more dignified than ever, and grave, so Mabel knew she had offended him. She said in explanation, "Well, you know how easy it is to get a cold from someone."

Tony said, "I think your heart take care of that if you let him . . ."

"Come here!" she cried, and she pulled him down and gave him a big kiss.

She continued: "But there was just a shadow of reserve in his touch now, a check. We both ignored it. We were used to each other's ways and sure, at bottom, even though our nerves and muscles still sometimes revolted at dissimilar attitudes of mind and custom. It seems as though we make a new adjustment every day!"

Tony was late coming home, and Mabel, listening to the howling of the coyotes, got into a state. She ran to meet him when she heard him coming.

"I was so afraid something had happened to you. Why are you so late?" she demanded.

Tony said, "What can happen?" He had visited his friends, he said, and gambled a few dollars, and had a nice time. Why was she so frightened?

"Such a night — the storm — " said Mabel.

Tony smiled and said, "Don't you know the moon is shining?" He pulled back the curtain to show her the peaceful desert.

Obviously Mabel, like the rest of us, didn't learn much from experience. But it is a good book, though it didn't attract the attention the others did. One is minded to agree with Spud Johnson, who declared it the best book Mabel ever wrote, but there were a lot of reviewers who didn't like it. The *Herald Tribune* approved, within reason; *Time* did not: "Those who enjoy, one way or another, author Luhan's slapdash mysticism and literary mirror-mooning will not want to miss *Winter in Taos*," said the reviewer.

"*Winter in Taos* is a chronicle of escape which makes pretty dull reading in times as rough and tough as these," said the *Forum Book Review*.

In autumn of the same year, 1935, the second *Intimate Memories* volume came out: *European Experiences*. Evidently some of her shock value had ebbed. Still, there was plenty of comment. Polly Ellicott in the Buffalo *Times* remarked that there was no cruelty, as there had been in the first memoir, and added, mystifyingly, "And what interests me most of all is that she did not write about the greatest romance of her life. Things which make the deepest impression are those which we never speak about." Did she mean the doctor?

Robert Briffault's *Europa* had recently appeared, and the *Christian Science Monitor* reviewer compared *European Experiences* unfavorably with it, saying, "On the whole, perhaps Mrs. Luhan reveals even more clearly than Mr. Briffault the reasons for the collapse of prewar society." There was on the part of several reviewers a disapproving feeling that the lady had talked too much about herself, which seems odd; after all, she *was* writing her autobiography.

"The flavor of this curious book is complex," said the *New Yorker*. "There is a good deal of salon reek, a touch of flighty mysticism, and a kind of skittish sexual frankness."

Bruce Catton in his column "A Book a Day" spoke without favor of the crowd of expatriates Mabel entertained at the Villa Curonia, adding, "It is a tribute to Mrs. Luhan's skill as a writer that she can make all of these antics interesting. Her book is eminently readable." "It may infuriate you, it may make you slightly sick in spots, but it will hold you," said May Lamberton Becker in the *Herald Tribune* book magazine.

Edwin wrote from Boston that though he was naturally interested in the book, he couldn't understand why she had published it. When she asked Carl Van Vechten why she hadn't heard from him, he replied that it was because he hadn't liked the book and saw no reason to write telling her so. She seemed to belittle everybody in it, he said, including herself. He felt when reading it that he was looking at life through the big end of opera glasses.

Chapter Fifteen

ADVANCE REPORTS that Frieda Lawrence was returning caused much excitement in Taos. The writer Paul Horgan, who then lived in New Mexico, described what happened. Everyone, he said, knew the day she would arrive at Lamy on the Chief. "A delegation was arranged to go to welcome her," he said.

She was the widowed Frieda, coming home — their hearts were open for her, and every consolation was prepared, overwhelming tact, visible love, the usual "understanding" of which Santa Fe was always capable for people who perhaps might prefer to be left alone. (The "understanding" are among Santa Fe's most trying types.) Anyhow, the station platform at Lamy was crowded with loving mourners primed to alleviate her desperate loneliness. Waiting for the train, the mood was noble. Nothing would be too great to do to help her forget or accept her sorrows in the best Santa Fe style of communal emotion. Hal [Bynner] had written an elegy to be read to her as she descended from the train. Hearts were heavy but valiant.

The train came around the last curve of the Glorieta passage, stopped, everyone moved to the proper car, grief and gallantry came up to the necessary pitch, and everyone strained for the first sight of her and her haggard misery. Suddenly there she was, in the vestibule. The door opened, the steps came down, all quickened on the brick walk, for the great sustaining moment had arrived, and her friends surged forward to console. But before anyone could do his sumptuous emotional duty, Frieda, beaming in the most robust pleasure, turned to someone behind her, and cried in her apple-frosty voice,

"Oh, Angie, look, they are all here, what darlings, they will love you!"

"With that, the widow, in genuine gaiety, brought DHL's successor down to meet all her old friends. Hal rapidly suppressed his ode. Everyone readjusted from solemnity to appropriate jolliness and a motorcade of a wholly different state of emotions returned bearing Frieda, Angelino and the rest to Santa Fe.

Angelino was Lieutenant Angelo Ravagli, a friend of the Lawrences who had met them in Italy. Frieda made no attempt to conceal the fact that they were living together. The affair was a nine days' wonder, but Taos gets used to practically everything, and Angie was accepted.

They went to the ranch immediately. Brett had removed herself and her belongings — later moving into a house she built not far from Mabel's grounds — and Frieda was eager to show her property to Ravagli. At first she felt a little ashamed of the primitive buildings where she and Lorenzo had spent so much time, because Angie, as an experienced landlord, was scornful of them. But the charm of the place won him over, and he admitted that it had "possibilities." An inveterate handyman, he was soon busy planning another edifice in which Frieda proposed to rebury Lorenzo's body, then he went to Vence to fetch the remains. There, however, he found that the complexities of transferring a corpse out of France into America were daunting, so he had the exhumed body cremated and brought the ashes back to Frieda.

The urn of ashes had many adventures on the way. For one thing, Ravagli nearly left it at the customs shed when he entered New York. Then it was actually abandoned on the platform at Lamy — the excitement of getting back and all that was responsible. He and Frieda had started driving back to Taos before they remembered it. Recovered, the urn accompanied its guardians to Santa Fe, where they attended a party and once more forgot it in their friends' house, but again they turned around and reclaimed it.

When Angie had finished rebuilding the tomb for Lawrence at San Cristobal (the official name for the ranch's locality), she meant to have a grand interment, or, as she described it to Paul Horgan, an *hommage à* Lawrence, which, in Horgan's words, was to be the place "to which the great intellectuals were to be and many actually have been invited for a certain date — Aldous Huxley, Maria, Thomas Mann, etc. etc.

"Plans went forward," said Paul. "Angelino was lovingly proud of making the garage-like structure on the hill above the little San Cristobal ranch house. When I saw it, (and Aldous and Maria were along, and Hal and Monte) Angie made biceps for me and said, 'I build. Sixty sacks of chement I build.' "

Frieda had well-worked-out plans for the ceremony of reburial in the chapel. In the meantime, however, all this had seriously displeased Mabel, who felt that as an old and very, very special friend of Lorenzo's she should have been consulted in the affair. Now, delving into her capacious and perhaps capricious memory, she came up with the story that Lawrence had wanted his ashes scattered over Taos mountain, and had told her so. If his friends really cared about his wishes, rather than setting up a tourist trap, said Mabel in effect, they would do their best to carry them out just as he had described them to her.

History doesn't tell us if she said all this in person to Frieda — even Mabel might well have quailed at such an act — but certainly she talked to Brett about it, and the Englishwoman, always ready to put one over on Frieda, was receptive. Between them they made a plan. Obviously in the interests of justice Lorenzo's ashes must be removed from his widow's possession and disposed of in accordance with his wishes. The plan grew swiftly, and seemed beautifully simple. Brett was helping Angelo and some Indians in putting the finishing touches on the chapel; she had been asked to decorate its interior. All she had to do was wait for a chance, when she and the ashes were together and alone, to grab them and make her escape. She had not succeeded in doing it, however, when Mabel sent a letter to Frieda in reply to a routine invitation to attend the ceremonies. In it she declared that though she had no legal right to Lorenzo's ashes, she wanted Frieda to know that she, Mabel, intended to outlive Frieda. The minute Frieda was dead, said Mabel, she would take the ashes and scatter them as Lorenzo had always wanted. In the meantime she would not come to the ceremonies, thank you very much, but she did send an enormous lot of flowers.

Paul Horgan now takes up the story again. According to him, an Indian woman friend of Frieda's came and told her of the plot to kidnap the ashes. "Knowing the mettle of Mabel, Frieda believed this, hastily cancelled the 'hommage,' and late at night (I thought of the burial of Sir John Moore at Corunna) the ashes were put into the poured cement ('cimento') sarcophagus in the garage where they still lie as the end of pilgrimage. Frieda said to me she vowed never again to speak to May-p-bel after that." (Frieda pronounced Mabel's name like that.)

Frustrated, Mabel turned her attention to the ceremony, which was to take place after this short delay. Some of Taos's dancers had been bespoken to dance for the occasion, but Tony went to them and said that if they did such a thing the spirit of Lawrence would lay a curse on them forever, so they sent their regrets. Frieda had to send to a more distant pueblo to find more Indian dancers. In one last malign stroke Mabel again managed to interfere when Judge Kiker, who had promised to read the eulogy, begged off — he just happened to be Mabel's lawyer. Here again Frieda coped. Her daughter Barbara and son-in-law Stuart Barr, a British journalist, were in Taos for the ceremony, and Stuart read the eulogy.

After all this one would suppose that the breach between Mabel and Frieda could never be healed, but one would be wrong, as Paul Horgan, among others, can testify. The war soon began, and he went into the army.

"After my return to New Mexico from military service," he said, "I was invited to a celebration at the University in Albuquerque of the publication of Tedlock's DHL bibliography. There was Frieda, vast and merry, and blue-eyed with gaiety. We embraced. Knowing few others, I stayed to talk with her. Small talk, in the course of which she offhandedly said something like, 'Ja, just last week I said to May-p-bel, I said —'

I interrupted with loyal horror. 'But you are not speaking to her?' Through over four years of war I had been faithful. But Frieda said,

" 'Ja, I know, I remember, but you know, there was the War, and we all did things, there was the Red Cross, we had to do things together, I saw *May-p*-bel, she was working too, we had to meet, I said to myself, we had a War, so I really had to speak to her, I spoke to her, we just kept on, then, after that.'

"My jaw dropped," continued Paul. "I saw that Mabel, actually, was Frieda's 'war work,' a sacrifice in the name of patriotism."

Toward the end of 1936, just in time for the Christmas sales, Mabel's third volume of *Intimate Memories* came out. *Movers and Shakers* was what she called it, from the poem by O'Shaughnessy about dreamers of dreams. The tumult surrounding its appearance could not have surprised her. She must have known that the book would bring down on her head the wrath of many labor leaders and former avant-garde thinkers because of her picture of their beloved Jack Reed, if nothing else. They didn't mind him being portrayed as a lady-killer. What they did mind was that he should have had an extended love affair with a rich bourgeoise like Mabel. It was something that many of them preferred, after Reed's apotheosis in Russia, to forget. Robert van Gelder said in the *New York Times* of November 19: "Her reports on the younger selves of many who are now famous are often not calculated to earn her much gratitude from the persons portrayed, but the general reader is more likely to be interested, and frequently amused."

Amusement and indignation were fairly well balanced, if the reviews are any criterion. "Don't read this book if you can't take it," warned the *Herald Tribune* on the fifteenth of November. "It's the most terrible showdown of Carol Kennicott, of Gopher Prairie, getting her wishes."

Quite a few commentators shared one inspiration and suggested that the title be changed to *Up in Mabel's Room*. Bruce Catton called the book dreary and tiresome, Floyd Dell liked it, and Clifton Fadiman of the *New Yorker* had a wonderful time making fun of it. "You can't explain Mabel in a phrase," he wrote. "She's a poser, right enough, and any way you define the word is OK with me."

In the Chicago *News*, on December 16, an unsigned reviewer said, "Our heart goes out in this charitable season to the Indian she married."

In the magazine *Midwest*, Ruth Suckow had a long article about Mabel, not a review of the book, but a study of her as a phenomenon. Cornelia Otis Skinner did a parody of *Movers and Shakers* called "Dithers and Jitters: A Brief Digest of the Intimate Memoirs of Mabel Rudge Truman." It began:

It is my gift to gather together the most brilliant personalities of my century. My soirees have become famous . . . My dynamic temperament attracted to the little house on Mott Street the titans of the day. Henry James, Picasso, Stravinsky, Oscar Wilde, and Ty Cobb, not to mention Ibsen and Loie Fuller. What evenings! . . . Freud would remark, "Mabel, you are extraordinary! The eternal hetaira." I can't help it. I was born that way.

But for all this, *Movers and Shakers* was on an occasional bestseller list in the hinterlands.

One evening in Pennsylvania, at a dinner party that included Paul Horgan and the novelist Joseph Hergesheimer, the talk turned to *Movers and Shakers,* and Horgan remembers that somebody asked Hergesheimer if he was mentioned in Mabel's book.

"No," said Hergesheimer, "thank God, I neither moved nor shook her."

Back in Taos, Paul found that Hal Bynner had produced a poem that was written, the poet assured him, of Mabel, though the title gives no hint of it:

GOURMANDE

Wishing to have a will, she wills a wish
That has no more to do with will than when
The eddy of a current turns a fish
And then as idly turns it back again —
Except that malice never actuates
The watery shifting of a spotted trout,
Unless an appetite for worms and baits
Happens to be the thing that, looking out,
For life, takes life as well. She is not that.
Her appetites are empty after all.
Though she is fed and surfeited and fat,
She does her best to drink a waterfall —
Not that she wants the water for a minute,
But she thinks she had better be round it than in it.

With a few others, they were sitting late in Bynner's library, drinking and talking, as people so often did, of Mabel — all their stories, in Paul's words, intended to reveal how sinister, ridiculous, destructive, she was. Suddenly, after it had gone on for what seemed forever, Hal said, "But why do we always sit around for hours and talk about her? It is all she wants!"

Bynner's animus is easy to understand. Not only had Mabel filched from him Spud Johnson, she took Henriette Harris too. Henriette had been a part-time secretary for him when Mabel came along and persuaded her to do some of her own work instead. Later, when Henriette decided to branch out and go into business for herself, she was very useful because she handled a lot of the possessions Mabel felt she had to sell.

"The day I met her," Miss Harris recollected, "I was a little nervous about it. I had been asked to go to her house, and while I waited for her to show up I remembered all the things I'd heard about her, and I didn't think it would work, really. Then she came downstairs and I was amazed. I don't know what I expected — probably a much bigger woman, sort of bullying, but she was small and sweet and nervous herself. She had the loveliest voice, too. I've never heard a lovelier. Well, we talked, and I agreed to do some of her work, and later I became a kind of agent for her: one thing led to another. I really did like her a lot. I've never had any patience with all the people who talked against Mabel: they just didn't know her."

Judging from Mabel's letters to Henriette, the younger woman did a bit of everything needed, from sorting her employer's thousands of old letters to taking care of the place while she was away, sending the odd articles of clothing that Mabel was always finding she needed, to selling pieces of furniture and once, even, trying to sell the house. There is an advertisement still in existence, from the Houston *Chronical:*

MABEL DODGE LUHAN'S

Fascinating big house in Taos, New Mexico. This famous and charming summer or winter home that has entertained many celebrities in its time, has just been placed on the market.

Handsomely carved gates open into a flagged and hollyhocked courtyard, bordered by tremendous cottonwood trees and a generous acequia. A long and beautifully proportioned portal leads into the quiet living-room. Through an arch can be seen a square sunny room. Extremely large dining-room with red tiled floor steps down from living room. Large kitchen and workroom.

Powder room and hall off living room. Four guest bedrooms. Bathroom off another hall. Attached to and part of main house is what Mrs. Luhan calls the Log Cabin. Additional patio, portal and patio bedroom off Log Cabin. Two large upstairs bedrooms and bath. Third floor sunroom with helioglass for sun-bathing. Oil furnace, deep well. Two garages and carpenter shop. Gardens.

Henriette Harris, Antiques
(sole agent)

It sounds mouth-watering, but nothing came of the project, just as nothing came of Mabel's idea of being a subsidiary colony to promulgate Gurdjieff's teachings.

Henriette seems to have served — many of Mabel's young female assistants did — as confidante as well as general dog's body. One long letter from her employer talks happily and at length about palmistry and the interesting lines to be found in her hand. A frontispiece for one of her books, she said, ought to be made up of a picture of herself and a close-up of her left palm, with the life line broken in half — very rare, said Mabel; "I have never seen another & palmists always shudder & exclaim over it." It was foretold all her life from childhood, she added, that it foreshadowed a complete break in her life halfway along her time, and no one ever knew what it meant. Violent death? Insanity? In fact, Mabel pointed out happily, at that moment what happened to her was coming to Taos and meeting Tony, which meant that her old life was abruptly broken off. In another letter written in 1936 we see how far the intimacy had gone: John Evans, she told Henriette, was not coming to Taos from Santa Fe because he had cold feet: he was afraid of the weather, Alice had refused to let the children visit Claire and himself for Easter, and he was upset.

Sometimes Mabel went to Santa Fe, and she always let Henriette know. Would Henriette like to drive back with her for Sunday? Or — if Mabel was away — would she see that everybody was prepared for the visitors who were expected: Evangeline, Adrian and Ronny, and Jeffers anytime afterward. And Stokowski. From California she wrote at some length about collecting her book reviews; the clipping bureau didn't cover magazines and she was especially anxious to have copies of Ruth Suckow's article and Granville Hicks's. It was worth doing, she said, for future reference. She went on:

"I and others firmly believe my adverse criticism will make a right about face some day, as Proust's did, & Lawrence's did, & in fact others whose writing *hurt* critics' feelings & was not truly estimated at the time, & it will be interesting to mark the change. I may sound vain — & maybe I am! but I believe I am right."

She told Henriette a good deal about her work in progress, naturally, since she was sending it to be typed as she finished it, chapter by chapter: "This one is hard because at any given moment I remember very little detail but if I start to write things unroll & write themselves. But away from work I feel quite blank & as tho' I have nothing to tell except those things I feel prohibited from telling! The problem is to let the book squeeze itself out somehow between the brakes: the conscious censor & unconscious one! Some job!"

From Carmel she wrote that she was thinking of bringing her

autobiography to a halt with the end of the book she was writing, *Edge of Taos Desert,* but she supposed her publishers wouldn't permit it. (They did.) Some of her letters were written from the Holy Cross Hospital, where she claimed to be enjoying a good rest. (Later she gave money to the hospital.) Her illness had been gathering strength, she decided, for months, but it did not really strike until the book was finished and on its way to the publisher.

"Do you suppose my new book is any good?" she demanded almost wistfully. "I am wondering!" She had anemia and perhaps diabetes, she said; anyway, she was weak and shaky, and had decided to rent the Big House and live during the time it was let in Tony's house, always known simply as "Tony house."

Edge of Taos Desert, the fourth and final volume of the memories, came out in September 1937, about a week after a columnist in the *Herald Tribune* had been west and described what could be seen in New Mexico, especially Taos:

Another sight . . . is Mabel Dodge Luhan on her recurrent hair-cutting pilgrimages from Taos to Albuquerque. First one sees Tony, in the Alvarado. He wears English riding clothes, tempered by long thick braids of hair over each shoulder. In the evenings, he wears boots, but in the morning, soft blue-beaded moccasins, the envy of tourists . . . Then there is a flurry in the hotel lobby, a small bull-dog dashes through on a leash, and holding the leash is Mabel, dressed like Mary Jane for a party; bangs, socks, strap shoes and smocked dress . . . She vanishes into the barber shop.

The book was greeted by less of a hubbub than its predecessors had been. Lorine Purette in the same *Herald Tribune* reviewed it on September 19, saying that it had two brilliant portraits, one of the author and the other of Tony Luhan.

Tony is the adolescent girl's dream of the perfect man, quiet, strong, tender, inexplicable and untrammeled. The trips made into the desert are likewise romantic even to the excessive discomfort accepted as heightening the experience. This is the way girls, and women, too, would like their love affairs to proceed. But perhaps only Mabel Dodge Luhan could make the attack of dysentery beside the dangerous waterfalls, and the Indians tending her, into a soul-stirring experience that is both believable and funny.

Harry Hansen of the *World-Telegram* began his review: "The most famous Indian captive in literary history is Mary Jemison, whose story, running into many editions, now lends fame to Elmer Adler's private collection. The most famous Indian captive in modern times bids fair to be Tony, of New Mexico, captured by Mabel Dodge Luhan, whose story, 'Edge of Taos Desert,' may run Mary Jemison's memoirs a close race among collectors."

After *Edge of Taos Desert,* Mabel published no more books for a while. This was not, one supposes, because she was discouraged, but because she had indeed almost caught up with herself. Instead she wrote a number of articles for newspapers and magazines, mostly local. Even so, her days were not idle. When all else failed, she could busy herself with pueblo affairs and do battle for the Indians through the Bureau of Indian Affairs, where she considered herself cozily at home because of John Collier being Commissioner. All went well for a while. She would telegraph him about matters that in her judgment needed attention, and Collier took action — sometimes. For example, she sent him a telegram on June 4, 1934, when the governor of Taos Pueblo was demoted: WHOLE PUEBLO RELIEVED, said Mabel. This sort of thing helped her to feel that she mattered, or, rather, that *Tony* mattered: she was well aware that in electing to live with her, Tony had sacrificed his position in the Pueblo Council. Again, in November that year, she put her oar in by telegraphing Harold Ickes, Secretary of the Interior, about a new irrigation plan for Taos. Ickes naturally handed over the affair to Collier, and a favorable conclusion was reached.

Inevitably, however, Mabel quarreled with Collier when he refused to do her bidding every time. In 1936, hearing a false rumor that she was going to divorce Tony, she blamed the Bureau and, especially, the Commissioner. Again and again she wrote to Ickes complaining about various officials, especially Collier, against whom she made wild accusations, until the Commissioner wrote wearily to Ickes:

... Mrs. Luhan has moved from extravagance to extravagance. The background is psychological. Mrs. Luhan, as you know, is a very old friend of mine. She expected to have a great sway in Pueblo affairs when I became Commissioner ... We should have chaos in short order if we permitted Mrs. Luhan to dictate policies.

He said that her allegations had been investigated and proved to be either trivial or unfounded. Mabel, he said, was campaigning among the other Pueblos, and when there was an All-Pueblo Coun-

cil meeting on June 6, 1935, he sent the officials there a long telegram aimed at frustrating her work. "Pueblos will be able to tell
the false from the true," he said at the end, and so it was: Mabel's
intrigues came to nothing.

Mabel told Ickes that Collier was sacrificing the Indians to his
own ends. Ickes replied, "I appreciate your deep interest in the
welfare of the Pueblo Indians, particularly those of Taos, but I find
it impossible to believe that Commissioner Collier is deliberately
sacrificing the Indians . . ."

On June 15 she wrote to Ickes offering to come to Washington
herself and talk things over with him in private. ". . . Please see
that it is not in your office but at your house because if John
should know I am going to talk to you he would again strike at the
Indians," she said.

"Allegations which it is proper to make at all should be made in
writing," replied Ickes.

The next excitement in Mabel's life was the matter of the Peyote
Church in Taos Pueblo. As Tony had said, some of the Indians ate
the drug regularly and considered their meetings in the light of
religious conclaves. Collier thought they had a right to do so: he
always believed in protecting Indian customs no matter how odd
they might appear to white Americans. Mabel, however, opposed
the whole idea. The Pueblo officials ignored her objections and
came to an agreement among themselves approving of the Church,
so that Collier was able to write to Washington, ". . . Although
Mrs. Luhan's name was never mentioned, and although I made no
reference to outside influences, I believe that Mrs. Luhan's sway
over the Pueblo officers has come to an end."

Her letters to Secretary Ickes, however, continued until he complained to Collier that he really didn't have time to answer them
all.

"The only way to stop corresponding with Mrs. Luhan would be
to stop altogether," replied the Commissioner, out of his wealth of
experience.

Stacy May, of the Social Science Department of the Rockefeller
Foundation, recalls a bit of trouble at Taos Pueblo with dissident
young Indians who were keen to change some of the old customs.
For example, they objected to the rule that no wheeled vehicle
could be brought into the compound. It made it hard on the young
workers, who argued that they cut the wood for the community,

hauled it back to the pueblo, and had to carry it in on their backs. It was a nuisance, they said. Then there was the question of the seat of the pants, which according to tradition had to be cut out. They paid for their Levi's, they argued. Why need they mutilate them the minute they got them home?

Because Pueblo men had always done so, replied the elders. Mabel was on the side of the traditionalists, working as usual through Tony at the meetings, and the young innovators resented her. They resented her anyway; she was always insisting on the virtue of tradition. Once she published an article in the local paper about the beauty of the way Indians had always used their water, carrying it in jars from the acequia rather than employing nasty-looking pipes and so forth, and a young dissident Indian replied in the same paper. If that was the way Mrs. Luhan felt, he said, he had a proposition to make to her. Let her hand over to him her house with its running water, its flush toilets and bathtubs, its electricity and its garage with cars in it, and he would cheerfully move into it with his wife and children. Mrs. Luhan could have, in exchange, his pueblo room, where she could tote water and observe all the other beautiful old customs, such as going out back to relieve herself in the open, to her heart's content. Mabel does not seem to have considered the article worth a reply.

Feeling ran high about the pants-seat controversy, so high that white officials became somewhat concerned. Hayricks were burned and there were a few scuffles. Indian bureau workers tried at last to get the traditionalists to give in to the young men, but it didn't work out. They argued that they could see the point made by the innovators; it was just impracticable to make people cut the seats out of their pants. Wind whistled through the hole, they argued, and froze a man's buttocks.

According to May, the chief listened patiently, then said, "Look. I notice white man goes around here with nothing on face. Indian's ass is just the same as white man's face."

Chapter Sixteen

AT FIRST Taos felt only a few reverberations from the approaching hostilities in Europe and Asia, but when at last the war was definitely started there was more excitement in the town. Many youths in both the white community and the pueblo went off to fight. John Evans was well beyond draft age, but he took part in the foreign service. He and Claire had two children, a boy and a girl. The girl, Bonnie, was small and dark, and Mabel believed fondly that she was a reproduction of herself, not only physically but temperamentally. Whether or not this belief was also held by Bonnie, the girl wore her hair in similar fashion, and her marital career in later life was nearly as variegated as her grandmother's. Mabel liked to have Bonnie around, though their relations were not always peaceful. When Bonnie was sixteen she was spending the summer with Mabel, and there was a fight of some sort. It seems to have been a stormy period generally, for Mabel had recently quarreled with Brett and forbidden her to come to the house. She told Bonnie, too, to get out and not to come back.

"I didn't know what I could do," Bonnie said. "My parents thought I was there for the summer and they'd gone away, and I didn't have any money to go anywhere, anyway. I was just standing out on the road wondering where to turn when Brett came over. She was always watching Ganny's house, you know, through a spyglass, and she knew I'd been kicked out. She said, 'Oh, nonsense, come on over and stay with me,' so that's what I did. I hadn't been there long, though, when Mabel stumped up and came in and said, 'Don't be ridiculous. Come on over to dinner, both of you,' and we did. That was the end of that. Ganny could be very difficult; you just had to ride it out."

Apart from such flurries between Mabel and Brett their relations were cordial. Mabel wrote often and affectionately to the younger woman when Brett went to New York for an exhibition of her paintings. Friendship apart, she had a strong proprietary interest in Brett's colleagues. In 1947 she published her last book, *Taos and Its Artists*, a beautifully produced volume with many illustrations.

During her later years her circle of acquaintance was enlarged by a new resident of Taos, Millicent Rogers. For some time the world had been discovering New Mexico, and Taos and Santa Fe had begun to fill up with strangers, more persistent than earlier tourists, who came to stay at the various dude ranches of the vicinity, saw the beauties of the countryside, bought land and remained. Mabel made friends with Millicent, but she was not sure she really enjoyed the presence, so close at hand, of a woman who seemed bent on outdoing herself in her own specialties. Millicent too had been much married; she too had a lot of money. Finally — the impertinence of it! — she too found a lover among the Indians of Taos Pueblo. One could hardly expect Mabel to welcome such a redoubtable rival, but she may have comforted herself with the thought that she had been the first.

She spent little time in the East. After the war there was a brief flurry of excitement among her old friends in New York because she came to stay for a while, took a large suite in a hotel, and permitted word to get out that she was going to start up her Evenings again. There was one such Evening when she invited a number of the old guard and some new ones. John Goodwin, the son of her friend Betty Sage, was asked to bring with him a number of his friends to take part in the discussion, but they made mock of the party, sitting by themselves in a closed group and refusing to take any of it seriously. It all went to prove, said Mabel, that the younger generation had neither brains nor manners. Thereafter she preferred to take her holidays in California or Mexico. At home, she found interest and amusement in something that never failed her: she built a new house, this time at Embudo. It may be recalled that Embudo in earlier days had been a stopping-off place for intrepid travelers on their way to Taos from Santa Fe. She herself had had to pause there on her first adventurous trip to the smaller settlement and she had not been impressed because of a very bad lunch. But now, hardened to some extent by experience, she was able to appreciate the beauty of the little Mexican village's surroundings, placed as it was at the edge of the river just before the beginning of the canyon drive. After the purchase of the land and building of the adobe house, her letters to Henriette from Taos or Carmel or Cuernavaca show a preoccupation with the gathering of money.

"The reason I would like to sell a good collection of furniture," she wrote to Miss Harris in June 1952,

is because I need money to drill a deep well at Embudo, & cannot wait till *winter,* as summer extra wages, animal food etc. etc. force me to live up to the margin of my monthly income, saving for *taxes* as I go! I would like to raise $1500 or $2000 for this. There is a chance I may be able to sell a slice of land on my other side of this house, to the contractor Montgomery but I don't like to. The pieces in the Bolognese Italian & *period* would be:
1. small sideboard (in dining room).
2. small cupboard (From Gisella).
3. one stool.
4. one straight-backed chair.
5. large carved mirror.
6. Two or three *Florentine* Medici chairs. (originals of course.)
7. one large table.
This makes a fine collection for some large room. It would be wonderful in a club room or living room, & it adds up easily to $2000. So please watch your chance. I would not care to sell piece meal but all together for a purpose.

By October she seems to have sold some, if not all of it, to Millicent Rogers. "Did Millicent agree to that Price?" she asked Henriette. "Who emties [*sic*] the chests and drawers?

"When?

"When does she pay?"

The never very even tenor of days in Taos was seriously ruffled for a time by Angelino, who for some reason was in Mexico alone and ran into trouble on the way back: the immigration officials were not ready to permit him to come in. The Italian was jumpy in any case because of what had happened just before the war when an immigration official had come to see Frieda and ask her a lot of questions. Ravagli was an Italian, wasn't he? What was he doing in the States, then? What were his relations with Frieda?

"Oh, they are intimate," replied Frieda with innocent cheerfulness.

But in that case, said the official, Ravagli was a gigolo, who had no business in the pure air of the United States. It was suggested that he could be deported on a charge of moral turpitude. The official then departed, leaving Frieda, already sensitized by her World War I experience with D. H. Lawrence, badly frightened. Nothing came of this in the end, probably because after Pearl Harbor American officials had more than moral turpitude to worry about, but anything was enough to send Frieda into another panic, and the affair of the immigration officials at the Mexican border caused a tremendous gefuffle in Taos. Hal Bynner, of course, made the most of it.

"I have been surprised to hear Hal is reponsible for the funny stories about me keeping Angellino [*sic*] out of the States!" wrote Mabel indignantly to Henriette Harris. "This was written to me by a Santa Fe friend! Heigho! What an unremitting enmity!"

"When I got back [from Santa Fe] I heard from Brett that Angellino had been kept in Mexico & couldn't get back in," wrote Mabel again to Henriette,

& that Frieda is saying I wrote a letter to Washington to bring this about. I am beginning to get mad! Enough is enough. She has blamed me for every single thing that her own actions are responsible for & pretty soon I'm going to take some legal action to stop her malignings. There are certain things I don't do. One of them would be this kind of backhanded meanness. I wish you would convey this to her if you see her there . . . However, it is probably Angellino's own stupidity.

Henriette seems to have tried to smooth things over, as Mabel wrote thanking her for her peace efforts. But, she added, "it doesn't matter much what Frieda thinks — I feel through with her. You asked where *Brett* heard the stories? Frieda told them to everyone here & at the ranch — also where she got the idea of them. Dear Henri — you try to help & make things nice but you can't in the face of the adversary!"

"What did you think of Frieda?" I once asked Miss Harris, who replied, "Well, Frieda had this loud laugh, you see, so everybody thought she was wonderful. But I didn't. I never liked her."

Paul Horgan, who usually referred to Mabel as the Morgan le Fay of Taos, made some notes on the subject. "My recollection is very strong that the socio-intellectual little world of Santa Fe–Taos was divided between advocates of either Frieda or Mabel," he said. "I have always comically referred to the factions as Friedonians and Mabellites. It may be simple justice to bear in mind that in any witness I offer I speak as a dedicated Friedonian." On the other hand, he saw Mabel only twice, recalling:

I avoided meeting her for years — not that she'd've noticed. I forget the first occasion. The second was for a fleeting minute in the Villagra Book-shop in Santa Fe, then managed by Miss Roberta Robey, and, I think, owned by Clifford McCarthy.

Mrs. Luhan came in one day while I was there looking at books. Miss Robey asked if we knew each other. Frigid nods. Then Mabel asked if a certain Mr. So-and-so had been in. Miss Robey said he had left just five minutes before. Mabel said, "I hope he falls and breaks his leg."

What struck me was the flat, malevolent earnestness with which she said this — not the expected or usual tone of comic exasperation at having missed an appointment. My blood chilled. She quite genuinely, I thought, hoped he would *really* fall and break his leg. She looked pale and puffy, with her wide-ish face, and her hair, black, cut in Pueblo bangs. She left the shop.

A footnote to the affair of Frieda Lawrence and Angelo Ravagli. The incidents of Angie and the immigration office, though they were only two, worried them both — Frieda probably more than Angie — until at last, in 1950, they decided to do something about it. Angelo acquired a divorce from his wife Serafina — no great task, as long as the Ravaglis did not expect it to hold good in Italy — and at last, when Frieda was seventy-one and Angelo fifty-eight, the guilty pair were legally married. It was rather like encasing Lorenzo's ashes in cement; the thing, once done, was irrevocable, at least as long as Frieda lived. Afterward, Ravagli returned to Serafina in Italy.

There was a slight, typical New Mexico flurry in 1951 when Bynner published his *Journey with Genius*, an account of his travels in Mexico with Lawrence and Spud. Wrote Mabel to Henriette,

If you want a real treat, a big exhibition of pure hatred, get & read Bynner's book: "Journey with Genius." Almost all falsified, mean to the Bynner end to Lawrence, untrue in all incidents to me (because I refused him permission to quote from my books when he started this one, because I distrusted his interpretation of Lawrence even before he wrote a word.) Get it! You'll have fun! Frieda is furious, I am disgusted, Brett is hopping! Such *meanness* . . .

Just before her sixty-fifth birthday, Mabel granted Henriette an interview for the Santa Fe *New Mexican*. "She looks young, very much alive and eager, her grey eyes luminous and observing as ever," wrote Henriette. "I asked her how she felt at 65 and she replied:

Just the way I've always felt, no different. One doesn't feel any different, that's the strange thing about life. The thing about that is that you are so constructed that you like all ages — you like the age you are in — like when you are facing death you don't mind it, nobody who is really about to die minds it. I don't think the dying have any fear of death at all. I think it is only the healthy who have. People who are getting older have no fear for old age or dislike for it. That's part of the same compensation that nature provides for the dying.

Her old age lasted a long time: she had always been a healthy, strong woman. One might say she simply faded. Before the end her old enemy Frieda died, in 1956, but she herself didn't come to an end until August 13, 1962, when she was eighty-three.

Brett has painted a picture of the funeral. A closed coffin with a sheaf of gladioli lying on it awaits burial in a corner plot of the very green Kit Carson Cemetery. Other sheaves of gladioli are propped against the railings in the background. Four white-clad figures stand in mourning attitudes. Seated in a row of chairs facing the coffin, their backs to the spectator, we see the members of Mabel's household. The faces of two veiled women, possibly Claire and Alice, are not visible, but in profile we can clearly see John Evans, Spud Johnson, and an aged Tony, bespectacled, with gray braids. Brett in blouse and blue Levi's stands to one side, facing the party. It is a bright picture, full of flowers and fun. Alice Rossin remembers the occasion well. She said:

"We'd all been to church and the cemetery. Tony had been very quiet through everything, then suddenly he started to talk, looking up at the sky. He said the sun had gone out, he said lots of other things. We were all staggered, because usually he didn't talk much at all. We tried to calm him down, and that worked to some extent, but through the rest of the proceedings he was apt to say to people, 'Where's Mabel?' or 'We can't start without Mabel.' It was awful, poor old thing. I still feel terrible about what happened later. John and Claire had come out for the funeral and to get everything sorted out, the will and the estate and so on, and they

were going to live in the Big House, so Tony was moved into another one of Mabel's houses. One night he got up, probably to go
to the bathroom, and he didn't remember where he was, and he fell
down the stairwell and died. Poor old Tony."

Bibliographical Note ⌫━━━━━

In Chapter One Mabel's recollections are from *Background* (New York: Harcourt Brace, 1933). In Chapters Two, Three, and Four they are taken from *European Experiences* (New York: Harcourt Brace, 1935). Hutchins Hapgood's comments in Chapter Four are from *A Victorian in the Modern World* (Harcourt Brace, 1939). Alice B. Toklas's from *What Is Remembered* (New York: Holt, Rinehart & Winston, 1963).

Mabel's life is recalled from *Movers and Shakers* (New York: Harcourt Brace, 1936) in Chapter Five. In the same chapter Muriel Draper's comments are from *Music at Midnight* (New York: Harper & Brothers, 1929) and Carl Van Vechten's from *Fragments*, Volume Two (New Haven: Yale University Library, 1955). Arthur Rubinstein's comments in Chapter Six are from *My Young Years* (New York: Knopf, 1973). In Chapters Six and Seven Mabel's recollections are from *Movers and Shakers* and Granville Hicks's comments from his *John Reed: The Making of a Revolutionary* (New York: Macmillan, 1936).

In Chapter Eight Hutchins Hapgood's *A Victorian in the Modern World* is cited, and in Chapters Eight, Nine, and Eleven Maurice Sterne's *Shadow and Light* (Harcourt, Brace & World, 1965) is quoted. Mabel's life as depicted in Chapters Nine, Ten, and Eleven is from *Edge of Taos Desert* (New York: Harcourt Brace, 1937); in Chapters Twelve through Fourteen from *Lorenzo in Taos* (New York: Knopf, 1932) and from *Winter in Taos* (Denver: Sage Books, 1935). In Chapter Twelve Mary Austin's *Earth Horizon* (Boston: Houghton Mifflin, 1932) and John Collier's *Indians of the Americas* (New York: Norton, 1947) are cited.

Index